Chicken Soup for the Christian Woman's Soul

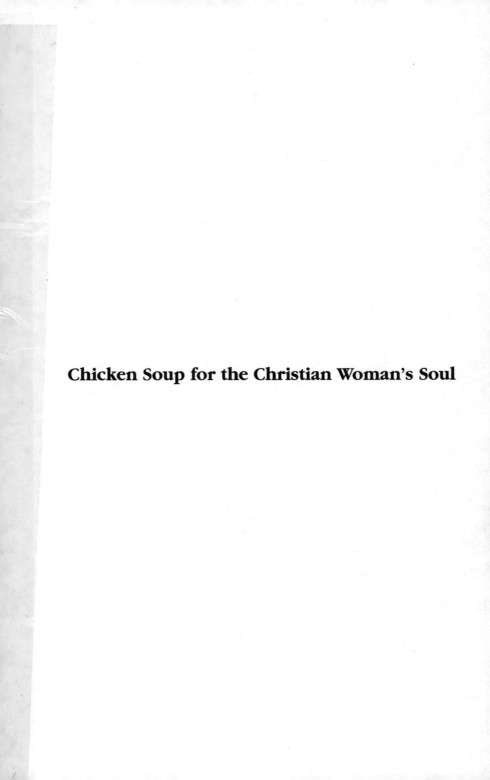

CHICKEN SOUP FOR THE CHRISTIAN WOMAN'S SOUL

Stories to Open the Heart and Rekindle the Spirit

Jack Canfield
Mark Victor Hansen
Patty Aubery
Nancy Mitchell Autio
LeAnn Thieman

Health Communications, Inc.
Deerfield Beach, Florida

www.bci-online.com
www.chickensoup.com

We would like to acknowledge the following publishers and individuals for permission to reprint the following material. (Note: The stories that were penned anonymously, that are in the public domain, or that were written by Jack Canfield, Mark Victor Hansen, Patty Aubery, Nancy Mitchell Autio or LeAnn Thieman.

The Piano. Reprinted by permission of Carla S. Riehl. ©2002 Carla S. Riehl.

The Ring I Really Want. Reprinted by permission of Rachel Wallace-Oberle. ©2000 Rachel Wallace-Oberle.

Seed Faith Money. Reprinted by permission of Patricia Lorenz. ©1991 Patricia Lorenz.

(Continued on page 384)

Library of Congress Cataloging-in-Publication Data
is available from the Library of Congress.

ISBN 0-7573-0019-7 (hardcover)—ISBN 0-7573-0018-9 (trade paper)

Publisher: Health Communications, Inc.
3201 S.W. 15th Street
Deerfield Beach, FL 33442-8190

Cover design by Lawna Patterson Oldfield
Inside book formatting by Dawn Von Strolley Grove

We dedicate this book to our mothers who not only
formed our lives, but our faiths:
Ellen Taylor
Una Peterson Hansen
Linda Mitchell
Berniece Duello

Contents

2. THE LOVE OF A FAMILY

3. GOD'S HEALING POWER

4. FRIENDSHIP

5. MAKING A DIFFERENCE

6. CHALLENGES

Acknowledgments

It's been an honor to write, compile, and edit *Chicken Soup for the Christian Woman's Soul.* What a privilege to read such outstanding stories from such loving people. So first and foremost, we must thank all of you who shared you heartfelt stories, poems, quotes and cartoons for possible inclusion in this book. While we were not able to use everything submitted, we know that each word came from the bottom of your hearts—sometimes from emotions or experiences that my have been difficult to share. We may have left out some of the names of those who contributed along the way. If so, please accept our apologies.

Bless our families for all of their love and support on this project: Patty, Inga, Mark, Kirk, Jeff, Christopher, Travis, Riley, Melanie, Elizabeth, J. T., Chandler, Molly, Christie, Angela and Mitch.

Our publisher and dear friend, Peter Vegso, for all of his love, support and commitment to the vision of this book and his commitment and faith to us as coauthors. Thanks, Peter. We love you!

Heather McNamara and D'ette Corona, our star editors who helped create this book and spent countless hours reading, re-reading and editing stories to bring this manuscript into its final stages. We appreciate you for your hard work in all that you do to keep the *Chicken Soup* books going! You are very dear to our hearts.

Thanks to Leslie Riskin, who managed and guided Veronica Romero through the permissions process.

Thanks to Veronica Romero, who secured all of the permissions, read the entire manuscript and helped acquire stories. You're the best!

And to Barbara Lomonaco, who helped read and grade hundreds of stories and who is always available for us whenever we need her.

As always, thanks go to Kathy Brennan-Thompson, Cindy Holland, Teresa Esparza, Vince Wong, Dana Drobny, Leslie Risken, Robin Yerian, Stephanie Thatcher, Michelle Adams, Dave Coleman, Irene Dunlap, Jody Emme, DeeDee Romanello, Gina Romanello, Brittney Shaw, Shanna Vieyra, Laurie Hartman, Dawn Henshall, Trudy Marschall, Maria Nickless and Lisa Williams for your commitment, dedication and professionalism in making sure Jack and Mark's offices ran smoothly throughout this project.

A special thanks to Health Communications for their ongoing support and faith in us: Terry Burke, Kim Weiss, Allison Janse, Christine Belleris, Lisa Drucker, Susan Tobias and Kathy Grant.

Tom Sand, Claude Choquette and Luc Jutras, who manage year after year to get our books translated into thirty-six languages around the world.

We are grateful to the following people who read and scored the final 200 stories and helped make the final selections: Madalane Bothma, Marla Bramer, Karen Briggs, Denise Carr, Sharon Castiglone, Helen Colella, Cheryl Cazer, D'ette Corona, Christine Dahl, Jennifer Dale, Maxine Dobbin, Berniece Duello, Teresa Esparza, Kerrie Flanagan, Karen Fehr-Rivera, Shannon Heath, Ellen Javernick, Sally Kelly-Engeman, Karen Kishpaugh,

Barbara Lomonaco, Carol McAdoo Rehme, Heather McNamara, Linda Mitchell, Tanya Motley, Linda Osmundson, Mary Panosh, Sharon Raffensperger, Veronica Romero, Kay Rosenthal, Carol Steward, Mary Streit, Christie Thieman, Dene Van Hecker, Tracey Worley and Jeannie Winstrom. We couldn't have done this without your feedback.

A special thanks to Naomi Rhode and Glenna Salsbury for sharing our call for stories with their wonderful networks of Christian women. You saw the blessings this book had to offer, and we love you more than ever for your help with it.

Our gratitude extends to Linda Shepherd and the Advanced Writers and Speakers Association (AWSA), a professional support group made up of the top 10 percent of Christian women in both publishing and speaking. Your assistance in collecting stories was invaluable.

All of Chicken Soup for the Soul Enterprises has come to appreciate LeAnn's writer's group. We have benefited not only from your excellent stories, but your professional expertise, wisdom, and loving support. We all join in thanking Jean Bell, Helen Colella, Debbie Dadey, Lynn Dean, Kerrie Flanagan, Margaret Hill, Ellen Javernick, Sally Kelly-Engeman, Linda Osmundson, Carol McAdoo Rehme and Carol Steward.

LeAnn eagerly thanks her assistant and marketing agent, Amy Williams, who managed her speaking business brilliantly while she devoted her time and attention to this project. And to LeAnn's mom, Berniece Duello, who personifies Christ's work on earth. A loving thank-you to her husband Mark, who supports her in her speaking and writing, but most importantly, her faith. And to Angela, Christie and Mitch, who are the answers to every mother's prayer.

And mostly to God, for His Divine guidance.

Introduction

Since the beginning of time and throughout biblical history, women have inspired and upheld one another by sharing their stories.

Sarah's desire for a child reinforces our own, and we find hope and promise in her story. We learn about the thrilling joys and devastating sorrows of motherhood from Mary, the mother of Jesus, who taught us the ultimate lessons in letting go.

During some phases of our lives, we draw strength from Ruth, who selflessly took in her mother-in-law. As we allow others to care for us, we find peace and strength in Naomi.

Like Miriam, we dance, sing and rejoice after triumphantly surviving life's difficult journeys.

When we step out in new adventures, feeling eager yet confused, we relate to lessons from Eve.

Tales of Mary Magdalene remind us to forgive ourselves as Jesus forgives us.

And how often have we wished for the wisdom and discernment of the prophetess Deborah?

As coauthors of *Chicken Soup for the Christian Woman's Soul,* we gathered literally thousands of stories from Christian women around the world to continue this legacy of sharing and to put together this collection. As you read how their faith in Christ has blessed these women's lives, you will be inspired to make Him the center of your life. These heartwarming, hope-filled stories will lift up your spirits and nourish your souls. Our wish is for you to savor each story and find inspiration and healing in each message. We believe you will draw strength from your fellow sisters in Christ as you practice these lessons of faith, love and forgiveness.

Together, we Christian women will continue our calling to share our faith to nurture and uphold one another.

It is with great joy, pride and humility that we are privileged to share with you—*Chicken Soup for the Christian Woman's Soul.*

Share with Us

We would love to hear your reactions to the stories in this book. Please let us know what your favorite stories were and how they affected you.

We also invite you to send us stories you would like to see published in future editions of *Chicken Soup for the Soul*. You can send us either stories you have written or stories written by others. Please send submissions to:

www.chickensoup.com or
Chicken Soup for the Soul
P.O. Box 30880
Santa Barbara, CA 93130
Fax: 805-563-2945

You can also access e-mail or find a current list of planned books at the *Chicken Soup for the Soul* Web site at *www.chickensoup.com.* Find out about our Internet service at *www.clubchickensoup.com.*

We hope you enjoy reading this book as much as we enjoyed compiling and editing it.

1

FAITH

Faith is to believe, on the word of God, what we do not see, and its reward is to see and enjoy what we believe.

Saint Augustine

The Piano

You pay God a compliment by asking great things of Him.

St. Teresa of Avila

During the early 1990s, being a Christian recording artist sometimes felt like one big struggle in a world of extremes. I would stand on stage in front of spotlights and thousands of people, only to go back to the hotel room with my family, wondering if anyone really cared about what I did at all. I would fall into bed in a small room shared by six, with one bathroom and suitcases piled everywhere.

We put on large contemporary Christian concerts in churches all over the country. I stepped into some of the most beautiful buildings equipped with state of the art furnishings and accoutrements, only to feel like I was on the outside looking in. For two hours I was the center of attention—lights dimmed, music played and God's presence filled all of our lives. Then moments after the concert ended, we packed it all up, rolled it out the back door into our trailer and disappeared down a lonely highway into the silence of the night.

I used to walk around those big, empty, church auditoriums as everyone scurried to get set up, wondering how they did it. How did these churches acquire all the wonderful facilities and resources they needed to make a difference in people's lives? What was the secret? I was doing the same thing they were, only I did it on the road and my "congregation" changed every night. I wondered how anyone ever acquired the unabashed boldness to just stretch their hands open, stand before God and simply receive from his overflowing abundance. It was easier to just believe that everyone else must be doing something right, and I must be somehow flawed. Maybe if I tried harder, worked longer and suffered a little bit more, I would finally be "worthy" of receiving what I needed.

One afternoon in between concerts, my husband and I walked into a huge music store filled with the most impressive collection of grand pianos I had ever seen. Row after row of black-and-ivory concert grands sat there waiting for someone with the gift of music in their soul to sit down and play them. I pulled a bench up to one of the pianos, touched the keys and smiled.

"Nice piano," I said to the salesclerk.

"Are you looking for a grand or a baby grand?" He perked up, thinking he had a customer.

"Oh me?" I laughed. "Well, I can't really buy a piano now," I said sheepishly.

My husband walked over and spoke up without hesitation. "Honey, you've been wanting a real piano for years. These are incredible instruments!"

I gave him the are-you-out-of-your-mind? look.

"Let me show you a baby grand over here that's really special," the salesclerk said moving us to the back of the store.

My husband followed him excitedly. I trailed behind,

dragging my feet, wishing we could just get out of there and save ourselves any further embarrassment. We didn't belong in an expensive music store. I felt like I was trespassing and any minute I was going to be found out.

"This is a brand-new baby grand," the salesclerk gushed. "It's the only one of its kind, and we're clearing it out. It's on sale—and I'll tell you, it's one of the most fabulous pianos I've ever seen."

"Sit down and play it, " my husband urged.

I wished he'd leave me alone. Why should I play it if I couldn't have it? To save face in front of the salesclerk, I sat down at the clean, white keys. They felt like smooth silk and sounded like a symphony. The salesclerk propped the lid open.

"Press the pedals and play hard," he said. "You can't believe how this thing resonates and fills up the whole room."

He was right. It was incredible. It moved and inspired me to just sit and play it in the store. I could have written a song right then and there.

"How much is it?" my husband asked casually—as if he had just won the lottery.

"It lists for ten thousand dollars, but since we're clearing it out, we're giving it away for only five thousand dollars." He grinned.

"Wow!" my husband cheered and turned smiling at me.

Wow yourself, I thought, rolling my eyes. What did it matter if it was five thousand or five million! We were struggling musicians who didn't have the money. I couldn't have this. I was nobody. We weren't the pastors with the big buildings. We didn't have a record company financing our tours. Who was I to spend that kind of money for a music ministry? Still, I wanted that piano, and my husband knew it.

"Let's put some money down on it and hold it," he

whispered to me frantically. "If we can't pay for it in thirty days, then we won't get it, but let's take a step of faith and try."

He handed the salesclerk a check for $500.

The salesclerk smiled. "See you in thirty days!" he said, waving good-bye.

As the days passed, I wanted that piano more than anything. Each day on tour I started my day with prayer time, and from somewhere deep down in my spirit, faith rose. Unabashed boldness seemed to come out of nowhere and I talked to God.

"God, if I were a pastor, and I needed one of those million-dollar buildings to share my message, you would provide it without question. If I was a medical missionary, and the 'tool' I needed was an airplane, it would come to me. Well, God, I'm a musician, and that's a God-given calling as worthy and as important as any other calling. I'm not asking for a building or an airplane; I'm just asking for a piano to write my songs. I'm ready to believe that my gift of music is as important to you as the gift of being a pastor or a medical missionary or a brain surgeon. I know you won't fail me because I'm important, too."

Every morning I prayed that prayer and as I did, I began to realize that I was just as "worthy" as anyone else, because God had given me my musical gift. In a few weeks, I believed it wholeheartedly and the doubt that I didn't deserve anything began to fade. I began to tell my friends about the piano I had "on hold."

Our concert tour ended twenty-nine days later. As we pulled into the driveway and started unloading our gear, my parents, who had been watching our house, appeared in the front yard with a letter in their hands.

"Here's the weirdest letter," they said, handing us the stack of mail. "It's addressed to you, honey, but your last name is spelled wrong, and there's no street address. I can't believe it got here."

I stared at the wrinkled, stained envelope with just my name and my small town and state scribbled across it.

I opened it up curiously and saw a yellow check inside. There was no letter or note, just the yellow check. As I unfolded it, I almost fainted. It was for $5,000, and it was made out to me from my great-uncle Britt. I hardly knew him and hadn't spoken to him in many years. My parents looked at the check in shock.

"Honey, what in the world?" my mother gasped.

"My piano," I whispered.

"Uncle Britt did that to me once," my dad laughed. "Sometimes he just likes to start getting rid of all the money he has. I guess your number came up today!" He giggled at his eccentric uncle and hugged me.

The next morning, exactly thirty days later, I called the music store, wired them the full amount of $4,500 and gave the leftover $500 to a worthy ministry. My shiny, white baby grand piano was delivered and placed in the middle of my living room where the sun streamed down on it from a skylight.

There are still times in my life when I feel like "I'm on the outside looking in," and I question whether I'm "worthy" enough. I sometimes wonder if God only blesses big names and big buildings. On those days I sit down in front of the most extravagant concert piano that I have ever played, and I remember that whether anybody else thinks so or not, God believes I am "worth it," and He got a ninety-year-old, eccentric great-uncle to help Him show me.

Carla Riehl

The Ring I Really Want

The manner of giving shows the character of the giver, more than the gift itself.

John Casper Lavater

"Oh, I love your diamond," Janet said admiringly as we served lunch to the children in the school gym. "It's beautiful."

"Thanks," I said, and then I confessed. "It's not real; it's just a cubic zirconia."

Her eyes widened. "Wow. I would never have guessed."

I have always had a passion for collecting fine jewelry, but I also own a few quality fake pieces, which generally fool everyone. Janet eyed my large sparkling ring. "I've never owned anything like that," she sighed, looking down at the plain thin wedding band on her hand.

We finished serving the children their Thanksgiving turkey lunch, but Janet's words stayed with me. I knew she and her husband could not afford even the small luxuries of life; they are a Christian family who lives down the street with four boys, and they work hard to make ends meet.

The idea of giving my ring to Janet came to me the next day. I pushed it away immediately. Although the 14-carat gold ring was only a cubic zirconia, I liked it and wore it often with my wedding band. The thought of knocking on Janet's door and presenting her with my ring seemed ridiculous. I try to shrug the notion off, but the thought persisted. It bothered me for a week. I had no peace until finally I prayed: "Lord, if this is something you want me to do, I'll do it, but please go with me and let her be home when I go." I reasoned that if I knocked on the door and Janet wasn't home, which she often wasn't, I would take it as a sign that I didn't have to part with my ring. I felt a little better but was still unenthusiastic about this errand.

The next morning I put the ring in its little blue velvet box, wrapped it up in tissue paper and walked down the street to Janet's house, my heart pounding. *She'll think I'm crazy,* I thought. *What kind of neighbor gives someone a 14-carat gold ring? I don't even know her that well.*

I felt like turning around and going home but forced myself to climb the steps to Janet's house. I knocked quietly on the door. No one answered. I stood on her porch, waiting uncomfortably. Knock again, God's spirit prompted. Reluctantly I knocked again. No one answered.

I felt the stirrings of relief. Maybe she was away and I could forget about this whole thing. Just as I stood there contemplating my escape, I heard the doorknob rattle. Janet looked incredibly surprised to see me. "Hi," she greeted me.

"Good morning," I said, struggling not to blush with discomfort. I handed her the small package. "I have something for you."

She looked astounded. "For me?"

I nodded. "The Lord has been telling me all week to give this to you."

She took it and as her fingers closed over the contours

of the box, she realized what it was. To my immense surprise, her eyes filled with tears and her hands began to shake. "No," her voice quavered. "I can't accept this. It's too much. I can't accept this."

An immense peace and joy descended upon me there on Janet's front porch. "You're my sister in Christ and I want you to have it," I said, unable to keep the delight from spreading over my face.

Janet unwrapped the ring and cried. I hugged her, my eyes full of tears. She hugged me back. It took a bit of convincing on my part, but she finally agreed to keep the ring. "If you ever change your mind, just tell me and I'll give it back," she promised. It was a few sizes too small for her, so I told her to have it adjusted at the nearby jewelry store, which had extremely reasonable prices.

I thought that was the end of the story, but several weeks later as I was walking past Janet's house, she flew out the door, across the porch and out to the sidewalk.

"I have a present for you," she said breathlessly. She thrust a little package at me.

"Janet, you don't have to do that," I protested.

"Open it," she said, grinning.

I opened it and found a little blue velvet box with my ring in it. I looked up at her, puzzled and slightly disappointed that she had chosen not to keep it.

"I went to the jewelry store you told me about to get it sized," she explained, "but the clerk didn't think it would be good for the claws and setting to enlarge it that many sizes. I was devastated. I finally had something beautiful and I couldn't even wear it."

Janet's smile was incongruent with her story.

"I don't understand," I admitted.

On the sidewalk, in the late afternoon, with the sun slanting through the maple tree in Janet's yard, she told me what had happened. For years, her set of wedding bands had lain in a dresser drawer in her bedroom. She had lost the diamond solitaire, and the rings needed repairs and sizing. It was a gorgeous antique set but she had been unable to wear it. Every Mother's Day, birthday and Christmas, she had quietly gone to that dresser drawer and examined her rings, hoping her husband had surprised her by getting them fixed. And every time she went to the drawer, she was disappointed. Repairing and restoring the rings were simply too expensive. She and her husband had received estimates from jewelers of nearly one thousand dollars for the work. They couldn't afford to spend their money on something so frivolous. My gift had touched her heart, but what she wanted most was to wear her own wedding bands.

On a whim, Janet asked the clerk in the jewelry store about getting her wedding rings fixed. She had given up hope that it would ever happen. It had never occurred to her to consider a synthetic gem—until now. Janet's rings were sized and repaired and the center stone replaced with a cubic zirconia for under $100. She held her hand out to show me. Her rings sparkled in the sunlight. Rows of glittering diamonds encircled a solitaire that flashed with brilliant fire. They were stunning.

"For the first time in seven years, I am wearing my rings again," she said, her voice breaking. "Thank you for your gift. Thank you more than you'll ever know—but these are the only rings I really want."

I walked home in a daze. It took quite a while for the whole extraordinary sequence of events to sink in. I have concluded that God's intricate plans are altogether too incredible to anticipate or comprehend. The next time He wants to entwine my life with another, I will do as He asks—without questions, without doubts—and with trust.

Rachel Wallace-Oberle

Seed Faith Money

He that gives all, though but little, gives much; because God looks not to the quantity of the gift, but the quality of the givers.

Francis Quarles

My friend Rosemary was newly divorced and overwhelmed by the awesome responsibility of raising two daughters alone. There were many weeks when she had less than fifty dollars to her name.

At Easter time, Rosemary's daughter Theresa discovered a pea-sized lump on her collarbone. Tests showed Hodgkin's disease and a tumor that filled 40 percent of her chest cavity.

In addition to the terror of watching Theresa suffer, Rosemary was also distraught over the enormous medical bills piling up. The hospital was demanding a fifteen-hundred-dollar payment.

A few weeks later, quite unexpectedly, Rosemary was named "Employee of the Year" at work and received a prize of fifteen hundred dollars: exactly the amount she needed. *What a stroke of luck!* Rosemary thought.

At church that Sunday an overpowering inner voice was so loud and clear she shook her head to make sure she wasn't dreaming. The voice said, "Give Maggie a hundred dollars."

"What?" Rosemary demanded.

"Give Maggie a hundred dollars."

Maggie? The Maggie whose job I took over when she quit at work? She was the only Maggie that Rosemary knew. *Why does this woman need me to give her a hundred dollars?* Rosemary asked the inner voice. *I'm the one struggling financially! At least Maggie has a husband to help her.*

Rosemary thought about her recent windfall. After tithing and paying taxes on it, the amount she actually cleared from that prize was less than a thousand dollars—not even enough to cover the hospital payment. Now someone—*was it God?* Rosemary wondered—was asking her to give a hundred dollars to a woman she hardly knew.

This is ridiculous, she said to herself. *Why, it's total fiscal irresponsibility!*

At home that afternoon Rosemary kept hearing the voice: Give Maggie a hundred dollars.

She dug deep into her faith reserve and remembered the verse from Matthew 28:20 that says, "And surely I am with you always, to the very end of the age."

Rosemary thought back to the last few months of Theresa's struggle with Hodgkin's disease. By now, she was well on the road to recovery. She hadn't even gotten sick from the chemotherapy. Yes, God had been with them throughout the whole ordeal, but Rosemary also knew that God didn't ask for paybacks.

It didn't make sense, but Rosemary reached for her checkbook. Shaking and sweating, she wrote the check and mailed it to Maggie. A week later Maggie stood on Rosemary's doorstep. Smiling, Maggie handed the check back. "I can't accept this, Rosemary, but I want you to know that you certainly did God's work when you sent it. My husband was getting so bitter about God and religion. He was so touched by your generosity, he's acting like a whole new person. Thank you so much," she beamed as she pressed the hundred-dollar check back into Rosemary's hand.

The next Sunday, Rosemary tithed an extra ten dollars for the hundred dollars Maggie had given back to her. On Monday, Rosemary received a check in the mail from her Aunt Joey for a hundred dollars for no particular reason—something her aunt had never done before.

On Tuesday, Rosemary tithed ten dollars of that money to the church.

On Friday she received a hundred-dollar check in the mail from her good friend, Sharon, who enclosed a note that said simply, "I'm sure you can use this." Sharon had never done such a thing before.

That's when it hit Rosemary square in the eye. She thought to herself, *When God asked me to give Maggie a hundred dollars for no apparent reason, I listened—a bit grudgingly, I'll admit. Was it a test, like when God instructed Abraham to sacrifice Isaac, his beloved son? And just as God spared Isaac at the last minute, did He "spare me" by bringing back that one hundred dollars three times in six days?*

Several years later, Rosemary's finances were again extremely grim. Her older daughter, Claire, was getting ready to go back to college, and Rosemary was frantic over how she would come up with the money for her tuition. In faith, she reluctantly sold some antique jewelry that had been given to her years earlier.

The next Sunday Rosemary slipped into the pew next to Margaret, a struggling single parent. The familiar inner voice said, *Give a hundred dollars to Margaret.*

Rosemary almost wailed out loud. *Now just a minute!* she

said to that inner voice. *I took a loss on the jewelry when I sold it, because I have faith in You! And You're* still *asking me to give Margaret a hundred dollars?*

Rosemary knew it was useless to argue. The world says "Hang onto your money." But sometimes God says "Give it away." She gave Margaret a hundred dollars.

Within five days, the bank suddenly approved an "iffy" college loan toward Claire's tuition. In addition, the following week Rosemary received a generous and quite unexpected raise at work.

The next week in church she quieted herself and prepared to "listen" to what God had in mind for her now—more out of curiosity at the absurdity of it all than with real eagerness. Within a few minutes, she was directed to give another struggling single parent whom she barely knew one hundred and fifty dollars. This time there was no, *Aw, come on, God, You've got to be kidding!* By this time, she was a believer. She'd been taught more than once that if she just put out a seedling effort, God would return His bounty in bushels.

Patricia Lorenz

The Song in You

And the song in you can make hopes and dreams come true.

LaDonna Gatlin

Back in the summer of 1976, in Nashville, Tennessee, I came to a crossroads in my life, and I had a decision to make. Should I stay with my brothers, the Gatlin Brothers, and sing their country music—or follow God's leading in my heart and sing a different song? Although the prospect of stardom lay just ahead for the Gatlins, I could not get away from that tug in my heart. So, after much soul-searching, I chose to sing God's song.

That song has taken me on an incredible journey. It has taken me from the Grand Old Opry to the splendor of the Crystal Cathedral and every place in between. I've sung it in the spotlight with hundreds of people looking on. I've sung it by the nightlight as I sang lullabies to my babies. I've sung it in the halls of corporate powerhouses, and I've sung it in the halls of death row prison blocks. I've found one thing to be true in all those places—people need to hear my song.

Oh sure, the melody and the lyrics change from place to place. Sometimes I sing, "I'm on Top of the World." Other times, however, I sing a far different tune. Like the day that a young female inmate walked up to me in a prison yard and said, "LaDonna, I can remember living in only two places in my entire life—under a bridge in Dallas and behind these prison walls."

I had no idea what to say to that young woman. So I cradled her precious face in my hands and with tears streaming down both our cheeks, I did the only thing I knew how to do—I sang her my song. "Amazing Grace, how sweet the sound that saved a wretch like me. I once was lost, but now I'm found, was blind but now I see."

I didn't have the power to reverse the young woman's sentence—to sign some document that would set her free. But I did have the opportunity to offer her something that I believe supercedes the constraints of any circumstances—hope—a hope that gave her strength.

My journey has shown me that there's a whole world full of people out there who feel just as imprisoned as that young inmate—imprisoned by their circumstances, their failures, their fears. They have no hope, or so it seems. We all have a God-given song to share, and just as I sang my song to her, we can each sing our songs of hope every day. It may be as simple as a smile, a kind word, a pat on the back or a handwritten note that says, "I'm here for you, I'm praying for you."

None of us should be afraid to sing our songs—we never know who needs to hear the music.

LaDonna Gatlin

God Listens

Faith is the pencil of the soul that pictures heavenly things.

Thomas Burbridge

"God, if you ever want a man in my life, you will have to put him there. In fact, he will have to be standing at my front door wearing a T-shirt that says you sent him." Those words, spoken from bitterness and disappointment for the crushed relationships in my life, stated exactly how I felt about men, as a single mother.

Years passed, and my busy life centered around church, my four sons and my job. My parents lived out of state, so our church became our family.

Slowly, I turned all my joys, heartaches and triumphs over to God.

During those healing years, my youngest son established a friendship with a man who assisted our youth music minister. Dean was a quiet, somber man, but one who lived a life modeled after our Lord. He urged youth to find their identity through God's unfailing love. I admired Dean's patience, understanding and giving ways. More so, I appreciated his friendship with my sons.

At first I felt suspicious of him spending time and effort on them, and I researched his background to ensure my sons' safety and well-being. He received glowing reports for his integrity and devotion to God. I decided he had been sent to fill the void in my sons' lives and to be the role model they so desperately needed.

Over the next year and a half, Dean spent more and more time with them. He took the youngest to Cancún during Christmas break and took two of them to Branson, Missouri, shortly afterwards. He purchased one of the boys a car so he could take a part-time job. Dean showed him how to pay for gas and insurance and still have spending money. He listened to my sons' escapades and problems, and he never judged or condemned their behavior. He and I were great friends. I felt no threat because Dean was twelve years younger than I.

One summer day the doorbell rang. Dean stood in the doorway wearing a T-shirt with the logo "God Listens." At that moment I remembered the words I had uttered years before. I felt the color rise to my cheeks, and my stomach knotted. Dean handed me five additional shirts with the same "God Listens" logo printed on the front.

"I got these at the Christian bookstore, and there's one for each of you," he said.

All I could think of was, *Oh no, Lord, not Dean. He's not the right one. He's too young, and he's—well, he's my friend.* Naturally, I said nothing, but thereafter the "God Listens" logo haunted me. I attempted to rationalize the entire incident, and I asked God to handle the matter for me. He did.

Two months later, Dean proposed. The boys were excited, and I realized how happy our lives had become since he first began a relationship with us. Still, I felt nervous and fearful of being hurt again.

Dean and I talked a great deal about a Christian marriage

and the value of open communication. We made a budget, attended premarital classes, prayed together and talked about our future.

Neither of us had family nearby, so my sons and a few close friends were all we wanted to attend the ceremony. We scheduled the wedding for ten o'clock on a November morning. Shortly before 9:30, the boys and I drove to the church where one of Dean's friends waited outside to video the whole thing. I'm not very comfortable in front of a camera, but I tried to relax and act normal—whatever that is.

Once inside I stared amazed at the number of friends who had come to share in our vows. My best friend, my sons and I stood in an empty office while a photographer snapped various poses of us. Of course, the video rolled on.

Promptly at ten, the pastor stepped in and announced it was time for the wedding. We walked down the hallway to find even more friends waiting.

But Dean did not stand among them.

The pastor reached inside his suit pocket and produced a folded piece of paper. "Dean could not be with us this morning, but he did leave a letter for DiAnn."

A hush fell over the room, and I teetered between hysterics and sheer bewilderment. *Why couldn't the pastor have pulled me aside to break the news?* My heart pounded furiously as I stood there in total humiliation and disappointment. Too stunned to even utter a protest, I watched in horror while the pastor unfolded the letter. Suddenly, the thought of fainting held merit. If only I could stop him—but it was too late.

With heartfelt words, Dean began his letter explaining how he had gradually fallen in love with each member of my family. He stated how his friendship with me had grown from admiration to a deep love. His first love was

Jesus, and he knew I shared the same feelings. Together we would establish a loving, Christian marriage and realize the blessings of our Lord. His love and commitment extended to my sons as well.

The letter concluded that he waited for us at a secret destination. There, he awaited me at the altar.

The pastor tucked the letter back inside his suit coat and escorted me to a church bus. I didn't know what to say for fear the lump in my throat would explode into a pool of tears. *Where could Dean be?*

We boarded a church bus, with the video still filming my every emotion, while I searched futilely for a possible wedding location. Each time I thought I knew where Dean intended to meet me, the bus drove right on by. We continued driving, and my mind raced with the possibilities. Then the bus turned into a lovely subdivision. There stood my husband-to-be in front of a beautiful and spacious new home. In the front yard, a sign leaned against a huge pine tree. It read: *The Mills Residence, established November 24, 1993.*

Inside, in the dining room, I found a wedding cake and food for all our friends. Candles and baskets of pink flowers surrounded a kneeling bench in front of a marble fireplace. Dean stood there, arms outstretched. A black grand piano filled the room with the music of love.

Dean's T-shirt had been right—God does listen.

DiAnn G. Mills
Submitted by Linda Evans Shepherd

"I truly believe that if we were meant to be, there would be a sign from the heavens."

A Thousand Ways

God has a thousand ways where I can see not one,
When all my means have reached their end,
Then His have just begun.

Esther Guyot

Heavy snow fell outside the home of Dick Osborn's parents in Boise, Idaho. Dick sat quietly in his room brooding about a dating relationship that had ended. Reaching for his Bible, he read Proverbs 16:33: "The lot is cast into the lap, but its every decision is from the Lord."

Normally Dick wasn't the type to give God an ultimatum, but this particular evening, he felt lonely and depressed thinking about his ex-girlfriend, Sandy. He reached in his pocket for a quarter and flipped it up in the air, saying, "Lord, if it lands heads up, I will get back with Sandy and marry her someday. If it doesn't, I know that isn't your will." The coin landed *tails* up.

"No, Lord," Dick said, "that's not the right answer. Let's go two out of three." He tossed the coin into the air once more, and it landed *tails* up again. After the fourth time, Dick groaned, "Well, this is just a bunch of hokey anyway."

Glancing around the room, Dick's gaze fell on a magazine lying upside down on the rug. On the back was an advertisement for the book *Parables for Young Teens.* He pleaded, "Lord, who am I going to marry, then?" Staring at the book's picture, he read the author's name and said, "Susan F. Titus?" Again, he flipped his coin up in the air, but this time it landed *heads* up.

"Well, that just proves that this really is a bunch of hokey. I don't even know anyone named Susan F. Titus, let alone what state she's in. How could I possibly marry her?" He soon forgot the incident and tried to move on in his life.

Months later, Dick sat laughing and talking with his church group.

"The thing I miss most from my previous marriage is the baseball tickets to the California Angels," one young woman said.

"It happens that I've got season tickets to a box seat. Maybe we can go sometime," Dick said.

She whispered discretely, "I'd like to, but I'm dating someone."

Dick smiled and responded glibly, "Let me know if you ever change your mind."

Several months later, Dick was disappointed to learn that his old girlfriend, Sandy, was engaged to someone else. The following Sunday he walked with his baseball-fan friend from the church sanctuary to the parking lot. She stopped and said, "Dick, remember what you said about my telling you if I ever changed my mind about going out with you?"

"Yeah."

"Well, I'd like to."

A smile lit his face. "Okay."

They had lunch the following Wednesday, and soon their romance blossomed. Before long, they were engaged.

One day, while Dick was carrying some of her son's things upstairs, he noticed a framed poster hanging on the hallway wall, which read: *Parables for Young Teens by Susan F. Titus.*

He stared openmouthed, then turned to his fiancée. "Sue, did you write that book?"

"Yes," she answered. "Why else would I have it hanging on my wall?"

He didn't respond, but just stared incredulously.

Later on their honeymoon, one evening Dick squeezed Susan's hand and said, "I have a story to tell you, and you're going to find it hard to believe. " Before he started the story, however, Dick took a coin from his pocket and flipped it. "Heads. I won," he said, and then he began.

Susan Titus Osborn
submitted by Linda Evans Shepherd

A Special Lady

We must take our troubles to the Lord, but we must do more than that; we must leave them there.

Hannah Whitall Smith

I rushed out of the feed store, eager to get home, when I heard her. "Wheee . . . eee . . . eee!" I turned to see a darling little filly in a small, fenced-in area in the parking lot. It seemed cruel to keep this beautiful animal penned up in a four-by-nine stall. Drawn by her beauty, I walked over to her. Her soft, warm nuzzle against my bare arm that hot summer day almost made me cry.

"Hi! You're a pretty lady!" I rubbed her nose and she immediately responded with a series of neighs that seemed to say, "Buy me . . . eee . . . eee."

I hurried home and tried to go about my business as usual, but I kept hearing an echo in my thoughts. "Love me . . . eee . . . eee."

About this time, I had begun to seek a closer walk with God. I had a yearning in my heart to know God in a deeper way. My husband, Emmitt, did not understand my new commitment and worried I'd go "overboard with religion."

Dear Lord, I prayed, *please don't let me turn Emmitt away from You. Draw him toward You. More than anything in the world, I want him to love You with all his heart.*

I took Emmitt to see the horse, which I already called "Lady" in my thoughts. Emmitt had a very tender spot for animals, especially horses, and we bought her right on the spot!

Since we lived at the edge of town and had an acre of backyard, we thought caring for her at home had more advantages than taking her to our small farm. Emmitt never admitted how much he cared for Lady, but I caught him many times talking to her from the window. He spent all of his extra time outside with her. He curried her mane and tail and led her around the backyard with her halter. When he took her halter off, she followed him anyway. Lady became a privileged character, and she knew it. She ran around inside the yard with the dogs, shaking her beautiful head and prancing like a circus pony.

One day I found her chasing cars with the dogs. *Oh no! She thinks she's a dog!* I thought. We kept our animals safely enclosed inside a chain-link fence, but Lady and the dogs ran the length of the fence every time a car went by.

As we loved, enjoyed and laughed at our playful filly, she grew into a very beautiful animal. Summer came, and she ate everything that grew through the chain-link fence—and everything she could reach over it. Rose bushes, trees—nothing within her reach was safe. The last straw occurred when she pulled the window screen off the bedroom window. She peeped in and called, "Whee . . . eee . . . eee."

I finally persuaded Emmitt to take Lady to the farm. Although he couldn't spend as much time with her there, my yard improved considerably.

What a thrill to see her in her newfound freedom. She

held her magnificent head and tail high and ran like a racehorse.

Then it happened. Emmitt came home from the farm with sorrow written all over his face. "Lady's suddenly gone lame. I can't figure out what happened. She was all right this morning. The vet just left and he can't find anything wrong."

I'll admit that at times I had been a bit jealous of Lady because Emmitt spent so much time with her. But the thought of her hopping around on three legs made my heart ache, too.

Three weeks later, after shots, liniment rubs and many anxious moments, she had not improved at all.

I am always amazed at God's perfect timing. A friend just "happened" to loan me a tape about a man who prayed for his horse, and the horse got well. We listened intently to the tape and discovered that God cares about what we care about, even animals. Emmitt immediately lost all of his inhibitions.

"Come on," he shouted, jumping up. "We're going to the farm right now and pray for Lady!"

It was a balmy summer night. The moonlight reflected on Lady, and the three of us seemed to sense the awesome beauty and wonder of God. A myriad of stars twinkled overhead, and the distant cooing of doves gave the midnight peace a holy hush. Lady neighed to us in her usual way as we walked up to her. She put her velvety soft nose against Emmitt's shirt and stood motionless on three legs.

Then Emmitt poured out his heart to God. I sobbed, knowing that no matter how God chose to answer Emmitt's prayer for Lady, He had begun a new work in Emmitt's life.

"Thank You, Lord," he prayed aloud, "for showing me how real You are. Whether You heal Lady or not, my life will never be the same. And how I praise You for that!"

From that moment on, I had a brand-new husband. He awakened the next morning with a new zest for living, grateful for everything in this wonderful world that our God has made. We could hardly wait to get to the farm. As we pulled into the gate I saw Lady, still hobbling around on three legs. I hurt most of all for Emmitt's sake.

"I don't care if Lady is crippled the rest of her life, I praise God for everything!" he said.

I silently shot up a prayer of thanksgiving as Emmitt expressed his newfound faith to me.

It was a gorgeous day at the farm. Lady neighed to us in her loving way. Even the birds seemed to say, "Bless you!"

"No use keeping Lady shut up in the lot like this. I'll open the gate. At least maybe she can limp around and eat a little green grass."

The instant Emmitt opened the gate, something seemed to quicken in Lady.

She shot out of that gate with her head and tail held high, running like the wind! A racing thoroughbred could not compare with Lady's beauty. She galloped the full length of the pasture and back to us on four strong, sturdy legs.

It was then that I looked at my husband. I shall never forget the scene. Tears streamed down his face and his arms stretched toward Heaven in thanksgiving. My heart leapt; the feelings I felt for this man overwhelmed me and I loved him more than ever.

Not only had God answered Emmitt's prayer for Lady, He had answered my prayer for Emmitt.

Lady foaled last spring. Her baby is another darling. Many people have wanted to buy Lady, but Emmitt just smiles. "She's not for sale. She's a very unusual horse, and God meant her just for me. Let me tell you about it!"

Joan Clayton

Living on the Ledge

Three months before my husband, Mel, was diagnosed with terminal lung cancer, we went on vacation to Glacier National Park in Montana, a place I had wanted to see since I was ten years old.

Within six months, my husband of thirty-five years was dead, and I was left with a shattered heart. Before he died, I made him promise that he would somehow let me know he was with God and that he was with me in spirit. I had his body cremated, knowing that someday I'd want to put his ashes down in Montana. I dreamed of one day having the courage to go back without him at my side. Mel had always believed I could do anything. He was always encouraging, always cheering me on to greater heights, but I never had his faith in me. How could I possibly do this alone now?

Two-and-one-half years passed before I could call the funeral home and arrange to pick up his ashes. Another six months went by before I could muster the courage to arrange a trip with Elderhostel to return to Glacier.

When we finally assembled at Big Creek for the first day of hiking, every one of the seventeen mountain hikers was experienced—except me. I was a flatlander who had walked only at sea level all her life. If I had known what hiking in the Rocky Mountains was like, I never would have signed up. I just knew I was going to die on those mountain ledges. Every step of the hike, I kept saying over and over, *I can do all things through Christ who strengthens me.* By lunchtime I was sitting on the top of a mountain peak, looking down at Two Medicine Lake on one side and a wide prairie on the other.

After lunch we continued climbing with an elevation gain of 2,300 feet in just three miles—and a temperature of at least 95 degrees. One of the most empowering moments of my entire life was when I reached the summit and finished in the top ten. I felt energized with faith, and I knew that with God's help, and the memory of Mel's faith in me, I could face any challenge life had to offer.

Of course, then I had to hike back down—but that's another story.

I had previously arranged with the director of Elderhostel in Montana to put down my husband's ashes. After four days of classes and hiking, the time and the place were set, and eight of the eleven women on the hike wanted to be part of the ceremony.

On Thursday, July 12, the same date that Mel and I had visited Glacier, the group went for our final hike together. The trail was twelve miles long at 6,700 feet. The last four miles descended 2,400 feet to our pickup point. We literally traversed the Continental Divide and the scenery was spectacular. When we returned to camp, however, I wondered how any of us would have the strength to carry out the plans for that evening's ceremony. To make matters worse, for the first time that week it had started to rain. I checked with the instructor after dinner, and she agreed we should carry on as planned, but take our umbrellas.

We met on the banks of the creek that eventually flowed into Glacier National Park, where I wanted the ashes to end up. The banks were too steep, and I knew I would slip if I tried to go down to the water's edge. I suggested that we go farther down the road to a clearing I had been to the night before.

As we approached the clearing, a large deer stood looking at us. Mel had had a fascination with deer and he often took me to watch them. I knew then that Mel was there with me and that I had chosen the right place. The deer retreated back into the forest, and we all gathered into a circle just a few feet from the creek's rocky edge. As we joined hands and closed our eyes, the instructor told everyone how important this week had been for me, that Glacier was the last vacation spot for me and Mel, and that, after several difficult years, I was putting the past behind me. She remarked that although life was a challenge, I could do anything I set my mind to do—even hike twenty-six miles in the Rockies at 7,000 feet.

We opened our eyes and the instructor, who was standing across from me, told me to slowly turn around. I turned and looked straight into the eyes of the same deer standing about twenty feet away. After it saw me, it retreated into the woods. We were all flabbergasted. At the next moment, the woman on my left told me to look to my right. At that moment, the sun came out and everything turned golden. There below the mountains, between two trees and stretched across the creek, was the loveliest rainbow I have ever seen.

I finally collected myself enough to open the black box with the ashes, walk out into the creek and put them into the water. But it was nearly anticlimactic as I watched them flow down the stream to Glacier National Park.

Denise Mizell

Startled by a Dream

He settles the barren woman in her home as a happy mother of children.

Psalm 113:9

I woke from a restful sleep and lay in bed thinking about the day ahead. Soon I drifted off again and dreamed: A teenage boy who looked about fourteen years old sat at a large cherry wood desk, concentrating on a book. Though I had never met him, I felt a sense of intimacy and familiarity with him. Then the Lord spoke: "This is your son."

Startled by this message, I moved in to get a closer look at this studious young boy with brown hair and glasses. The Lord spoke again. "I have a plan, a special purpose for him."

Then a feeling like cold water hit my face and I woke.

I shook my husband. "Stan, we're going to have a baby, a son!"

"Huh?" he said and rolled over, unimpressed. But as I thought about the dream, seeds of hope grew in my heart.

At forty-two, despite major surgery and other medical

interventions, I had never been able to conceive. My husband had two grown children, but not having a child of my own grieved me.

My husband and I directed a ranch at Vista, California, for street men from Los Angeles trying to get their lives back together. Part of the summer program included a camp for kids. Under close supervision, teenage counselors shared kitchen duty with the street men.

One day, Jack, a thirty-year-old former Los Angeles street gang leader and drug addict, told us about a sixteen-year-old junior counselor named Robert who shared kitchen responsibilities with him. Robert's foster mother, exasperated by her inability to control him, abandoned him at the ranch. Since she suspected he stole and lied, she turned him over to the police and they hauled him off to a boy's detention home.

Jack pleaded with us. "Robert's mother abandoned him at age eleven. He has been shuffled from home to home since then. He needs a stable place. Please take this boy in, otherwise he will end up like me. I want him to have a better chance than I did."

Our hearts went out to Jack and Robert, but homes for troubled teenagers are almost nonexistent. The staff at the ranch prayed and searched for a month but nothing happened. Jack persisted. "How can you not take care of him when you call yourselves Christians?"

My husband became convinced that God wanted us to take Robert into our home. I didn't have parenting experience. I wanted to start out with a baby, not a teenager. Additionally, I battled chronic fatigue syndrome. I didn't think I had the strength to handle the challenge of a teenager, let alone an abused and troubled one.

Finally, after discussing my fears with my husband, I prayed. *Lord, if this is Your will, then I will yield to it. I know that every path You lead us on is fragrant with Your loving kindness and truth, even if it is a hard path. I don't want to miss the blessing You have in mind.*

One week after this prayer of surrender, we took Robert in. We faced many challenges working through his problems with him, but ultimately we adopted him. A few months after the adoption, I remembered my dream and wondered if this was the son it had promised.

Robert grew up, married and became the proud father of two little girls. Two years after he left home we thought about adopting another child. We had learned a great deal during the difficult challenge of raising Robert, and he was worth it. After what we had been through with him, we thought we could handle anyone!

We asked the Lord to show us if He wanted us to have more children. Few people adopt older children, yet these older kids yearn for the love of a family as much as the younger ones. We contacted a Christian international adoption agency since we learned that some foreign countries have fewer time and age restrictions. Since my husband is fifteen years older than I, we decided to explore this option, and they accepted us. Three weeks later, they sent us a picture and information about Alex, a fourteen-year-old boy from Brazil.

Alex had a tough background. His father had abandoned him at birth and his mother had abused him and later abandoned him. Despite these negative influences, he had many good characteristics, such as being caring, considerate, a good student and cooperative.

We decided to adopt him—and then the mountain of paperwork began. When we discovered the costs of an international adoption, we blanched. We did not have those kinds of resources.

Discouraged, we talked with a friend who had adopted two older children. She adamantly told us, "Don't let the lack of money stop you. God has ways of providing. Go forward. Begin the process with what you have."

So we began the adoption process, trusting God to provide. Through a series of miracles, and help from others, God made a way for us.

After six months of paperwork, we received approval and flew to Brazil to claim our son. We arrived at the airport and hastened to the courthouse. I wondered how long it would be before we met Alex. A thousand questions went through my head. *Is this really God's will for all of us? Are we sure this is the right boy for us—and are we right for him? Will we bond? Will he like us? Will we like him? How will we manage to communicate with the language barrier?*

Finally, after lengthy preliminary visits with the social worker and psychologist, they ushered Alex in. He anxiously hugged us and sat down. We talked through an interpreter for forty-five minutes and then we all rose to leave. My husband and the social worker walked out of the room ahead of me. As Alex got up to leave, he put on his glasses for the first time. I gasped. Stunned, I ran out of the room to catch up with my husband. I blurted, "It's him! Alex is the boy in the dream I had years ago!"

During our stay in Brazil, as the three of us spent time with one another, our hearts knit together, and we became a family. About a month later, back in the states, a friend who spoke Portuguese asked Alex, "Weren't you worried that you were nearly sixteen, the cutoff age for international adoptions, and hadn't been adopted yet?"

Alex said, "No. I told Jesus the kind of parents I wanted, and He gave them to me."

Sharon Gibson

"I'm lucky. When I was a baby, I got to pick out my parents. I'm adopted."

Hanging On to Hope

Be strong and take heart, all you who hope in the Lord.

Psalm 31:24

I was thrilled to be pregnant within the first year of our marriage. My husband, Russ, and I were so excited, we went out to a department store the night we found out and bought two little shirts. We were certain it was going to be a boy.

But our excitement was short-lived. The pregnancy ended in a miscarriage after three months. Following doctor's orders, we waited six months and tried again. This time, the pregnancy made it past the first trimester. It made it to the second and then the third trimester. It made it all the way to a week before my due date, but then, during a routine examination, the doctor failed to pick up the baby's heartbeat. I was admitted to the hospital where labor was induced, and after spending most of the night in labor, I finally delivered a ten-pound, two-ounce stillborn son.

We named the baby Hugh Leon, and although we

received cards, flowers and words of encouragement, unless someone's been there, there's no way to describe the overwhelming disappointment and grief a stillbirth can bring. Realizing that losses like this either make or break a marriage, we leaned on each other. And we leaned on God.

They say time heals all wounds, but being inundated with advertisements for everything from diaper services to baby insurance seemed to slow the healing process. I packed away all the brochures and samples, believing that someday we would use them.

The next several months were spent applying to every adoption agency we could find. They all had waiting lists longer than the *Congressional Record,* so we did the only thing we could do—we applied and we waited.

After several discouraging years, we decided to take a step of faith. Believing that God would give us a family someday, we moved from our two-bedroom home into a four-bedroom one. We didn't know when God was going to answer our prayers and fill the extra bedrooms, but we knew He would. Someday.

When I called the adoption agencies to give them our new address, several of them informed me that since our move had taken us out of their area, they would drop us from their waiting list. We were stunned. Our hopes crashed and burned before our eyes. Were we going to have to start all over again? Had our giant step of faith turned into a giant step backward?

We had been in our new home one week, and we were still living with wall-to-wall boxes. We decided to start fixing up the nursery first, thinking it would be the easiest room to arrange. We hung baby clothes, moved furniture around and nailed up wall decorations. It seemed a bit futile to spend so much time arranging a room that wasn't being used, but we were driven to finish it. Russ was driven until midnight. Then, because he had to go to work early the next day, I stayed up to complete the job—although I ended up doing more crying than unpacking.

I couldn't understand why God was allowing this ongoing tragedy in our lives. At two o'clock in the morning I finally decided to "give up." I'd been blaming God since the stillbirth, and I was tired of being bitter and hurt and angry. After a few more hours of licking my wounds and being mad at Him, I finally surrendered. I knew I couldn't go on harboring bitterness and resentment. He had a plan for our lives, even if it wasn't our plan. I vowed I would remain faithful to God even if He didn't answer our prayers for a baby. Then I went to bed, feeling at peace for the first time in a long while.

At six A.M. the phone rang. It was one of the adoption agencies. I thought they were calling to get our new address to update their records, but they told me they had a three-week-old baby boy waiting for us. All I could do was cry and jump up and down on the bed, waking my husband!

We named our son Russ II, after my husband, and within the next few years, we adopted a second son, Matt—when I was six months pregnant. Our third son, Tony Shane, was born three-and-a-half months later. Two years after moving into our new home, God had filled every bedroom.

Our step of faith turned out to be a step forward after all.

Martha Bolton

The Egg

I know no blessing so small as to be responsibly expected without prayer, nor any so great but may be attained by it.

Robert South

It was a tense day around our home. That morning, when my daughters, Becky and Lisa, returned from an overnight outing with their Sunday school class, they discovered that the egg their pair of pigeons had been sitting on was missing. A quick check around the outside of the cage had revealed pieces of the egg—someone had broken it and tried to hide it.

It didn't take a detective to guess that the culprit was four-year-old Hailey. The pigeons had fascinated her. She hadn't realized that the egg had been a developing baby bird. To her it was just a smaller version of what I cracked and cooked every day.

That night Hailey approached her sister Becky. "I'm sorry, Becky," she said. "I prayed to God tonight and asked Him to bring you another egg. I told Him I wouldn't touch it this time."

"Yeah, right," Becky quietly responded as she turned and headed to her room. She was not ready to forgive.

In a few moments Becky was back. "Momma, you're not going to believe this." She was speaking to me but staring at Hailey. "There's an egg in the cage. It wasn't there before." She couldn't say aloud the thought that was racing through her mind.

But Hailey did. "Becky, I told you. I prayed to God, and God laid an egg."

Dorothy M. Hill

It Can Happen

Hope is the thing with feathers, that perches in the soul and sings the tune without words, and never stops at all.

Emily Dickinson

The mechanic made his prognosis, patting the van as if it were a sick dog. The ailing transmission would take eight-hundred dollars of our hard-earned vacation fund. I was more than disappointed. We had scrimped for months to earn money for our first "big" vacation. This trip wasn't going to be the usual campouts at local lakes or theme parks with wild rides and sticky cotton candy. This was a special trip born of wishes.

The family newsletter had announced the reunion in Tehajapi, California. I laid it in the cast-off pile of old bills. It just wasn't possible. I had been sick the year before, and the treatment had taken every spare penny. Cancer did not come cheap.

My husband found the newsletter. "Are we going?" he asked.

"I wish," I said, teasing back.

He pulled me tight. "It can happen."

Somehow it did. We saved the money.

Disappointment choked me as I wrote the mechanic's check. We told our kids the bad news. They were becoming champions of receiving hard facts. They begged us to try again. "We'll help, Mom," they pleaded.

The teamwork began. My husband and I both worked overtime. We held the world's fastest garage sale. We sold everything but the dog and the kids. Somehow, once again, we raised the money.

On the day of departure, the kids secured their seatbelts, their excitement barely contained. We sang as we pulled out of the driveway. Thirty minutes into our journey, the van sputtered—a red light flashed—and everything went dead.

We stood on the highway like mourners at a funeral. My children held back tears and I said good-bye to my California dream. We called a tow truck and rode in the front seat, our hopes towed behind us.

This wasn't fair.

As we pulled in our driveway, we passed the little red Tercel I used in my daily commute to work. We unpacked the van. The stack was easily as tall as I was. I kept looking over at the little red car. *Was it possible?* My husband followed my gaze. He shook his head. How could we fit two adults, three kids, six pieces of luggage and a cooler in a car designed to fit two adults, one kid and a map?

"It can happen," I said. The kids cheered.

In two hours, we pared our luggage down to three suitcases. A neighbor found a shell that we anchored onto the top of the small car. We packed every nook until we had it right. I now knew how a sardine in a can felt, all snug and tight. We moved the sign from the van, taping it in the back window of the Tercel: *California or Bust* now had a whole new meaning.

We rotated seating as adults took their turns in the back. I found out what real leg cramps felt like—man-sized leg cramps. I sat by my son on all my rotations. When my daughters had complained about sitting next to him, I'd said, "He's not that bad." Now I changed my mind. His sharp elbow poked me in my side and once in my eye.

"Can't you sit still?" I asked. One daughter giggled in the front seat. The other snuggled quietly against my side.

We must have been a ridiculous sight on our frequent stops—like clowns emerging from a circus car. I unfolded from the back seat, decompressed my spine, brushed crumbs from my clothes and walked like an old lady for the first few minutes.

It was easily the best trip we've ever taken. We picnicked on the side of the road in several states. We saw the world's largest thermometer and ball of twine. It was summertime, but we played in the snow at the highest elevations in the Colorado mountains. The closeness of the car forced us to abide by the rules for avoiding bloodshed: Be nice; no body noises; definitely no body smells. The kids were especially good. I believe they would have ridden unicycles if it meant we could go on this trip.

As we pulled into the reunion, my relatives gaped. *They had come all the way in that?* I hugged people who looked like me. My parents, brothers and sisters joined us, fresh and rested from their plane trip.

Sissies, I thought.

When it was time to leave, relatives shook their heads in dismay. We grinned, winking at each other. We were veterans of small car travel.

Fifteen hundred miles later, we arrived home, happy and tanned. My sleeping son pressed into my shoulder, his elbow sticking in my ear.

"We're here," I said, shaking the kids gently. They stumbled into bed with contented smiles on their faces.

I went outside and patted the little red car, loaded down like a pack mule. I thought about all the obstacles that had been thrown in our path during the past week—and especially the past year. They had been challenges, financially and emotionally. This trip reminded me of God's grace through those times. It seemed that the darker things became, the more God shined. My busy life had been altered and my faith challenged, but there was a peace that could only come from God.

Contented and happy, I headed in. "It *can* happen," I whispered to myself.

T. Suzanne Eller

"Remember the safety rules: Stay buckled up and don't say, 'How much farther, Daddy?'"

The Wedding

A block of granite which was an obstacle in the pathway of the weak becomes a stepping stone in the pathway of the strong.

Thomas Carlyle

Jack and Jean were among our earliest friends when I began ministry in my very first church as full-time pastor. Their friendly faces and warm smiles were a great encouragement to a young preacher with the Sunday morning pulpit jitters. The smiles were genuine, and that was a surprise to me. They had been through more trials than almost anyone I'd known.

Jack had been a chemist with a successful company. Over a period of ten years, a diagnosis of severe rheumatoid arthritis took Jack from being a healthy workingman to someone confined to a wheelchair and living on a disability pension. By the time I met him, he could move himself from the wheelchair only with great difficulty, and then, only to shift to another chair, or to stand for a moment. Pain and effort showed in his face when making these transitions, which were usually few and far between.

He and Jean got around well in a new van, converted for the wheelchair. A small elevator installed in their townhouse moved Jack between the floors, and despite his misshapen, arthritis-bent fingers, he learned to use a computer and assisted us at the church with some of our financial work.

Through Jack and Jean, I came to know their now-adult daughters. When Susan, the eldest, arrived at my office to ask me to perform a wedding for her and her fiancé, Eric, it was no great surprise. Her father had hinted only a few weeks earlier that this might be coming.

The counseling and the planning of the ceremony seemed to go by very quickly, and soon it was almost time for the wedding. One day Susan made an unscheduled stop at my office. From the look on her face, I knew that something was seriously wrong. She came straight to the point. "My dad wants to walk me down the aisle," she said, close to tears. "He really thinks he can do it. He absolutely insists on it."

"I'll practice until the wedding. I'm going to do this," he told me adamantly while we sat at his kitchen table drinking tea the next day. "Please pray for me!" I knew there was no changing his mind when he was determined to do something, and so I let the subject drop. I did, however, pray.

When the evening of the rehearsal arrived, we set up several scenarios which would allow Jack to "present" the bride. Only one of the three involved him walking, and we included it only to please Jack. A brief experiment that evening seemed to deflate Jack's determination as he only took a few steps before he had to sit back down. From the platform, I watched sadly as he hung his head where he sat. Again I prayed.

The wedding day arrived. Everything was going as planned. At the top of the hour, I found myself standing on the steps of the platform with groom and groomsmen awaiting the bridal party.

The music began playing and the bridesmaids proceeded down the aisle. Each paused and turned as they passed the front row of pews and took her place opposite the groomsmen. The maid of honor was last to walk and as she turned in her appointed position, the music softly concluded.

After a brief pause, the organist played the dramatic opening notes of the wedding march. "Will you all please stand," I instructed.

I found myself thinking of Jack. He had been brought up the steps to the sanctuary earlier, and now waited in the wheelchair by the door. With the struggles of the previous evening still in mind, I was sure that Jack would not be walking the aisle today. I was disappointed for his sake, but I couldn't imagine his hurt. This had meant so much to him.

The doors to the church sanctuary opened to the side at the rear. This meant that the bride would have to walk behind the last row of pews before turning into the center aisle. I could just make out Susan's progress above the heads of the now standing congregation because of the puff of white taffeta that stood up from her veil.

I saw that puff of white stop, and then murmuring began near the back of the church. A moment later, the beautiful bride made her turn into the main aisle. It took a second to realize what was happening. Susan was being escorted by her father, and he was walking!

Slowly, and painfully, Jack took a few steps and then paused to catch his breath. With a cane in his left hand and her arm on his right, father and daughter moved toward me. It seemed as if the entire congregation was holding its collective breath, all of us fearing that the next step would be the last. I believe, in that moment, that we were all unified in prayer for Jack.

The organist looked at me with panic in her eyes as the music came close to its conclusion. I motioned for her to continue playing, and a few more minutes inched past before the bride and her father finally arrived at the front.

As the music concluded, I quickly gathered my thoughts. Still awestruck, I voiced a rather shaky introduction. I almost choked up when I asked, "Who presents this woman to be married to this man?" Jack's voice came back clear and strong, and not without some measure of pride: "Her mother and I do."

As Susan hugged her father and then took her place alongside her soon-to-be husband, I noticed that her face was wet with tears. I noticed my own face was wet. In fact, it seemed like the whole congregation had been deeply moved.

The wedding reception which followed was a wonderful affair. It was one of the grandest I had ever attended. But whatever the charm or excitement of the post-wedding celebration, the highlight of the day, in everyone's eyes, remained the miracle we had witnessed shortly before. The miracle of Jack, with determination born of love, and with faith in the living God, escorting his daughter down the aisle on her wedding day!

No truer words express the miracle of that day as those written in Mark 10:27: "With man this is impossible, but not with God; all things are possible with God."

John P. Walker

Bringing It to Pass, Football and All

If you believe, you will receive whatever you ask for in prayer.

Matthew 21:22

It was a crisp fall day in Madison, Wisconsin, when our University of Wisconsin football team defeated the University of Illinois in the final Big Ten Conference home game of the season. Now Wisconsin was headed to the Hall of Fame Bowl in Tampa, Florida, over the Christmas holidays. My twenty-two-year-old son, Michael, a senior at University of Wisconsin at Madison, was a four-year member of their marching band, famous for their wildly entertaining high-stepping antics that dazzled crowds.

I'd desperately wanted to go to the Rose Bowl game the year before to watch him perform, but the trip was too expensive. I didn't know anyone in Pasadena to stay with, and airfare was out of the question. On New Year's Day 1994, my house was full of relatives as we all watched Michael on TV. He played his drums with such precision during the Rose Bowl parade and game that my heart nearly burst with excitement and pride.

When the Wisconsin Badgers won the right to play in the Hall of Fame Bowl the very next season, I realized that that game would be Michael's last time ever to march with the band before he graduated. I had to be there. Right!—a single parent with a small income and bigger-than-life dreams; that's me.

In late November I mentioned my dream to my airline pilot friends who use the extra bedrooms in our home as their Milwaukee-area home away from home. One said he had a couple of low-cost "friend" passes that my fifteen-year-old son Andrew and I could use to get to Tampa and back.

"The passes are only about ninety dollars each, round-trip," he said. "But you'll have to fly standby."

I jumped at the chance as he set things in motion. Next, I had to find housing. I looked on the map and saw that our retired friends, Wally and Shirley, lived just forty-five minutes from Tampa. I was sure they'd put us up for the week in their Florida condo.

Everything seemed to be working smoothly until I called my dad in Illinois to tell him the good news. Dad planted my feet back on the ground when he said, "You're going to Florida between Christmas and New Year's? That's the busiest tourist week of the year down there! And you're flying standby? What do you think your chances are of getting on a plane that week?"

My bubble of optimism burst again when I heard on the radio that nearly thirty thousand Wisconsinites had already bought tickets to the Hall of Fame Bowl. Our chances of getting down there flying standby certainly didn't look good. In fact, they looked impossible.

Besides, there was another glitch in the plans. The airline we'd be flying on had only one flight a day to Tampa. How could I even think there'd be empty seats on that plane during the week between Christmas and New Year's?

I told myself disgustedly, *How could you be so stupid? This will never work!*

In addition to decorating for Christmas, buying gifts, cleaning house and planning meals for the holidays, I now had an additional stressor in my life.

I commiserated with my friend Heather, who told me, "Pat, stop worrying. Do something for me. Look through the book of Psalms. Read it until you find a verse that seems to be speaking to you."

"Psalms? What am I going to find in there?" I asked Heather.

"Just do it. You'll find what you're looking for."

That afternoon I opened my Bible and read the first two psalms. Nothing hit me. The third verse said something about a tree yielding "its fruit in season," which only depressed me more. It made me think of ruby-red grapefruit and large, juicy oranges hanging on trees all over Florida—fruit that I certainly wouldn't be enjoying.

This can't be the verse that's supposed to make me feel better, I thought. I closed the book and opened it again at random. This time my eyes went directly to Psalms 37:5: "Commit thy way unto the Lord; trust also in Him; and He shall bring it to pass."

Two things about that verse threw me for a loop. The part about committing my way to the Lord—my way to see my son perform in his last game, perhaps? The other was the notion that the Lord would "do this." If I did my part, then God would do His. In other words, if I really, truly trusted in the Lord, then He would bring all things to pass. That was the clincher, since Andrew and I would be flying standby on a "pass."

I thought, *Okay, Patricia, this is it. If Heather can be so deadbolt certain of her faith, why can't you? You have to put it on the line. Do you truly believe that this is in the hands of the Lord and that He will bring it to pass?*

I only had to ask myself that question once. I sat down that moment and memorized verse 37:5. It was the first Bible verse I'd ever memorized in my life. I've been a long-time Bible reader and student, but memorizing is very difficult for me. I chanted the verse at least a hundred times a day during those weeks before Christmas: "Commit thy way unto the Lord; trust also in Him; and He shall bring it to pass."

The minute I turned the problem over to the Lord, I relaxed completely and virtually sailed through the preparations for Christmas.

Never again did I worry about whether or not we'd get on the plane, not even when I learned every flight had been greatly oversold with the exception of Christmas morning. And even for that flight, eighty of the eighty-four seats had been sold, with three weeks still to go before Christmas.

For the next three weeks, I repeated my newly memorized verse a thousand times: before I got out of bed in the morning, before each meal, during the day, in the car, in my home office, walking down the hall, in bed at night. I repeated it to all my friends and family and assured them that Andrew and I would be in Tampa for the Hall of Fame Bowl on January 2, and that we'd be flying down there on Christmas morning.

Christmas Eve day dawned holy and cold in Milwaukee. Andrew, my grown children, son-in-law, granddaughter, and friends Rusty and Heather and their two little daughters, all celebrated Christ's birth amidst my giggling excitement as I packed our bags for Florida. I shared my memorized Bible verse from Psalms with them as part of the grace before our Christmas Eve dinner.

"So Mom, are you just going to keep going back to the airport every day all week until you get on a plane?" my daughter Julia asked during dessert.

"No, honey, we'll be getting on the plane tomorrow morning. I'll send you postcards and bring you seashells!"

Never before in my life had I been so sure of something—something that to all the sensible people around me seemed to be the folly of the century.

Bags packed, car loaded, Michael drove us to the airport at 7:30 A.M. Christmas Day. The gate agent said there'd been four people with emergencies in Florida, and they'd been given priority standby status.

It didn't matter. I knew that when that gate closed we'd be on the plane.

That afternoon, Andrew and I picked grapefruit from the tree next to the hot tub in the backyard of our friends' house in Florida. Nine days later, after sunning ourselves on Gulf beaches, exploring exotic wonders and following the Wisconsin marching band as they performed all over Tampa, we watched as the University of Wisconsin defeated Duke in the Hall of Fame Bowl on a beautiful, sunny, eighty-degree day.

Michael's last performance with the band was stellar.

But not quite as stellar as my faith in the Lord—who brings all things to pass.

Patricia Lorenz

2

THE LOVE OF A FAMILY

Perhaps the greatest social service that can be rendered by anybody to this country and to mankind is to bring up a family.

George Bernard Shaw

You Did Good

My dad grew up during the Depression and later fought in World War II. When he was born, his own father was too old and tired to invest any time in his only child, so my dad learned early on how to work hard and make money. And no matter how bad things might be, my dad always knew how to look strong. In the postwar era, when everyone wanted to erase their horrifying memories and emotions, my father became a master at burying his feelings. After liberating the concentration camps and seeing the worst that any war had to offer, keeping his feelings inside was the only way my dad knew how to survive.

Without realizing it, my dad became domineering and controlling. As a parent, he did anything for his children and worked hard to provide the best for us. However, if he didn't agree with us about something, our feelings didn't interest him; his opinions always prevailed—"case closed." When it was time for emotional intimacy or vulnerability, my father played his cards close to his chest. He kept his feelings locked in a vault that no one, including himself, had the combination to.

Still, despite our being very different emotionally, my dad was my hero.

He was a world-class businessman, a marketing genius, an entrepreneur, a singer and a true visionary. When I was learning how to dream, he taught me how to dream big. "Broaden your horizons, sweetie," he used to say. "There's a whole world out there and nothing's stopping you." I emulated him, quoted him and listened for every nugget of wisdom I could glean from him.

I was a musician, actress and writer. Somehow, those occupations just didn't fit the bill with my father; what I did never seemed to meet his approval. Poetry and songwriting were intangible and involved an area unsafe for him: emotions.

"What are you doing out there in the backyard with your guitar and your journals, anyway?" he would ask me sarcastically when I was younger.

"I'm just writing songs," I answered, trying not to feel ashamed.

"Writing songs? How are you going to earn a living? What are you going to have to fall back on?" he demanded, exasperated.

There were things we could never talk about, things that were painfully left unsaid. I wanted with all my heart to tell my dad what a hero he was to me. I wanted him to understand who I really was. I began to wonder if the reason he couldn't approve of me was that he never really approved of himself. He was so hard on everybody, but he was the hardest and most unforgiving on himself. I tried to crack the door to his heart on many occasions. I tried so hard to share my feelings and create a bond of intimacy, but it was too awkward for him, too frightening. I often sent him sentimental cards and told him I loved him. He would hug me, but then crack a joke and cover it. There was so much that I needed to say to him, but I didn't know how to do it.

One Friday night I came home late for dinner and my son announced, "Grandpa's been trying to call you all day and is waiting for you to call him."

How strange, I thought. It was always my mom who did the long-distance calling while my dad sat in his recliner and read the paper, calling out things that she was supposed to remember to tell "the kids." Why would my dad be trying all day to reach me? I was tired and hungry and thought about calling him in the morning, but decided to dial him then. He answered right away and was relieved to hear from me.

"I've got a problem, sweetie," he said directly, "and I need your advice."

My advice? When had my father ever approached me as an adult for advice?

He was upset about some things going on among our relatives and actually wanted to confide in me about it. I was shocked. He was thoughtful and introspective and it drew me in.

"Oh, I probably shouldn't worry about them," he said trying to appear strong, "but it just drives me crazy."

We talked a long time and as he opened up to me, I felt that door to his heart crack open, something I had waited for my whole life. The more he shared his frustrations and reached out to me, the more I felt I could cross the line and tell him how I really felt.

"Dad," I began. "You know, you're not only a great person, you did a great job as a father. Did I ever tell you that?"

He didn't say anything, but I knew he was listening intently. "You did a great job," I exhorted. "I know you're upset now, but things will work out with everybody. The main thing I just want you to do is to give yourself credit—you never give yourself enough credit, Dad. You sent me to college, you gave me a vision, you supported me."

I'd finally said it.

He laughed good-naturedly. I continued, "I owe you a thank you, and I hope you realize how much you did for me as my dad."

I could almost hear him smiling on the other end. I knew he was touched and felt a little awkward. His voice sounded shaky. "Well, we got you educated," he said, laughing nervously.

"You did more than that," I said. "You did *good*."

"You like your house now, and your life?" he asked quietly, catching me off guard.

"Yeah, Dad, I'm happy. You don't have to worry—things are going great for us."

"That's good," he said, with a sigh of relief. "So everything's okay, then?" he asked, almost as if he were checking it all off a list that would allow him to rest easier.

"Everything's great, Dad."

I told him I loved him and he told me he loved me and I hung up the phone. As I got ready for bed, I thought about what an amazing conversation we had. I was high with the emotional intimacy, which had been long overdue.

Ten hours later, my mother called, waking me. I could hardly understand what she was trying to say.

"Your father's dead!" she screamed. "I found him lying on the dining room floor. He had just opened the drapes to let the sun in, and he fell over dead."

Suddenly I was standing straight up beside my bed, clinging to the phone and sobbing.

"Where are you right now, Mom?"

"I'm sitting here waiting for the police to come."

"Are you there alone?"

"Yes, but the neighbors are on their way over."

I was a thousand miles away. All I could think about was how many hours, minutes and seconds it would take me to jump on a plane and get there. I thought about my mother sitting there alone with my father, and I couldn't move fast enough.

The flight was long and painful, like a slow-motion dream. I had planned on going home to see my dad and mom in another month, and I wept aloud, thinking I was too late. Then I suddenly realized the incredible miracle of it all: I hadn't been late at all. Actually, everything had been right on time.

Carla Riehl

The Plan

In his heart a man plans his course, but the Lord determines his steps.

Proverbs 16:9

Bob and I pulled into Kirksville on a hot summer afternoon. "So what's the plan?" he asked.

"Plan? What plan? I thought *you* had a plan."

"I don't have a plan." He gave me the teasing, big-brother grin. "I thought *you* had a plan!"

We'd come to find our lost forty-five-year-old little brother. Keith had severed all ties with the family five years before. No one knew why. I suspected that when his wife left him without warning, he vowed that his broken heart would never be hurt again, and he let go of everyone he loved, simultaneously.

His absence, however, was breaking my mama's heart. Our mother personified unconditional love, but her letters to Keith were always unanswered and often returned as "addressee unknown."

"Let's start at the Wooden Nickel Café," I suggested. The last word on Keith had been three years ago, when a friend of a friend said he frequented the local café on Main Street. "We can have a late lunch there and ask if and when anyone's seen him. While we're eating, we can make a plan."

"Plan? I thought you had a plan?" Bob teased again.

It was easy to find the Wooden Nickel in the quaint downtown. We walked in and sat at one of the half-dozen tables. As we ordered the home-cooked daily special, we questioned the futility of our escapade.

I had driven from Colorado to Iowa to visit my six brothers and sisters and my mom. While I was there, Bob and I had concocted this day trip to find Keith. Bob's cows had gotten out earlier that morning, however, and by the time he got them back in, we were three hours behind schedule. We had even debated about canceling the four-hour drive altogether. But here we were in Kirksville.

"I'm not kidding myself," Bob said while we had our lunch. He tipped his farm-feed cap back on his head. "I think the chances of finding Keith are slim to none. But maybe we'll at least get some news about him we can share with Mom. There can't be that many independent carpenters in a town this size. We'll just ask around all day and into the night and ask some more tomorrow if we need to." Bob pulled a toothpick out of his denim shirt pocket and chewed on it. "He doesn't want to see us, you know."

"I know," I said glumly. "But we have to try. I can't explain it, Bob. I just know we're supposed to try."

"What'll you say if you see him?" Bob asked.

"I've rehearsed a dozen different things, yet I have no idea. I'm counting on God to give me the right words at the right time."

A kitchen door opened at the rear of the café—and in walked Keith.

I grabbed an open menu and held it in front of my face.

"Oh dear God, Bob! It's Keith!" I hissed. "Don't turn around—he'll see you and I don't know what he'll do!"

Bob stared at me in disbelief. "You're sure it's him?"

"He's thinner than the last time I saw him, his hair is graying, but that's our Keithy."

"He likely won't be glad to see us," Bob whispered.

"What if he runs?"

"He can't run faster than me," Bob smirked.

I looked at Bob's receding gray hairline. "Right."

Keith was carrying on a quiet conversation with the man at the next table. Bob and I decided to wait until Keith's food was served before we approached him—maybe if he was eating, he wouldn't leave.

When the waiter placed a burger and fries in front of Keith, I signaled to Bob: "This is it!" Keith didn't see us get up and walk six steps to his table. I sat next to him, put my arm on his shoulder and said, "Can I buy you lunch?"

Keith turned to see me with shock—almost terror—on his face.

"What are you doing here?" he asked curtly.

"We came to have lunch with you," I said, my heart beating in my temples.

"Nothin' to do on the farm," Bob grinned. "So we decided to take a drive—and find you."

The waitress was obviously confused as she delivered our food to Keith's table. Keith politely introduced us to her and her husband behind the counter. The owners, he said. Then he finally forced a smile and said to me, "How're the kids?"

I began chattering like a chipmunk about our three grown children, adding funny stories of misadventures. These reminded Bob of mischievous antics we shared on the farm and Keith laughed with us as we recounted them.

I ate my sandwich in tiny slow bites, fearing that when the meal ended, so would the moment.

Then I could suppress it no longer. "You seemed to have let us go, and we don't know why. Did any of us say or do anything?"

"No," Keith snapped.

"Christmas isn't the same without you. We miss you so much."

"I don't need that in my life anymore." His voice was terse.

"Mom went to Africa," I beamed.

"No kiddin'?" He smiled again. So I jabbered about tales of Mom bouncing along in a Jeep in Nairobi.

Then I nibbled while he told us about his work. He was remodeling the back room of the café into a bar and lounge. He always ate in the kitchen—he didn't know why he had come into the dining area today.

"Want to see what I do?" he asked.

Proudly he took us through the back kitchen door and into the lounge, filled with saws, lumber and tools. Small strips of inlaid wood fanned in a beautiful pattern on the wall. Bob and I marveled at the mastery of his work as he showed us around.

Too soon Keith said, "Well, I better get to work."

"Can I call you?" I ventured.

"Sure."

"Can I write you?"

"Sure."

With his carpenter's pencil, he scribbled his address and phone number on scratch paper. I wondered if they were true—if I'd ever see him again.

He shook Bob's hand, slapped him on the back, then pulled him into a bear hug.

He kissed me and held me to his chest. As I left the room, I turned to look back and said, "I love you, Keith."

His lips silently mouthed, "And I love you."

As we headed home to tell Mom, Bob and I giggled and laughed.

"I'm so glad your cows got out and we were late, or we'd have missed him!"

"Can you believe he just came walking in there?"

We recounted every word and moment shared with our brother—so grateful that the Mighty Someone had a plan.

LeAnn Thieman

Come to Our House

Whoever welcomes one of these little children in My name welcomes me.

Mark 9:37

I saw them nearly every day from the window of my home office: a young boy and girl passing our home on their way to school. Busy working at my computer, I would look up only to see them trudging by, never seeming to speak a word to each other. The boy appeared to be about eight; the girl slightly older, although it was hard to tell as she always walked with her head down, her long hair sweeping forward to hide her face.

The girl's name was Sarah, I came to discover; the boy's was Matthew. Our daughter Amber relayed this information when she arrived home from fourth grade one day with news to share.

"I have a new friend, Mom! Her name is Sarah and she's in class with me. She's moved in just down the street from us. And guess what? She even has my same birthday!"

The next day Amber arrived home with her new friend in tow. Sarah was a quiet child—too quiet, I feared. When I inquired as to what the girls would like for an after school snack, Sarah looked up from beneath her bangs at Amber, and then quickly echoed Amber's choice. She began to visit us more often and seemed to like coming to our home, but she rarely spoke and she stayed right on Amber's heels at all times. Her brother Matt was a year behind her in school, and sometimes he'd come over as well to play with our two sons. Matt said little, though, and rarely smiled.

Sarah was easily frightened, particularly, she said, when they arrived home only to find no one there. We learned that the children had not seen their father in several years, and the caregivers their mother hired never seemed to last long. After an anxious phone call from Sarah one afternoon, I instructed her to leave a note on the door telling her mother that she had come to our house. "I work at home," I assured her, "and there is almost always someone here. If you are alone and afraid, you just leave a note and come on down to our house anytime."

In the next few years the children visited us often. Then, some trouble in their family caused them to move out of our neighborhood, seventy-five miles away to the city of Boston.

One night we received a frantic phone call from Sarah. The police had come to their house, she sobbed, and her mother had been arrested. After posting bail, her mother had returned to tell the children that they would be leaving the country. Gripped with fear, Sarah hopped on her bike and didn't stop riding until she found a phone booth, where she placed a collect call to our home.

"Sarah, where are you?" my husband queried. "Do you think you can find a police station?"

He heard a long pause, and then a small surprised voice. "I'm right in front of one!"

"Go inside, Sarah, and the officers will help you. We'll be right there!"

Several hours later my husband and daughter arrived in a driving rainstorm to find the two frightened children being cared for by a compassionate police officer and a social worker.

"Kids," explained the officer, "if we have to take your mother away, do you have anywhere to go?"

"When we lived on Cape Cod," Sarah quickly responded, "these were our neighbors and they said that if we were ever alone, we could come to their house." After running a background check on our family, the police released Sarah and Matthew into our custody.

Sarah and Matt did indeed "come to our house," and they stayed for many years. My husband and I went through foster care approval in order to keep the children, and they became full-fledged members of our household, sharing possessions, rooms and yes, even birthdays with our other three children. One year we drove to Florida to visit Sarah and Matt's grandfather. Another year, when all five kids were teenagers, we raised money and the seven of us went to Nairobi, Kenya, to donate our services to a mission school for the summer.

There were difficult times, too. Blending a family is never easy, and the children grieved at times for the life that had been taken from them. For several years we appeared to be on "speed dial" with the principal of their high school, and with four teenagers in braces at one time, we were given our own parking space at the orthodontist's!

There were far more times, however, when we felt incredibly privileged to have been entrusted by God with the care of these additional children. My husband taught Matt how to drive a car and fix a faucet. They climbed a mountain together and talked about what it means to be a man.

As for me, I experienced the joy of buying Sarah her first prom dress—a lovely lavender gown that complimented her slim figure and enhanced the long blonde hair she wore piled high. I taught her cooking and computer skills, and talked with her about what it means to be a woman.

Sarah is in college now, and Matt is finishing high school. When Sarah walks down the street, her body straight and erect and her head held high, she commands attention. Matt is a confident, quick-witted young man who can hold his own in any adult conversation.

Our foster children will soon be on their own, as will our other children. Our home has been a launching pad for all of them—not a permanent resting place. One day we know they will have homes and families of their own. When they do, I trust that someday they will share the story of their growing-up years with their own children. I hope they will tell them that families come together in many ways, and that homes can always stretch to make room for another hand to hold. Most of all, I hope each of our five children will remember that both life and love are for sharing.

Perhaps a needy child will one day walk down the street and through the doors of their hearts as well. I know what they will say: "If you're ever alone, just come to our house."

Maggie Wallem Rowe

"Melanie and Buddy came over here to play 'cause their mommy is readin' a book."

Reprinted with permission of Bil Keane.

Love Lives Forever

Train a child in the way he should go, and when he is old he will not turn from it.

Proverbs 22:6

My mouth felt dry as I followed my mother into the doctor's private office and sank into a padded chair next to hers. This doctor didn't carry a stethoscope. He had a room full of gadgets and gizmos to analyze the learning abilities of failing students. That day he had analyzed me.

He shuffled papers and jabbed his wire frame glasses with a forefinger. "I'm sorry to tell you this, Mrs. Dow, but Peter has dyslexia. A fairly severe case."

I swallowed and tried to breathe. The doctor went on. "He'll never read above the fourth-grade level. Since he won't be able to complete high school requirements, I suggest you enroll him in a trade school where he can learn to work with his hands."

I didn't want to go to trade school. I wanted to be a preacher, like my dad. My eyes filled with tears, but I forced them back. A twelve-year-old was too big to cry.

Mom stood up, so I jumped to my feet, too. "Thank

you, Doctor," she said. "Come along, Peter."

We drove home without saying much. I felt numb. Dyslexia? I'd never heard the word until last week. Sure, I was always the slowest kid in my class. During recess I had a special hiding place behind a shrub. There I would cry because I couldn't do my lessons no matter how hard I tried.

Of course, I never told my mom about that part of school. I was too ashamed. I didn't want to worry her, either. She had enough on her mind with teaching school full-time and taking care of Dad, my two brothers, my sister and me.

Mom and I arrived home before the rest of the family. I was glad. I wanted some time alone. With my chin almost touching my chest, I pulled off my coat and hung it in the closet. When I turned around my mother was standing right in front of me. She didn't say anything. She just stood there looking into my eyes with tears running down her cheeks. Seeing her cry was too much for me. Before I knew what was happening, I was in her arms bawling like a big baby. A few minutes later, she led me into the living room to the couch.

"Sit down, honey. I want to talk to you."

I rubbed my eyes with my sleeve and waited, plucking at the crease in my trousers.

"You heard what the doctor said about your not finishing school. I don't believe him."

I stopped sniffling and looked at her. Her mild blue eyes smiled into mine. Behind them lay an iron will. "We'll have to work very hard, you and I, but I think we can do it. Now that I know what the problem is, we can try to overcome it. I'm going to hire a tutor who knows about dyslexia. I'll work with you myself evenings and weekends." Her eyebrows drew down as she peered at me. "Are you willing to work, Peter? Do you want to try?"

A ray of hope shone through the hazy future. "Yes, Mom. I want to real bad."

The next six years were an endurance run for both of us. I studied with a tutor twice a week until I could haltingly read my lessons. Each night, my mom and I sat at my little desk and rehearsed that day's schoolwork for at least two hours, sometimes until midnight. We drilled for tests until my head pounded and the print blurred before my eyes. At least twice a week, I wanted to quit. I had the strength of a kitten, but my mom's courage never wavered.

She'd rise early to pray over my school day. A thousand times I heard her say, "Lord, open Peter's mind today. Help him remember the things we studied."

Her vision reached beyond the three R's. Twice I won at statewide speech competitions. I participated in school programs and earned a license to work as an announcer on a local radio station.

Then my mother developed chronic migraines during my senior year. She blamed the headaches on stress. Some days the intense pain kept her in bed. Still she'd come to my room in the evening, wearing her robe, an ice pack in her hand, to study with me.

We laughed and cried when I passed my senior finals. Two days before graduation I talked to my mother and father about Bible college. I wanted to go, but I was afraid.

Mom said, "Apply at the Bible Institute in our town. You can live at home, and I'll help you."

I put my arms around her and hugged her close, a baseball-sized lump in my throat.

A week after graduation, my mom felt a stabbing pain in her head. She became disoriented for just a moment, but seemed to be all right. It was another migraine, she thought, so she went to bed. That night Dad tried to wake her. She was unconscious.

A few hours later, a white-coated doctor told us Mom

had an aneurysm that had burst. A massive hemorrhage left us no hope. She died two days later.

My grief almost drowned me. For weeks I walked the floor all night, sometimes weeping, sometimes staring at nothing. Did I have a future without my mother? She was my eyes, my understanding, my life. Should I still enroll in Bible school? The thought of going on alone filled me with terror. But, deep inside, I knew I had to move on to the next step, for her.

When I brought home the first semester's books and course outlines, I sat in the chair at my little desk. With trembling fingers, I opened my history book and began to read the first chapter. Suddenly, I looked over at the chair she used to sit in. It was empty, but my heart was full.

Mom's prayers still followed me. I could feel her presence. I could sense her faith.

In my graduation testimony I said, "Many people had a part in making Bible college a success for me. The person who helped me most is watching from Heaven tonight. To her I say, 'Thank you, Mom, for having faith in God and faith in me. You will always be with me.'"

Peter Dow
As told to Rosey Dow
Submitted by Linda Evans Shepherd

READER/CUSTOMER CARE SURVEY

We care about your opinions. Please take a moment to fill out this Reader Survey card and mail it back to us.
As a special **"thank you"** we'll send you exciting news about interesting books and a valuable **Gift Certificate.**

Please PRINT using ALL CAPS

First Name ______ MI. __ Last Name ______

Address ______

City ______ ST ___ Zip _____ – ____

Phone # (___) ___ – ____ Fax # (___) ___ – ____

Email ______

(1) Gender:

______Female ______Male

(2) Age:

______12 or under ______40-59

______13-19 ______60+

______20-39

(3) Marital Status

______Married

______Single

______Divorced/Widowed

(4) Did you receive this book as a gift?

______Yes ______No

(5) How many Chicken Soup books have you bought or read?

______1 ______2-4 ______5+

(6) How did you find out about this book?
*Please fill in **ONE.***

1)______Recommendation
2)______Store Display
3)______Bestseller List
4)______Online
5)______Advertisement
6)______Catalog/Mailing
7)______Interview/Review (TV, Radio, Print)

(7) Where do you usually buy books?
*Please fill in your top **TWO** choices.*

1)______Bookstore
2)______Religious Bookstore
3)______Online
4)______Book Club/Mail Order
5)______Price Club (Costco, Sam's Club, etc.)
6)______Retail Store (Target, Wal-Mart, etc.)

(9) What subjects do you enjoy reading about most? Rank only ***FIVE.*** *Use 1 for your favorite, 2 for second favorite, etc.*

	1	2	3	4	5
1) Parenting/Family	O	O	O	O	O
2) Relationships	O	O	O	O	O
3) Recovery/Addictions	O	O	O	O	O
4) Health/Nutrition	O	O	O	O	O
5) Christianity	O	O	O	O	O
6) Spirituality/Inspiration	O	O	O	O	O
7) Business Self-Help	O	O	O	O	O
8) Teen Issues	O	O	O	O	O
9) Sports	O	O	O	O	O

(14) What attracts you most to a book?

(Please rank 1-4 in order of preference.)	1	2	3	4
14) Title	O	O	O	O
15) Cover Design	O	O	O	O
16) Author	O	O	O	O
17) Content	O	O	O	O

TAPE IN MIDDLE; DO NOT STAPLE

NO POSTAGE
NECESSARY
IF MAILED
IN THE
UNITED STATES

BUSINESS REPLY MAIL

FIRST-CLASS MAIL PERMIT NO 45 DEERFIELD BEACH, FL

POSTAGE WILL BE PAID BY ADDRESSEE

CHICKEN SOUP FOR CHRISTIAN WOMAN'S SOUL
HEALTH COMMUNICATIONS, INC.
3201 SW 15TH STREET
DEERFIELD BEACH FL 33442-9875

FOLD HERE

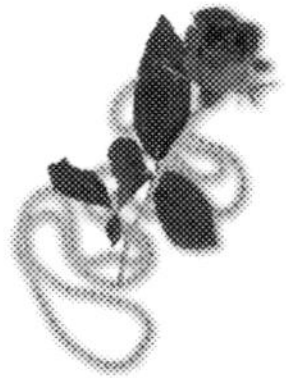

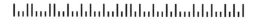

Do you have your own Chicken Soup story that you would like to send us? Please submit separately to:
Chicken Soup for the Soul, P.O. Box 30880,
Santa Barbara, CA 93130

Comments:

Love That Lasts

A happy marriage is still the greatest treasure within the gift of fortune.

Eden Phillpotts

It's six A.M., gray and still. Thelma Wright, a sparrow-sized woman of seventy-seven, sits on the back step watching the sunrise. Overhead two purple finches circle. Thelma is often up before the birds. Up at midnight to care for her husband, Wilbur, she seldom drops back to sleep. Instead, she scrubs the bathtub or dusts a few shelves. In the ten years since Wilbur's stroke, she's had little time for chores in daylight.

Indoors, there is a bit of sparrow in her movements, the plucky hip-hop of arthritic joints. On the kitchen counter, the coffee machine gurgles. Thelma peers at it through her thick-lensed glasses. By instinct more than sight, she navigates the familiar kitchen spaces, cupboard to refrigerator to drawer, mixing Wilbur's strawberry drink, carrying his bran flakes and white-scalloped bowl.

When Thelma enters the front bedroom, the clock on

the mantle ticks toward seven. Her husband's breath puffs in-out, in-out, his eyes closed.

From an apparent sound sleep, Wilbur says, "I'm awake."

Thelma smiles. "I'll get your washcloth and eyedrops."

One-handed, Wilbur rubs the wet warmth over his face. Since 1961, when his left arm was severed in an industrial accident, Wilbur has done everything one-handed. Then six months ago, poor circulation reduced his right foot to pain so incessant that the leg was amputated.

"There really isn't much of me left, is there?" he said one day.

"Hey, buddy," replied Thelma, patting his chest, "the best part is right here."

Bathing done, she says, "Ready to get up?"

Wilbur nods, and his eyes fix on Thelma as she starts to operate the Hoyer lift. She pumps the hydraulic lever on the hoist, her husband rises from the bed, then he is lowered into his wheelchair.

Nowadays Wilbur and Thelma need each other. She is his movement. He is her reason for moving.

"You okay?" she asks.

"You haven't dumped me yet," Wilbur says.

"No, sir. After thirty-three years I'm not about to dump you."

"One of these days," Wilbur adds, "I'm going to get up and give you a ride in this machine."

In the bathroom, Thelma shaves and grooms her husband. Together they arrive at the kitchen table in a swirl of scent—hot coffee and cool aftershave. Wilbur shoves the right wheel lock into place. Thelma locks the left.

Over bran flakes and milk, Thelma and Wilbur link fingers and pray in unison, "Our Father, who art in heaven, hallowed be Thy name. Thy kingdom come, Thy will be done . . ." Halfway through, tears track down Wilbur's cheeks.

Two quiet cups of coffee later, he says, "If you'd known all this—how bad it was going to be—maybe you wouldn't have said 'I do.'"

Thelma looks at him through double-ringed lenses. "You know something? Just to see your smile and those blue eyes looking at me, it's worth it all. I wouldn't change any of it—except maybe one thing. If I could take six months of the year—and divide it up with you—I'd take your place and let you switch with me."

Barbara Seaman

Crisis on the Court

That July 25th was hot and humid at Parris Island Marine Recruit Depot in South Carolina. Our younger son, Rick, was competing there in the Marine East Coast Championship Tennis Tournament. Rick's dad and I, along with his older brother Randy, had determined this would be a splendid time to vacation at our favorite spot, Hilton Head Island, a short drive from Parris Island. We could watch Rick's matches, and, when he wasn't playing tennis, he could spend time with us at the beach.

That morning, in our rented condo, Rick gathered his tennis rackets and utility bag. "Mom, are you coming over with Dad to watch today's matches?"

"Matches!" I exclaimed. "You mean you're playing more than *one?* In this *heat?"*

"Yep," he said, giving me a big bear hug. "Doubles this morning and singles this afternoon."

I returned his hug. "I think I'll stay here where it's cool. But I'll be there for the finals tomorrow, so hang in there." Then I added the standard reminder of parents everywhere: "Drive carefully."

Rick didn't know the real reason I was staying behind.

Today was his birthday and I planned to surprise him with an old-fashioned, home-cooked meal—something he missed in the Corps. I'd brought along all his favorite foods, even a chocolate layer cake.

I spent all afternoon in the tiny kitchen, preparing a feast, humming a happy tune. I had just turned the fried chicken when Randy came in from a swim.

"Everything's just about ready. They should be here soon," I beamed.

Two hours later, I was trying to keep dinner from drying out as my eyes kept darting toward the kitchen clock. Randy headed back out the front door, trying without success to hide his own uneasiness. "I'll see if they're coming," he called over his shoulder.

By then, my mind had pictured all the worst possible scenarios of highway accidents. I had to *do* something. I shut off the burners on the stove and walked out onto the back deck. I leaned against the wood railing and stared into the shadows. Beyond the sand dunes and sea oats silhouetted against the horizon, the Atlantic Ocean continued its rhythmic sway. Overhead, stars hung like millions of tiny lights in a black, velvet sky.

"Lord," I began, "please let Rick and Joe be safe." All at once, I was seized by a heavy feeling of regret. Regret that I hadn't prayed for them this morning—I had just told them to be careful. And now, maybe it was too late to pray. I whispered, "Forgive me, Lord."

After some while, the answer came. As softly as the ocean breeze, I sensed God say to me, "Gloria, I knew what you meant this morning when you said, 'Be careful.' What *I* heard was, 'God go with you and protect you.' Remember, Gloria, *I* know the heart."

My concern lightened, I hurried back inside and once more, I warmed up dinner. "Randy, get ready to light the candles," I called out. "They'll be here soon and they'll be starved."

Within minutes, the door opened and the two of them trudged in—completely bedraggled. Joe carried Rick's tennis gear. Rick stood there, pale and exhausted-looking, wrapped in a blue sheet stamped U.S. NAVAL HOSPITAL.

"What in the world?" was all I managed. As I collapsed onto a chair and Rick folded into another, Joe recounted the events of their terrifying afternoon. "The day turned out to be a scorcher with no breeze," he started. "Even where I stood in the shade the heat was oppressive. Rick and his partner had just won a hard-fought doubles match, and when Rick was in the second set of his singles match he screamed out and fell to the asphalt surface, writhing in agony. Severe leg cramps. They put him into a Jeep and sped away. I jumped in our car and raced after them. At the base, as they were helping Rick across the parking lot to his quarters, a new wave of spasms struck, again knocking him to the pavement. He had difficulty breathing. 'I need help,' he gasped.

"'Call the medics!' the sergeant shouted. Soon a military ambulance careened across the field and whisked Rick to the base hospital."

As Joe continued his story, *I* could barely breathe. "In the emergency room," Joe said, "they plunged Rick into a tub of ice and water, up to his chin, in an effort to lower his dangerously high temperature. They gave him shots; they forced liquids."

At this point, Rick joined in the telling. "All this time, Dad and several medics rubbed as I called out first one muscle, then another."

Joe added. "I worked feverishly and prayed silently, *Please, God, don't let a cramp hit his heart.*"

When, at long last, the pains had subsided and Rick's temperature returned to normal, the doctor explained that due to excessive perspiration, Rick had become gravely dehydrated, which had depleted essential elements in the blood and thus caused the cramping.

On top of that, his other symptoms indicated heatstroke—a critical emergency that is often fatal. The cramping might have saved his life because it resulted in his getting early medical treatment.

"Oh, by the way," Joe added, "the doctor said for Rick to eat a good meal tonight."

As the four of us gathered around that little table, the twenty-four candles on Rick's chocolate cake held special significance. I didn't hesitate to pray out loud, thanking God for sparing Rick's life—and for bringing us together as a family once again.

Then, I breathed yet another unspoken prayer: *Thank You, Lord, for knowing the hearts of moms and dads. When we say "Be careful," we really mean, "God go with you and protect you."*

Gloria Cassity Stargel

A Mother's Intuition

There is no instinct like that of the heart.

Lord Byron

An orange-sherbet sunrise heralded the day as I reached for my morning tea. Glancing at the clock I knew Amanda would soon be on her way home, tired from her night shift at the coffee shop in the city.

I went about my usual morning routine and thought how determined my daughter was to earn enough money to help put herself through college. It was a challenge for her to juggle two jobs but she managed. As I drifted from dishes to dusting I felt an unusual surge of concern for my now late-arriving daughter. I tried to keep busy, but I found myself watching out the window and listening for the familiar sound of Amanda's car pulling into the driveway.

A wave of nausea washed over me and my heart raced for a moment. I closed my eyes and prayed for her safety, then chastised myself for being a paranoid mother. Amanda often jokingly reminded me about my smothering-mothering tendencies. I countered with the "Wait until you have children of your own" lecture. Was this one of those moments? I called Amanda's cell phone. No answer.

Something was terribly wrong. I felt an urge to jump in my car and look for her. First, though, I called out to God for direction. I cannot say I heard an audible voice—it was more like a gentle nudge, but I truly felt God wanted me to leave the house.

My heart raced as I followed the likely route Amanda would take home. I kept pushing the redial button on my cell phone, but Amanda was not answering. I felt a sudden grip of fear and pulled over to the side of the road, wondering what to do. I remembered the countless times I had told Amanda to pray—how it was the most important step to take when fear crouched on the doorstep. So I prayed. I prayed that God would send His angels to protect my daughter.

My fear, thankfully, did not turn into panic, as I still felt compelled to drive. I drove for forty minutes but there was no sign of Amanda. Then my cell phone rang. My heart jumped to my throat. It was a female voice. The connection was so poor that I could hardly make it out: "*. . . accident . . . Bethel Sideroad . . .*" I thought it was Amanda's voice, but I couldn't be sure. I was about fifteen minutes away from the Bethel Sideroad, so I did my best to keep my composure and drove, praying without ceasing.

A sickening sight awaited me. An ambulance and two police cars blocked the path of oncoming traffic. I saw Amanda's little grey car wrapped around a broken hydro pole. The whole car was crushed. I gasped in horror and knew Amanda had surely perished in such a wreck. Feeling faint, I jammed on my brakes. A policewoman approached me and I wailed in agony. I jumped out of my car, frantically screaming for Amanda. Just then, she stepped out of the ambulance. "Mom!" she called. I raced to her and clung to her with my arms and heart.

How had she survived? The paramedics kept saying it was nothing less than a miracle. The police officers, after they had calmed me down, told me they had expected to pull a body out of the car. In their estimation, no one should have survived such a horrendous accident.

Amanda had apparently fallen asleep at the wheel and as she hit the side of the road, her car had flipped twice and hit the hydro pole. The entire car was crushed—except for the driver's seat. She was taken to the hospital for observation, but other than a few scratches and bruises, she was fine.

I still marvel at the power of prayer and the sense of urgency that flooded my mind and heart that morning. The Almighty Protector shielded my Amanda—and sent His angels to protect her, just as I had prayed.

Glynis M. Belec

Daddy's Gift

The family you come from isn't as important as the family you're going to have.

Ring Lardner

It's Christmas and I'm worn out. All the activities are draining, depleting me of energy, enthusiasm and confidence. Looking for a way to leave it behind, I wander outdoors and straddle my bicycle. It's a regular old bicycle, nothing fancy, but just the right vehicle to free my spirit. As I pedal up the driveway toward the street, I wander back in time.

It was 1955, on the eve of the first real Christmas my sister, Mary, and I ever had, and Daddy was determined that his two new daughters would find it filled with love and joy. I was four, Mary was two and the entire process of "coming to live with" Daddy, Mama and Lamar, a big brother, took place without their ever laying eyes on us. When asked how he could adopt two children sight unseen, Daddy answered, "It doesn't matter to me what they look like. If they need a home, we want 'em."

Our first two months with them were joyful, but

expensive. We brought with us a lot of "needs": tonsils to remove, medications to take, clothes to buy. But our greatest need was for emotional support and reassurance that this was indeed our home—for life. I knew there was a chance that our birth parents would reclaim us—a right they could exercise for up to a year.

The townspeople pitched in. Neighbors hosted a "children's shower," the local pharmacist donated the required medications and someone even provided a new tricycle for Santa to bring Mary. My little sister and I were so excited about our first Christmas. We learned about Jesus and how much He loved us. For the first time in our lives, we listened to Bible stories and sang "Jesus Loves Me." We learned to say the blessing and our prayers.

As the holidays approached, Aunt Florice secretly put the finishing touches on a set of matching mother-daughter dresses that Daddy knew would leave Mama in tears. Lamar, at fourteen, helped plan the details of how Santa would deliver the new baby dolls and the blocks that had been fashioned in the shop from leftover bits of wood.

Everything seemed to be in order for the wonderful Christmas celebration—yet Daddy was restless. He couldn't forget about the small blue bicycle Santa had been offered for just ten dollars, even though he and Mama had agreed they had spent enough.

On Christmas Eve Daddy paced and thought, and thought and paced. He sensed that I had the most profound scars from our past. I was afraid of the dark, afraid of enclosed spaces, even afraid to go to the bathroom alone. In fact, I could not speak an intelligible sentence and often needed little Mary to interpret for me.

As dusk fell, he told Mama he had one last errand to run. On Christmas morning, my eyes grew wide when I saw the beautiful blue bicycle beside the tree. I couldn't wait to take it outside to the sidewalk. Daddy eagerly helped me learn and quickly recognized that I didn't need the training wheels after all. When they were removed, I pedaled and Daddy released his hold on the bicycle, sending me off for the first time on the road to freedom. But even as he let me go, he ran alongside me, there to help me if I wavered too far off course.

Now as I ride into the wind, calmed and recharged, I realize that long-ago bicycle trip had been the first of what would be a lifetime of send-offs. And with each one, whether I was attending my first day of school, learning to drive a car, heading off to college or landing my first real job, Daddy provided me with a way to soar along with the "training wheels" of a Christian home. And he and Mama were there, running alongside me whenever I questioned my course.

The melody plays in my head—"Jesus loves me, yes I know." I enter a straightaway, rediscover my center of balance, release the handlebars and lift my hands to the sky in jubilant celebration and gratefulness for Daddy's gift.

Shirley Garrett

Make a Wish, Mommy

The heart of the giver makes the gift dear and precious.

Martin Luther

Sometimes life's greatest lessons are the ones we would never be able to have learned without difficult circumstances leading us there to them.

It was my twenty-eighth birthday, and I was depressed. Divorced, raising two children alone, and too poor to even afford a telephone, I was going through the most dark and depressing time in my life. I hadn't lived in Utah very long, and I was still trying to adjust to the snow, and this particular January was one of the most brutal in years.

The snow outside was literally thigh-high, and it was a daily struggle to leave the house, which added to my isolation. My son Nicholas was in kindergarten, and I was a junior at nearby Weber State University. I had taken the quarter off because my five-month-old, Maya, had been very ill, so I had little social interaction. It was a winter of loneliness for me, but also of incredible closeness with my children. My small son, with his enormous child-sized heart, taught me the greatest lesson.

The day before my birthday, I was a grouch. I was used to celebrating it with the friends I had moved away from. I was used to presents and phone calls, none of which I would be receiving this time. Feeling sorry for myself was becoming comfortable for me. Depression became so second-nature that I didn't even remember the happy, laughing person I used to be. I was so wrapped up in my own problems that I couldn't even see that the greatest joys, blessings and sources of laughter that I would ever know were right there in front of me.

Tucking the children into bed that night, I was in a cloud of hopelessness. My little Nick wrapped his chubby, six-year-old arms around my neck and said, "Tomorrow's your birthday, Mommy! I can't wait!" His blue eyes sparkled with an anticipation that mystified me.

Kissing his sweet rosy cheeks, I hoped that he didn't expect a birthday party to magically appear, like it did on his birthday. Life is so simple when you're six.

The next morning, I awoke before the children, and began making breakfast. Hearing noises in our tiny living room, I assumed Nick was up, and waited for him to come in to eat. Then I could hear Nick talking to Maya. He was sternly telling her to make Mommy smile today.

It suddenly hit me. Being so wrapped up in my misery, I didn't see how it affected my children. Even my little boy sensed I wasn't happy, and he was doing his best to do something about it. Tears of shame at my selfishness washed down my face. I knelt down in our little kitchen and asked for the strength to somehow find happiness again. I asked God to show me some beauty in my life. I asked Him him to help me see, really *see* the blessings I did have.

Putting a smile on my face, I marched myself into the living room to hug my children. There sat Nick on the floor, Maya on her blanket next to him, and in front of them was a pile of presents. A birthday party for three.

I looked at the presents with disbelieving eyes, then looked back at my son. His face was gleeful at my shock. "I surprised you, Mommy, didn't I? Happy birthday!" He grinned his toothless, adorable grin.

Stunned, I knelt down next to him and with tears in my eyes, I asked him how in the world he had possibly found a way to get me presents. He reminded me of our trip to "All a Dollar Store." I suddenly remembered him telling me he was spending the allowance he had been saving for ages. I had laughed at his bulging pockets and remembered thinking that he walked like John Wayne, his pants loaded down with his life savings. I had almost chided him for spending everything he had so carefully saved, but thought better of it, and did my shopping while he did his.

Looking again at the beautiful pile of presents in front of me, I couldn't believe that my small, darling son had spent everything he had in his crayon bank on me. On his mom. What kind of kid goes without the toys he wanted so that he could buy his mom a pile of presents? *There.* I heard the voice in my heart. *I am showing you your blessings. How could you ever doubt them?* My prayers were being answered. No one was more blessed, and no one had more to be thankful for than I did. I had been so selfish and petty to feel unhappy with my life.

With tears flowing, I gently hugged my son and daughter and told them how lucky I was. At Nick's eager prompting, I carefully opened each present. A bracelet. A necklace. Another bracelet. Nail polish. Another bracelet. My favorite candy bars. Another bracelet. The thoughtful gifts, each wrapped in gift bags and wrapping paper purchased with a six-year-old's allowance, were the most perfect I've ever received. The final gift was his personal favorite. A wax birthday cake with the words "I love you" painted in fake frosting across the top.

"You have to have a birthday cake, Mom." My oh-so-wise little one informed me.

"It's the most beautiful cake I've ever seen," I told him. And it was. He then sang "Happy Birthday" to me in his sweet little-boy voice that melted my heart and brought on more tears. "Make a wish, Mommy," he insisted.

I looked into my little boy's shining blue eyes and couldn't think of a single thing to wish for. "I already got my wish," I whispered through the tears. "I have you."

Susan Farr Fahncke

Unconditional Love

The sublimest song to be heard on Earth is the lisping of the human soul on the lips of children.

Victor Hugo

After Steve left for work, I gathered our three children to stand in a circle to pray. Todd, ten years old, held hands with his eight-year-old brother, Kevin, and his toddler sister, Kristin. They knew that after two years of suffering from muscle weakness, their daddy was going through a lot of medical tests. And they knew we were having an important meeting with his doctor today to hear the final diagnosis. As we held hands, I prayed: "Lord, thank You so much for the gift of Daddy. Thank You for the doctors who have been working so hard with him. And thank You for being in our lives. We ask You today to hear our prayers and to grant us the gift of hope. In Thy name we pray. Amen."

The kids and I hugged, the boys went off to school, and the babysitter arrived for Kristin. I picked up Steve at work and we headed to the hospital. The doctor called us into his office and gave us the news. "Steve, you have multiple sclerosis."

I was relieved because I knew the other alternative was fatal. I thanked God for answering our morning prayer for hope.

Steve, on the other hand, was totally devastated. He couldn't believe he had something going on in his body that he couldn't control or fix. It was the first time he had to face his own mortality—and it was terribly painful. We drove home without saying a word, and Steve went immediately to bed. I told our children that Daddy was discouraged, but that God had answered our prayers for hope and that as long as we all loved and supported Daddy, he would be all right, and so would we.

I tucked the kids into bed that night, and then went upstairs myself. When I went into our bedroom, Steve was fast asleep. I noticed a piece of paper sticking out from beneath his pillow. Quietly, I pulled it out and saw our son Todd's handwriting. I went into the bathroom and in the light, I read:

Dear Dad,

I know how discouraged you are about your problem. I just wish that it would get better. I don't know why God gave it to you, out of all the people in the world. I can't imagine why. Having the chanch [sic] to run might be great but it is more important for you to love us and care for us, then [sic] to just play a runing [sic] game. You can still do millions of things with us that is [sic] just as fun. I just wanted to say that I love you, and hope your problem will get better soon!

Love,
Your Son,
Todd

P.S. Even if your problem does not get better, don't worry about it. We'll love you just the same!

I went to the bedroom and fell to my knees, as I thanked God for the gift of our son's unconditional love and support of his father and for the realization that when we share our pain and our faith with our children, they can reach out to us in such simple, yet profound, life-changing ways.

Carol Hamblet Adams

My Turn

There is a time for everything, and a season for every activity under heaven.

Ecclesiastes 3:1

I got lost walking home from kindergarten on a stormy, raining, cold day. I was so scared. A very kind lady was letting her puppy out and saw me crying. I tearfully told her my name and where I lived, which was only a street away, but to a five-year-old it seemed as if I was at the other end of the world. This kind old lady (she must have been at least thirty-nine) took her puppy into the house and called my mother. Mom arrived with a warm sweater and a big umbrella. She gently took my hand, thanked the lady and walked me home. I will never forget the happiness and security I felt when I saw my mother coming to rescue me. It felt so good to be safe and loved.

Now, it is my mom who is lost, in a storm called Alzheimer's. Most of her days are unsettled and cold. I had raindrops, my mom has teardrops. But for her there are no kind ladies to call for help, no warm sweaters, no umbrellas, no hands to lead her home. She will never in this lifetime know the happiness of being found. I take her hand and hold her tightly, but I am frustrated because as hard as I try, I can never lead my mother to a place where she feels safe and loved.

Yet so many times, in the midst of her worst confusion, when she stops her meaningless chatter and says "I love you," her heart is talking to mine. And sometimes when I take her hand and say the Lord's Prayer, she joins in automatically. These two things are more powerful than a hundred other actions or a million sensible words.

Why do I bother to visit? friends sometimes ask. Though it breaks my heart, I never look at it as a bother. This very mixed-up person who doesn't know my name is the same gentle lady who once cared for me, comforted me, held me, cleaned me up, cheered me up, and nourished and nursed me through the roughest times. It was difficult for my mom. Knowing how much she loved me, I understand now that her heart must have been broken every time mine was. Before I was able to speak a word, she knew my every need and did all in her power to fulfill it.

Now it's my turn.

Barbara Jeanne Fisher

A Treasured Gift

The art of giving presents is to give something which others cannot buy for themselves.

A. A. Milne

"Grandpa's dying," Mom called to tell me. The hospital had sent her father home with little time left. My aunt and cousin had already moved in to provide around-the-clock care. Mom felt she should be there, but we'd been estranged from her family for more than twenty years. I agreed to go with her for moral support.

Instead of being tense and awkward, however, the visit turned out to be warm, loving and special.

After we arrived, my grandfather gestured at the wall. "Kimmie, see that?" he said, struggling to sit up. "I tell all my friends my granddaughter drew that for me!"

A framed piece of art hung over the television. I didn't recognize it. Keeping my smile as I crossed the room to get a closer look, I mentally ran through diplomatic ways of telling him he was mistaken. Getting closer to the drawing, my eyes widened. There was my signature, plain as anything! Stunned, I tried to recall any information about this picture. How could I have completed such detail but not remember it?

Like an open door allowing a flood of light into a dark closet, I suddenly remembered. I was sixteen when I'd drawn this chalk pastel picture of a goldfish for him—a man I didn't know well, except as my mother's father. Everything became clear, and I remembered why I'd drawn this for him. That Christmas I had purchased a Bible for my grandmother. I'd added a box of colored pencils with instructions for marking special verses. I felt excited about this personal, significant gift. Then I puzzled over what to do for my grandfather. It would look odd giving a Christmas gift to one grandparent but not the other. I prayed for a solution. Then I realized I could give him something personal as well—a gift of my artwork. I drew a goldfish on a black background, because that seemed adequately masculine. I worried over whether my grandfather would care about a silly fish picture. But as I worked on all of its colorful oranges, with a tinge of white in the flowing tail and a touch of blue in its darting eyes, I prayed that my gift would touch his heart.

With little contact before or after that Christmas long ago, I'd assumed my grandfather didn't care for my siblings and me. I wasn't offended, but accepted it pragmatically. Some men simply aren't comfortable around children. I assumed that was true for him.

Now I stared at the fish hanging on my grandfather's paneled wall. Shame filled me and tears blurred my vision. He had treasured my gift all those years, and I never knew.

Needless to say, I returned for several more visits, getting acquainted with Grandpa. He shared with me about his service in World War II. He told me about his work building prototypes for Boeing's commercial jet airplanes. He met my sons—his great-grandsons—before he died.

After the funeral, my aunt and cousin approached me. "We want you to have this," my aunt said, smiling through tears. In her hands she held the goldfish picture.

The treasured drawing now hangs on my kitchen wall. When I tell visitors about it, and I tell them about my grandfather, my voice always catches when I share about the error of assumption, the mystery of relationships—and the amazing power of a treasured gift.

Kimn Swenson Gollnick

The Breathin' Part

He will wipe every tear from their eyes. There will be no more death or mourning or crying or pain, for the old order of things has passed away.

Revelation 21:4

When my beloved Mama Farley died at age ninety, Don and I decided that five-year-old Holly and six-year-old Jay would attend the Kentucky funeral with us. During the long drive south, we talked about heaven and told our children that Mama—the part we couldn't see—was already with the Lord. Then I, a veteran of Southern funerals, told them about the part they would see. She'd be lying in a big box, called a casket, surrounded by flowers. A lot of people would be in the room, I said, and many would be crying because Mama Farley couldn't talk to them anymore.

Then remembering previous funerals, I explained that some people would touch her hands or kiss her forehead. Don and I stressed that no one would make them kiss her, but they could touch her hands if they wanted to.

I talked about the sad hymns the people would sing, what the minister would do and even about the procession to the cemetery after her adult grandsons carried the casket to the big car called a hearse. Then, most important of all, we asked if they had any questions. Jay wondered about practical matters, such as how they put the casket in the ground, but Holly just stared at me, her eyes round with silent wondering.

When we arrived at the funeral home, we held the children's hands and walked into the flowered area. I studied Mama Farley's dear, ancient face and thought of the godly example she'd been throughout my childhood. I remembered the family unity during our farm days and longed for a skillet full of her incredible biscuits. I thought of her faith-filled, pragmatic view of life. Still years away in my memories, I was startled by Holly's question.

"Is Mama breathing?" she whispered.

We hadn't anticipated that question, and it required more than just a quick, "No, of course not." Suddenly this business of explaining death to myself had become difficult. How could I make a child grasp what I couldn't?

"Well, Holly . . ." I stalled, searching for something both simple and theologically sound.

Jay then turned from flipping the casket handles to face his little sister. "No, Holly, she's not breathing. Remember? The breathin' part's in heaven."

Sandra P. Aldrich

Love Bugs

Along unfamiliar paths I will guide them.

Isaiah 42:16

My father-in-law leaned against his garden hoe and in his gentle voice warned, "If you don't do something with those bugs, you won't have any potatoes!" It was the summer of 1981, and we had just planted our first garden after moving to the farm from the big city of Toronto. Not having any gardening experience, I'd thought I could just plant and harvest. I didn't know there would be many long hours spent in the hot summer sun before we would reap what we had sown.

Standing at the edge of the garden, looking down those long rows of potatoes, I felt very inadequate beside my father-in-law who had been a farmer all of his life. I wondered, *Should I tell him I know nothing about getting rid of potato bugs?*

As if reading my thoughts, he said he would buy me a bag of potato bug poison when he went to town, and all I would have to do is dust the potato leaves with the powder. It wasn't long before I saw his truck coming back down our lane. Though I had seen him dusting in his own garden in his shirtsleeves, I read the instructions and precautions on the bag and donned long pants, a long-sleeved shirt, rubber boots, gloves, cap and mask. Up and down the rows I went on a hot summer afternoon dusting the rows with white powder. A week later the bugs were just as bad. We offered our two small sons a penny for each bug they could pick. After they filled a gallon ice-cream bucket, their interest dwindled. So again I went through the same dusting procedure over and over all summer, wondering, *Why did God make potato bugs?*

After we harvested our first crop of potatoes, I forgot all about the bugs. That is until planting time came around again. How I dreaded the idea of putting poison on our potatoes—organic gardening is what we had been dreaming about in the city. The second summer I decided it was time to tell Grandpa I would do away with dusting the potatoes forever. I took my gallon ice-cream bucket to the garden and began picking bugs.

I was surprised when one morning Grampie joined me there, with his own bucket and a shingle. "It will be easier this way," he told me. "Just tap the leaves gently and the bugs will fall into the bucket." Together we went up and down the rows. When I went back to the garden after supper, Grampie was there again. When we finished our garden we went to his garden. The next morning I looked out the kitchen window wondering if he would come again. Sure enough, I saw his truck coming down the lane. I met him at the garden, and with our buckets and shingles, we started down the rows. As we began our chore, Grampie began telling me a story.

"I remember when . . ." and with each row we walked, Grampie told me stories of the river, stories of how the Lawsons settled here, stories of his mother and father, stories of what it was like when he was a boy and how farming was in days gone by. Every now and then one of us would stop, wipe the sweat from our brows and say, "What good are these bugs anyway?" and then continue on.

Each gardening season, Grampie and I continued picking potato bugs. As his steps grew slower it took twice as long to finish a row but the, "I remember when . . ." stories became even more precious.

It wasn't long before my daughter Melanie joined us in our quest to rid the garden of potato bugs, and even at the age of eighty, there were not many days that Grampie didn't join us in the potato rows. One day Melanie asked, "Grampie, why did God make potato bugs?"

He replied, "I don't know, Melanie. They are nothing but a bother."

Then came the summer his cancer progressed. One evening as I went alone to his garden, he called from his lawn chair. I left my bucket in the rows and joined him at the front of the house. The river that he loved so much was calm and peaceful that evening and we sat for a long time as he told me still more river stories. We wondered where we would sell our beans tomorrow and discussed those useless potato bugs.

The next summer Melanie and I were alone in the garden.

Early mornings and late evenings found us there planning our days, wondering where she would spend her gardening money and daydreaming about the mountains. Every now and then one of us would say, "Remember when Grampie . . ." and more often than not, we would straighten our tired backs and scorn the potato bugs.

By the summer of 1999, Melanie was in Vancouver. I stood at the edge of the garden alone. With bucket and shingle in hand I started down the first row, and from days gone by I heard, "I remember when . . ." Only now I have my own memory stories. I remembered days spent with Grampie as we formed a rare and wonderful friendship, and days spent with Melanie as she daydreamed about life and the mountains.

I've planted my first garden of the new century, and this morning I start on the potato rows with a small boy at my side. My four-year-old nephew Jordan is visiting from Sherbrooke, Quebec. He only speaks French and understands very little of what I say to him, but he understands that I love him very deeply. So when I hand him a bucket and a shingle, he anticipates that Auntie has something exciting in store for him. We start down the first row, Jordan on one side and me on the other. As he reaches across the row with wonder in his eyes, he tucks his small hand in mine. I spot a bug and drop it in his bucket. He looks up surprised and chatters away in French. I explain to him in English why we have to pick these bugs. I continue to find more bugs and drop them in his bucket. He is now intent on finding some for himself—his little head close to the plants, searching. We continue down the rows, delighting in his ability to find as many bugs as he can. He bursts with excitement over all those bugs in his bucket—and so do I.

I finally know why God made potato bugs.

Darlene Lawson

"I planted peas, carrots, corn, squash, tomatoes, onions. . . ."

By Their Roots Ye Shall Know Them

After all, what is God? An eternal child playing an eternal game in the eternal garden.

Aurobindo Ghose

"Carrot, carrot, carrottop," sang my four-year-old son as he placed another wooden block on his teetering tower. "I'm a carrottop!"

Earlier that day, my friend Christi had patted him on his flaming head and said, "How are you doing, Carrottop?" When Koy looked blankly at me, I explained that his bright orange hair was nearly the color of carrots.

"I'm just like the carrots at the grocery store," he beamed.

"The grocery store!" I exclaimed. "Carrots grow in the ground."

It was at that moment I realized my little carrottop had had no exposure to gardening during his young life. I conjured a vision of sun-ripened vegetables growing in tidy rows and sighed.

My own experiences with gardening were limited. As a young child in Sunday school class, I planted flower seeds in a paper cup for a Mother's Day gift. I was told they were marigolds, but I can't know for certain. They withered. In a fourth-grade science class, I sprouted beans in a glass jar. Lima, navy, string, kidney . . . I never did find out what kind. They rotted.

Once, early in my marriage, I cleared and planted a small plot. But overnight my lush-leafed tomato plants were stripped bare; instead, rheumatic branches sagged with fleshy fruit. Upon closer investigation, I came eye-to-hideous-eye with my first tomato worm, and my career as a master gardener was nipped in the bud!

How I wished my own city-bred sprouts could experience the earthiness of nature and the awesome lessons I was certain only waited to be learned.

Decisively, I dialed Christi and explained my desire. She obligingly invited us for a series of visits to her small acreage. I was as eager as my four children—the joy of a garden without the bother of the bugs.

In the spring, Christi let us plot her garden by pounding stakes and stretching string. We crumbled moist clods of dirt, planted onion sets and patted tiny seeds into the fragrant soil. During early summer, we plopped belly down to marvel at the dainty green shoots that striped the garden. We learned how to thin radishes and hoe weeds.

What golden teaching opportunities this created. And, typically mother-like, I took advantage of each visit. By illustrating the importance of nourishment, maintenance and pruning, I emphasized the hand of the Master Gardener in the lives of my own precious seedlings.

On one trip to the plot, I applied the principles of faith. Another time I taught that we "reap what we sow." I found an opportunity to explain the parable of the mustard seed. I even told the story of *The Little Red Hen.* After all, I wanted the children to cultivate the full impact of this garden.

And how thrilled we were to reap the bounty of our

labors. With her thumbnail, Christi showed us how to split plump green pods and scrape the sweet peas into our mouths. The kids plucked ripe tomatoes, sun-warmed and heavy. While they played hide-and-seek between the stately, towering ranks of cornstalks, I bent low to fill a small basket with crunchy carrots.

"Here, Carrottop, this is for you!" I tickled my son's face with the feathery leaves.

Koy took the crisp, tapering vegetable and turned it end-over-end in his chubby hands.

"Hey," he said, and I saw revelation light his face.

He examined the fine, hairy roots.

"Hey," he repeated, and I felt his wonder.

He waved the ferny top through the air. I waited expectantly to learn which profound lesson of the harvest he had gleaned. What had most impacted his young life?

"Hey!" he finally said, slapping the green leaves against his legs, then pointing accusingly to the orange root. "Everybody is all wrong. Carrot tops are GREEN. I'm not a carrottop. I'm a carrot BOTTOM!"

Carol McAdoo Rehme

Blossoms for Belle

Lovely flowers are the smiles of God's goodness.

William Willerforce

Meg glanced out the window when she heard the screen door creak next door. She saw Belle heading toward the circus-bright blossoms in her flowerbeds. "Aunt" Belle was no one's aunt in particular, but she was claimed as such by everyone in this new neighborhood. Especially the kids—they all adored her.

Speaking of kids . . . Meg sighed. She needed to apologize for the way her own had acted. *What an embarrassing first introduction to a neighbor,* she thought. She headed out the door, praying that her apology would be accepted.

"Are your flowers this abundant every year?" Meg frowned at the dandelions freckling her own back lawn.

"Oh my, yes," answered Aunt Belle as she plucked a spindly weed and pinched a spent bloom. "They are my pride and joy."

"I can see that. You spend a great deal of time working with them and it shows. Your yard is beautiful! Obviously, my kids think so, too," Meg rushed to add. "I'm sorry my daughter picked your new bedding petunias, Belle. It won't happen again."

"Don't let it worry you, dear. Children are more important than flowers. The petunias will come back." Aunt Belle adjusted her frayed straw hat.

But it did worry Meg. As the weeks wore on, her kids quickly made new friends up and down the block. Now an entire army of children stormed the house and yard in summertime abandon. No matter how much she cautioned—and threatened—they overflowed into Belle's yard next door. Meg paid another visit to Aunt Belle.

"I noticed that our basketball knocked the blossoms off your prized peonies. I'm so sorry."

It didn't seem to frazzle Aunt Belle, however. "Children are more important than flowers," she said again. "The peonies will come back."

As the weeks wore on, her yard took a backseat when it came to the kids. In fact, she championed them, all the while encouraging their visits, laughing at their antics, plying them with homegrown nosegays and homemade treats.

One hot month melted into another. Meg's temper got shorter while her apologies grew longer.

"I see the kids have worn a path through the corner of your lawn. It's their latest 'shortcut.' I can't believe I didn't catch them at it sooner.

"I'm sorry, Aunt Belle. I saw tracks crisscrossing your violets, and I'm personally acquainted with the guilty party. I'll remind him to keep his bicycle on the sidewalk where it belongs.

"Sorry again, Aunt Belle. Honestly, you must be a saint to put up with all these kids tearing through your beautiful yard. What were they thinking to let the dog roll and dig in your marigold bed? Your beautiful flowers are ruined!"

But, no matter what, Aunt Belle's angelic smile never wavered and neither did her reply. "It's fine, dear. Don't worry so. Children are more important than flowers. The flowers will come back."

Meg thanked God for a neighbor as forgiving as He was. Meg tried not to worry. After all, the children didn't seem to. They knew Aunt Belle was always available to listen to *both* sides of a disagreement, kiss a skinned elbow and praise a slam-dunk. Her broom swept aside their capers along with her raining rose petals. In her patient way, Aunt Belle nourished both her garden and the blossoming children.

And so the summer passed, as did many summers after that. The pattern never changed: Aunt Belle serenely nursed bruised blossoms; Meg begged pardon for more "problems." By ones and by twos, all the kids grew up.

Today, Meg grinned as she walked into Room 33 at Four Seasons Manor. There sat her elderly friend, parked in a wheelchair, puttering with a row of posies.

"I can tell that it's summertime again, Aunt Belle, just by glancing at your windowsill. Why, look at all the flowers!"

An impressive collection lined the wall. Vases of fresh-cut roses and peonies, flanked by crocks of marigolds and jars of pansies, all haloed Aunt Belle's angel-white hair. Her delicate fingers tamped the rich, damp soil that molded a clay pot of nodding violets.

"Yes, aren't they lovely, dear?" Aunt Belle glowed. "I've had so many visitors lately, mostly children from the old neighborhood. My, my, how they've grown. And each one who visits brings me flowers." Delphinium-blue eyes watered. "What a beautiful surprise."

Inhaling the earthy, garden blend of fragrance and friend, Meg slipped an arm around fragile shoulders.

"Why, that shouldn't surprise you, Aunt Belle. Don't you remember? You always promised, 'They'll come back.' And you were right. They have."

Carol McAdoo Rehme

3

GOD'S HEALING POWER

Bless the Lord, O my soul.
And forget not all His benefits:
Who forgives all your diseases.
Who redeems all your life destruction,
Who crowns you with loving kindness and tender mercies.

Psalm 103:1–4

A Small Unsteady Light

Jesus said, "Let the little children come to me, and do not hinder them, for the kingdom of heaven belongs to such as these."

Matthew 19:14

My mother insisted one of us had to stay with the Turners, holidays or not. They should not be left alone. They were not only friends and neighbors, but belonged to our church, and Mrs. Turner, as far as anyone knew, had never refused a request to help anyone.

Now her family had been stricken, and my mother was determined to do whatever it took to stand by them. "It breaks my heart that they have to suffer this way," she said. "We'll do our Christmas early. I'm not leaving Jeremy and Ruth to struggle through Christmas. Each of you can spend a day there now and I will go over on Christmas day. Then you all will just have to fend for yourselves."

So three days before Christmas I went to stay with the Turners. I was to answer phones and do errands—whatever I was asked to do.

Their house, just two doors from ours, was the most

sorrowful place I'd ever been. There were no Christmas decorations and hardly any lights on in the whole house. I wanted to go through the house and turn on all the lights, but that wasn't up to me to do. I answered phone calls and cleaned up the kitchen. They ate mostly fried chicken or meatloaf or vegetable soup brought in by friends and neighbors. They rarely talked because there was nothing to say.

Almost a week earlier their son, Skip, who was nine, had taken his old bike to Jim Nelson's house to practice carols with Jim and two other boys in their quartet. He broke his chain as he struggled to pedal up their steep drive. When they were finished practicing, Punky Harkins rode Skip home on his bike. Fifteen minutes later, Skip was dead. They'd skidded on the streetcar tracks on Harrison Avenue and Skip was thrown. His head struck a piece of frozen sludge, fallen from a passing car. He never opened his eyes again.

Now, four days after the funeral, Ruth Turner often sat alone in the kitchen drinking coffee. The Turners had sort of a playroom with an old couch downstairs, and I was down there on Christmas Eve reading when I heard Jeremy Turner come in the front door. I heard him go into the kitchen. He moved around a little, then I heard him say, "Gonna make coffee. Want some?"

"I have some," she said. Her voice sounded as though it hadn't been used for a long, long time. I knew she was sitting at the oak table, hunched over, head bowed, looking at the picture of Skip she kept with her all the time.

Then Mr. Turner said, "I'm going to put that away."

"Give that back, Jeremy. It's mine!" She screamed this at him. That sound made me afraid and I didn't know what to do. Then she said, "If you'd bought him a bike when he wanted it! If you had just once listened!"

"Stop it, Ruth. Stop it. I loved him as much as you."

Then there was scuffling, and the crash of glass, and then no sound at all. None. I did not know what to do. I waited until I was certain they'd left the kitchen and then crept upstairs. The frame the picture of Skip had been in was smashed and there was glass all over the floor. I began to clean up the mess.

I could hear Mrs. Turner crying in their bedroom. It was a soft sound that somehow reminded me of a bird's wings. I cleaned up the glass, wrapped it in paper and put it in the trash. I thought of calling my mom, but the worst seemed to be over and there was nothing she could do. Nothing anyone could do.

I decided to make hot chocolate, just in case. I don't know what made me do it, except we always had it at our house when everyone needed to calm down. As I was heating the milk, I heard the sound. It was faint and strange. The sound was coming from the Turners' yard. It was soft and shaky—the sound of small boys trying to sing carols before the dark face of the Turners' house.

Then Mr. and Mrs. Turner came downstairs. He came first and she a few moments later. I moved back against the living room wall trying to stay out of the way. They stood together in the darkness, waiting, I thought, for the singing to end. But it didn't. The boys sang and sang until the Turners finally went to the door.

Mr. Turner turned the light on in the hallway and then quickly opened the door. On the lawn stood three small boys. Last year, there had been four. Last year they'd had to pretend they did not know they were going to be caroling. It always had to be a surprise in our neighborhood.

The three boys stood there holding candles, the tiny flames throwing a small unsteady light. The boys were trying to sing "O Little Town of Bethlehem." Their breath frosted in the winter air and rose above their heads like smoke. Mr. Turner looked down at his wife who was clutching her robe at the throat. She took his hand and shivered so badly I could see it. She leaned against him, and he put his arm around her shoulder. Then we all saw in the flickering candlelight, a small boy standing in the snow, trying to sing. Punky Harkins was trying his best to sing although his entire body was shaken with the terrible sorrow he must have felt.

Mrs. Turner put her hands over her eyes and said softly, "Oh Lord, Lord." I held my breath, hoping that the darkness in her would break, that somehow she would not feel so alone. She stood, with her husband, for a long time, leaning into his body. And then he, in a gesture so gentle, so soft, that it seemed to come from someplace he had never before touched, he reached his hand to her face and guided her gaze outward to where the three boys of Skip's quartet sang in the cold winter air—"and in the dark street shineth, an everlasting light."

She looked out at them and then she raised her head. "Oh, that poor little boy," she said, "That little boy. To think of how he must feel!"

And she ran down the walk, through the sparkling snow and swept him up in her arms.

Walker Meade

Meeting God at 30,000 Feet

Humanity is never so beautiful as when praying for forgiveness, or else forgiving another.

Jean Paul Richter

I did some dumb things in junior high school. I think it just comes with the territory. But one particularly dumb thing involved a theft. I didn't steal money or shoplift, and I didn't take anyone's boyfriend. I simply stole a few votes.

The scene of the crime was journalism class, where those of us on the yearbook staff sat counting ballots for the school superlatives contest. Suddenly someone yelled out, "Caron! It looks like you may get enough votes to win Most Talented."

Until that moment, I had been the epitome of average. Winning a category in the superlatives contest would skyrocket my approval rating at Glenridge Junior High. I was eking out a social existence because my friends had friends who were cool. Like a mere feeder fish, I hovered close to the big fish in hopes of sucking some algae off them.

I soon found out, however, that I was not the only one

up for Most Talented. Trailing close behind me was Cindy, our school's guitar-playing singer. Cindy had real talent. She was even asked to sing her original song, "Beauty," at a school assembly. My only claim to fame was the pen and ink drawings I did on notebooks and book covers. Hardly a class went by that I didn't get at least one request for "Judy & Johnny 4-Ever," or "S. M. loves T. P."

Clearly, my talent was no match for Cindy's. Someone important once said, "The pen is mightier than the sword." But no one ever mentioned how the pen would do against the guitar. Guitars were big deals. I knew if I didn't do something fast, I would live my whole life in obscurity.

So, while votes were being tallied for other categories, I secretly grabbed a handful of uncounted ballots and tossed them in the trash. I was pretty sure no one saw me. I should have felt guilty, but I didn't. At the end of the day, I had won. And suddenly the demand for notebook art increased a good 40 percent.

Why it took God fifteen years to confront me on this, I'll never know. But it was He who brought it up one morning in my prayer time. By then we were on a first name basis, and He had full permission to speak to me about anything that bothered Him. Here is an abbreviated version of our conversation:

Me: God, I want to be all I can be for You. I've searched my heart for anything that might be standing in the way of this, and I've come up empty. I think I've dealt with all the sins I've ever committed. But I'll just sit here and wait for You to go through your files and see if You have something there I may have left out.

God: Well, there was that time in junior high school.

Me: Which time?

God: Most Talented?

Me: You saw that? It was such a long time ago. Surely

You have a statute of limitations or some kind of cutoff date for people who do dumb things prior to high school.

God: Not really.

Me: But, I'm 1,200 miles away. No telling where Cindy is. Do You realize the difficulty I would have in finding her? Okay, here's what I'll do. If one day I'm walking down the street and I happen to see her, I'll know You sent her and I'll make things right with her. Fair enough?

God: Fair enough.

I felt pretty safe. I hadn't seen Cindy in years. The odds of running into her in another state were microscopic.

Six months later, my husband and I were racing through the airport trying to catch a plane. When we reached the door of the 747, it had just been shut. My husband, forever the determined optimist, banged on the door as the noise of the engines accelerated. Suddenly, a nice flight attendant with exceptional hearing came to our rescue and opened the door.

We made our way to the back of the plane, comparing our tickets to the numbers overhead until we found a match. I plopped down in the middle seat assigned to me. Using my polite voice I said "Hello" to a woman next to me who was looking out the window. When she returned my greeting, adrenaline shot through me. In unison we both exclaimed, "Oh, my gosh! I can't believe it!"

There was Cindy, the guitar-playing singer.

A boxing match began inside me. From one corner came the feeling of someone who had just been given a million dollars. And from the other came the emotions of a hunted felon. Immediately I began carrying on two conversations, one on the surface with Cindy, the other internally with God.

Me: You actually found her! This is an outright miracle!

I can't believe You are forcing me to do this. You really are into the details, aren't You?

God: Yes.

From takeoff to landing, Cindy and I chattered away but all I could think of was how, out of the hundreds of thousands of people on airplanes that day, God looked for a needle in a haystack, found it, threaded it and placed it in my hand.

My palms started to sweat. I swallowed hard. No use stalling any longer. It was time to let Cindy in on the whole story. "Cindy," I said. "You're not going to believe this, but it's no accident we met today. Several months ago, I promised God I would make things right if our paths should ever cross again."

As I explained, Cindy laughed. She easily forgave me. It barely fazed her. I felt like scolding God for orchestrating such an ordeal. Then a familiar quote popped into my mind, "To whom much is given, much is required." God knew that if I'd confess a small matter from the past, He could trust me with greater responsibilities in the future.

I felt far from the epitome of average.

Caron Loveless

The Healing Power of Forgiveness

So I tell you, her many sins have been forgiven; hence, she has shown great love. But the one whom little is forgiven, loves little.

Luke 7:47

I thought about her. I dreamed about her. I saw her in every woman I met. Some had her name—Cathy. Others had her deep-set blue eyes or curly dark hair. Even the slightest resemblance turned my stomach into a knot.

Weeks, months, years passed. Was I never to be free of this woman who had gone after my husband and then, following our divorce, married him? I couldn't go on like this. The resentment, guilt and anger drained the life out of everything I did. I blamed myself. I went into counseling. I attended self-help classes, enrolled in seminars and workshops. I read books. I talked to anyone who would listen. I ran. I walked the beach. I drove for miles to nowhere. I screamed into my pillow at night. I prayed. I did everything I knew how to do.

Then one Saturday I was drawn to a daylong seminar on the healing power of forgiveness held at a church in my neighborhood. The leader invited participants to close their eyes and locate someone in their lives they had not forgiven—for whatever reason, real or imagined. Cathy. There she was again, looming large in my mind's eye.

Next, he asked us to look at whether or not we'd be willing to forgive that person. My stomach churned, my hands perspired and my head throbbed. I had to get out of that room, but something kept me in my seat.

How could I forgive a person like Cathy? She had not only hurt me, but she'd hurt my children. So I turned my attention to other people in my life. My mother. She'd be easy to forgive. Or my friend, Ann. Or my former high school English teacher. Anyone but Cathy. But there was no escape. The name, and the image of her face, persisted.

Then a voice within gently asked, "Are you ready to let go of this? To release her? To forgive yourself, too?"

I turned hot, then cold. I started to shake. I was certain everyone around me could hear my heart beating.

Yes, I was willing. I couldn't hold on to my anger any longer. It was killing me. In that moment, an incredible shift occurred within me. I simply let go. I can't describe it. I don't know what happened or what allowed me at that moment to do something I had resisted so doggedly. All I know is that for the first time in four years I completely surrendered to the Holy Spirit. I released my grip on Cathy, on my ex-husband, on myself. I let go of the rage and resentment—just like that.

Within seconds, energy rushed through every cell of my body. My mind became alert, my heart lightened. Suddenly I realized that as long as I separated myself from even one person, I separated myself from God. How self-righteous I had been. How arrogant. How judgmental. How important it had been for me to be *right,* no matter what the cost. And it had cost me plenty—my health, my spontaneity, my aliveness.

I had no idea what was next, but it didn't matter. That night I slept straight through until morning. No dreams. No haunting face. No reminders.

The following Monday I walked into my office and wrote Cathy a letter. The words spilled onto the page without effort.

"Dear Cathy," I began. "On Saturday morning . . ." and I proceeded to tell her what had occurred during the seminar. I also told her how I had hated her for what she had done to my marriage and to my family, and, as a result, how I had denied both of us the healing power of forgiveness. I apologized for my hateful thoughts. I signed my name, slipped the letter into an envelope, and popped it in the mail, relieved and invigorated.

Two days later, the phone rang. "Karen?"

There was no mistaking the voice.

"It's Cathy," she said softly.

I was surprised that my stomach remained calm. My hands were dry. My voice was steady and sure. I listened more than I talked—unusual for me. I found myself actually interested in what she had to say.

Cathy thanked me for the letter and acknowledged my courage in writing it. Then she told me how sorry she was—for everything. She talked briefly about her regret, her sadness for me, for my children and more. All I had ever wanted to hear from her, she said that day.

As I replaced the receiver, another insight came to me. I realized that as nice as it was to hear her words of apology, they didn't really matter. They paled in comparison to what God was teaching me. Buried deep in the trauma of my divorce was the truth I had been looking for all my life without even knowing it. No one can hurt me as long as I am in God's hands. Unless I allow it, no one can rob me of my joy.

Karen O'Connor

Healing at Columbine

For just as the sufferings of Christ flow over into our lives, so also through Christ our comfort overflows.

2 Corinthians 1:5

Screaming sirens. Hovering helicopters. Flashing lights. Yellow crime tape. No amount of training could have ever prepared me for what I was about to face.

Frightened students streamed out of Columbine with hands on their heads like criminals. Mothers cradled shell-shocked daughters in their arms. Fathers frantically ran to embrace their sons. The scenes on the television mesmerized us. Our assistant principal broke our fixed gaze. "All school district counselors need to report to Columbine immediately. Go."

I hurried to my office and grabbed my coat and purse. I ran to my car, turned on the radio and headed toward Columbine. Screeching tires pierced the tension as I swerved to miss a car that cut me off. Cars swerved recklessly while drivers were transfixed by the radio updates. The typical twenty-minute drive felt like an eternity. As I got to the main road leading to Columbine, I prayed out of desperation. *Lord, what do I say to these people? Please give me the right words for each person.*

Columbine was completely blocked off so I was detoured to Leawood Elementary. The streets were bombarded with four times as many vehicles as they could hold. Streams of people heading toward Leawood darted between cars. Media vans jumped the curbs to park on the grass. Police from every jurisdiction swarmed the area on ground and in the air. I parked in the closest spot, three blocks away. The magnitude of it all penetrated deeper with each step I walked toward Leawood. *Lord, give me wisdom for each situation.* My heart raced. *Help me to calm down, Lord. Please help me.*

I arrived at 1:30 P.M. and squeezed my way through the hordes of people and media. I flashed my ID card and pushed my way through the main doors. Chaos reigned inside. A familiar face directed me to the gym. Lines of parents, reunited and clinging to their kids, signed their names feverishly to get out of the pandemonium.

Confusion and frenzied activity now enveloped the gym—such a stark contrast from elementary children's laughter and joy just a few hours earlier. Students sobbed and hugged each other. Parents paced with eyes darting throughout the gym searching for their sons and daughters. Buses began arriving with the precious cargo from Columbine. When they entered the gym, students were corralled up to the stage at the far end. As parents saw their frightened teenagers, screams of joy and relief raised the rafters. For other parents, their wait continued.

As I mingled to see how I could help, I spotted her. She had gentle eyes and an unpretentious demeanor. Her wind-blown, short brown hair suggested she had probably been snatched away unexpectedly from her daily routine. She had the look of a mother who could relate to and understand teenagers. The man with her was dressed in business attire and must have rushed from his job to the scene. I eased my way over to them and my eyes met hers. I introduced myself and asked who they were waiting for. "Our son." I asked his name. "Jake Thompson.* I'm Karen—and this is my husband, Jim." I sensed that they didn't want to talk, so I respected their privacy and didn't press any further. I told them I would be listening for Jake's name, too. They personified the reserved hope mixed with fear that filled the room. I prayed as I walked to another area of the gym. *Lord, be with Jake wherever he is, and be with Karen and Jim, too.*

I talked with many other parents and students. The lists of names from the buses continued to ring out. Students came off the buses whooping and hollering. At times when I missed hearing the names being called, I would look across the gym to the Thompsons with a look that asked, *Was Jake's name called?* And they would shake their heads to the contrary. The hours dragged on, fewer buses came and the atmosphere in the gym became more solemn. I checked in with the Thompsons as often as I could to see if they had heard Jake's name.

The gym was swarming with more and more volunteers bringing food, drink and help. All was appreciated, but as the hours wasted away, everyone lost their appetites. At about 6:30 P.M., a question rang out from the far side of the gym. "Are any more buses coming?"

A deafening silence fell on the crowd. After a pause that seemed like forever, the answer pierced the stillness. "No."

I looked over at the Thompsons, and their heads dropped. They had several friends around them now, and I was glad they had familiar faces to support them. There were circles of people in chairs throughout the gym with

*name changed

about seventeen families still waiting for word. Of the eight families I'd worked with most closely that day, six saw their children enter the gym—two did not.

Now there was a circle of praying people around the Thompsons. I moved over behind them, yet stayed removed enough not to intrude. I prayed with them from where I was. When they were finished, they encouraged Karen to go home since it would still be hours before they would know anything definite. She left with several supporters at her side.

At 9:30 P.M. I left Leawood, exhausted. The streets were dark and foreboding. The heaviness in the air thickened and remained over the next few days as I spent long hours counseling students and parents.

Four days after the shooting, I saw a picture of Karen and Jim Thompson at their son's funeral on the front page of the morning paper. All the emotions from that day at Leawood came flooding back. I couldn't get the Thompsons off my mind. For the next several months, their faces and that day at Leawood flashed before my eyes. I prayed every day for them. I was very guarded about dealing with my own grief from the tragedy, because I was continually in situations where I had to be strong for others. I planned to counsel in the Columbine area throughout the summer. I was afraid that if I allowed the grief to come, I could lose control and be overwhelmed by it. I would have time for my own healing later.

In the middle of the summer, I wrote Karen a letter to let her know that she was in my thoughts and prayers every day. I knew that typically the most difficult times after a tragedy are three to four months after the event. The shock wears off, the grief is more intense than ever and the constant support from friends and loved ones subsides. I wrote the letter to validate Karen and the grieving process she was going through.

A month or so later, I was delighted to see Karen at a luncheon at a women's conference in Denver. I was anxious to see how she was doing, though seeing her brought back my own memories of our hope-shattering day. To my surprise, I couldn't hold back my tears any more. But this time Karen counseled me. "Sandy, your letter was a great encouragement. It came just when I needed it. Knowing you were praying for me was such a comfort."

Her words inspired my heart. It comforted me to know that I had helped her, and I was glad to see how well she was doing. She had courageously faced her pain, and her example gave me strength to face my own pain as well.

As I brushed away the tears, I knew that my time for healing had finally come. It was time to let go of my pent-up emotions. I had gone to the luncheon thinking I could reach out to Karen again, but instead God used her to reach out to me. She was the catalyst to my own healing process.

Before that meeting, the sound of police sirens and helicopters made me cringe as I remembered that day at Leawood. But now when I hear them, they remind me of God's faithfulness and provision, and that He will provide me—and others—with the words and strength to do what He calls us to do.

Sandy Austin
Submitted by Linda Evans Shepherd

Mercy's Time

His heart was as great as the world, but there was no room in it to hold the memory of a wrong.

Ralph Waldo Emerson

She was almost my mother-in-law. I was nineteen, and she was in her late fifties.

She welcomed my presence into her son's life and treated me like a daughter. Our mutual love for her son was our commonality and created a strong bond between us. Invited into their world, I shared meals and trips to the family cabin. A year and a depleted box of Kleenex later, we left her son at boot camp.

To fend off long winter nights I visited her after work. We had warm talks of possibilities. She, a patient right-hander, taught me, a left-hander with dreams of marriage, to crochet a bedspread. I helped her pick out a puppy at the Humane Society; Doris named her Precious.

When the engagement was announced, she started my hope chest with gifts of a silverware chest and milk-glass butter dish. Though she often said she was a terrible cook, my first recipe of Mexican stew, which I still make, came from her.

Sadly, when I broke the engagement, I broke my friendship with Doris. Awkward and young, I didn't know how to say good-bye. So I didn't.

On occasion, in the twenty years since, she came to mind. As hard as I tried, I could not put her out of my head. I knew I would never forgive myself if something happened to her before I said I was sorry for my rude behavior.

On a Florida vacation as I read a novel filled with estrangements and reconciliations, she visited my thoughts again. Whether Doris chose to forgive me or not, it was time to apologize for the abrupt severing of our friendship. I had no idea where she lived, but I knew that her sister, Elsie, lived in town. Through the phone directory, I found Elsie's telephone number. It took me two weeks to muster the courage to call.

Elsie informed me that the years had been harsh to Doris. She had gone through a divorce, suffered through several seizures and then brain surgery, and was now in the final stages of emphysema. Elsie gave me Doris's address and said it would be fine if I wrote to her.

Now that I had permission I was terrified. I had broken her son's heart and shattered a seemingly perfect dream of togetherness. Surely she must hate me. Certainly no good could come from a simple, handwritten apology.

A sleepless week went by. It was no use—until I put pen to paper, there would be no peace in my heart. *Lord, give me the words to convey how sorry I am,* was my quiet plea.

"Dear Doris," I wrote. "I know it's been many years since you and I last had contact." It took until page three to get to my reason for writing. "I know when I broke your son's heart, I broke part of yours," I continued. "Knowing you like I once did, you probably forgave me years ago, but what good is an apology that no one hears? I'm sorry for the pain and the way I ended it all," I wrote. I asked for forgiveness; if she found it in her heart to do so, I wanted to hear it.

Two weeks went by before her familiar curly handwriting appeared in my mailbox. The envelope was heavy. My fears resurfaced. I prepared for a severe lecture.

"You can't know what your letter has done for me," she wrote. "Came at the right time, too." Her letter was delightful. She gladly accepted my apology and forgave me, recalled some happy times and even asked for a recipe.

Her words lightened a burden I had carried for too long.

As I put the letter back in the envelope, a picture of Precious slipped out. On the back she had written, "Remember when you went with me to pick her out? She died last year. I miss her so." That dog, like the Mexican stew, was a part of our togetherness that had carried into Doris's life, too.

God's merciful timing taught me it's never too late to say you're sorry. Two months later her sister called to tell me Doris passed away. I'm grateful God knew I needed to say good-bye.

Julie Saffrin

Forgiveness Tastes Sweet

For if you forgive men when they sin against you, your heavenly Father will also forgive you.

Matthew 6:14

In the prewar Soviet Union, few Russians would openly call themselves Christians. People disappeared for lesser slips of the tongue.

In their crowded communal apartment in Leningrad, only my grandmother's children could occasionally hear her whispering prayers early in the morning behind closed doors. The state would take away her children and place them in an orphanage if her "religious influence" on them became known. It was in her best interests, and her children's, to keep her faith to herself.

That's why the prewar census worried my grandmother. Everybody was told to report to census centers organized at schools, hospitals and other public places. Many dressed up for such a festive occasion; few people knew that the state used the information collected to prosecute its own citizens.

Grandmother watched her neighbors standing in line,

answering the census clerks' questions. Piles of completed questionnaires towered on the desk. Age, education, place of birth, native tongue—religion? "Atheist," people answered without fail. Few of them were truly atheists, and some even ventured to church, making sure no one saw them enter. But they all chose the safe answer.

Finally, my grandmother faced the census clerk. Breathless, she could feel her heart beating in her ears. His questions seemed to last for an hour. She prepared to lie, for her children's sake.

"Religion?"

She looked at the other people in the room. All the census officials needed from her was a statistic, a figure to add to others. God knew the truth—so she wasn't really telling a lie, was she?

"Atheist," she said.

After that, her life changed. Once a cheerful young mother of three, she grew depressed and quiet. In her disturbed mind, she kept asking herself whether she still had a right to pray to God, and whether she still belonged to Him.

World War II started. In September 1941, the Germans surrounded Leningrad and bombed the city's food stores. The 900-day siege of Leningrad had begun. By December, the townspeople's daily rations consisted of four ounces of smelly bread made of bran, starch and sawdust. The winter temperatures fell to a record 40 degrees below zero. City plumbing collapsed and frozen sewage covered apartment floors. There was no water, no food, no heat. People died by the thousands—daily. They passed away in their beds, on the street, in offices and factories. They all quietly shared one silent resolve: not to let the enemy enter their city.

One December evening, as her children fell asleep fully dressed under layers of quilts, my grandmother knew her time had run out, too. She was going to die before morning. By that time, all people had learned the signs of approaching death from starvation—a sudden bout of appetite, bloody diarrhea, lethargy. Grandmother wanted to spare her children the horror of waking up next to their mother's dead body. She desperately needed to survive until the morning. And she knew of only one power capable of stopping death. She prayed.

She didn't think she had a right to ask for God's help. But a mother will do anything to save her children, even face God's wrath. That night, my grandmother screamed her heart out, begging God to let her live until the morning. As she finished praying, she remembered one thing that was said to delay death from starvation: movement. She looked around the room. They had already burned most of the furniture for fuel, but a few pieces remained—a nineteenth-century carved oak bed and mahogany bookcases weighing hundreds of pounds. Now a dying, emaciated woman was going to push and pull them around in a desperate attempt to prolong her life with exercise.

Afraid of waking the kids, my grandmother started with the kitchen. She felt her way through the dark apartment and forced an oak table away from the kitchen window. She barely moved the buffet from the corner. Sacrificing a match, she investigated the floor behind the buffet. Not a crumb of bread. Not even a dead mouse—the townspeople had eaten the mouse population a long time ago.

As the flame was dying out, she noticed something in the corner by the wall. She squeezed her frail body into the crack to check it. She lit another match to see what it was. A brown bag sat in the corner, covered with cobwebs, lost and forgotten since the happy prewar days. She took it out and placed the heavy pack on the kitchen table.

Sugar.

In the morning, she woke her children and gave each a

see-through slice of heavy, moist bread sprinkled with strange white powder.

"What's that, Mom?"

"Eat it. It's cake."

The elder daughter doubted the answer as she remembered fancy cream cakes in the prewar shop windows. But this one tasted a hundred times better.

Their mother laughed with them now, as happy and beautiful as she was before the siege.

Two pounds of sugar can save quite a few people. My grandmother didn't die that winter, and neither did her children, nor most of her family and neighbors. Sometimes, she said, it seemed the brown bag had no bottom at all.

Yet, my grandmother forever grieved that, just like Peter, she'd had to answer the question about whether she knew Christ or not. And she'd answered, "I do not know him."

Grandmother never forgave herself—but she knew God did.

Elaine Freeland Galaktionova

The Ride

Peace I leave you; my peace I give you. Not as the world gives do I give it to you. Do not let your hearts be troubled or afraid.

John 14:27

Since both of my parents worked, Dad frequently shared in the parental duties of raising his daughters. It was often Dad who met us at the bus stop after school, ripped old Band-Aids off of our skinned knees, and taught us how to ride our bikes without training wheels. He snuck quarters into our pockets when the tooth fairy forgot, made up funny stories, and attended school plays that I knew broke in to his work day. Often on his days off, he joined us in a game of hide-and-seek, finding creative and original places to hide my younger sister. I was certain the safest place in the world was being wrapped in my dad's strong arms. His hugs melted away all my fears.

Dad wrote notes on the back of my artwork and other school projects, saying such things as, "I love you more than you'll ever know," or "I'm so proud of you."

The summer I was fourteen, my father did something

totally uncharacteristic of the other fathers in the neighborhood: he bought a motorcycle. We were amused at first, never realizing that owning a motorcycle was a lifelong dream of my dad's.

"I used to have a bike when I was in the Navy," he reminisced. "I've waited years for another." He beamed proudly at the bike parked by the side of the house, its chrome exterior flashing in the sunlight. My father drove it every chance he could, often taking my sister or me along for the ride. He bought us helmets and took time teaching us the rules of the road as they applied to motorcycle riding. I knew this was not just a passing phase with Dad, he truly enjoyed this motorcycle. The shiny bike and my father were a perfect fit. One day, while we were on a road trip, he confided in me that when his time came to die, he hoped he would be on his bike.

The following spring, my dad dusted the winter dirt off his bike and went for a ride. I never saw him alive again. He was killed instantly when a drunk driver collided into him. The grief and terror of the following days were a blur. Many nights I woke up and discovered my pillow wet with tears. I was inconsolable; I was convinced I would never feel joy again.

The grieving my family and I endured seemed endless, yet we mysteriously held each other up at the same time. On one difficult night, my mother shared with me a vision that consoled her: "I saw your father taking that last trip on his bike down a beautiful country road that lead straight into heaven."

That image was a healing balm for my aching heart. Whenever I felt insecure about losing my dad, I would retrieve that soothing image.

I was in my late twenties when I met John. He was in his early forties, the same age my father was when he died. John had warm eyes, a ponytail, a leather jacket, and—you guessed it—a motorcycle that he enjoyed as much as my father had enjoyed his. John and I became friends through our shared faith in God. I never told him the circumstances of my father's death, and I secretly prayed for his safety every time I saw him riding his bike. John frequently went on extended road trips, and I often didn't see him for months at a time.

One day, after an absence of several months, John caught up with me at a church gathering. He was excited about a recent road trip. He looked healthy and his eyes were sparkling.

"Come with me, I have something to show you." He took my hand and led me out the door. I had no idea what he was up to. We walked past the rows of cars and turned the corner of the building. There stood his huge, shiny new motorcycle.

The familiar sense of terror and grief returned.

"Come closer and take a look at this," he said, completely unaware of the emotions I was fighting.

I took a deep breath and walked up to the bike. The leather seat, paneled instruments and shiny chrome were all reminders of an innocent past. My heart began pounding loudly in my chest. Hidden memories of a cherished childhood surfaced in one bittersweet swell. How vividly I remembered traveling on that bike, my arms wrapped tightly around my father's waist, and my head buried in the back of his shoulder as the sharp wind snapped against us.

At John's urging, I walked closer to the bike and stopped. I couldn't believe my eyes.

"My son painted this," John said. His smile spread across his face.

The beautiful scene, skillfully hand-painted on the upper body of the bike, depicted a man riding a motorcycle down a beautiful country road leading into heaven.

The clouds held an image of Jesus with arms outstretched, ready to meet the rider. It was an exact representation of the vision my mother had shared with me over a decade before.

"It's beautiful," I said to John.

The old grief and terror melted away, and peace filled my soul as I finally let my father ride into the waiting arms of Jesus.

Michelle Beaupre Matt

The Purpose of My Soul

Have a purpose in life, and having it, throw such strength of mind and muscle into your work as God has given you.

Thomas Carlyle

The view of tree-lined, snowcapped mountains, with Mt. Lassen towering above all, was majestic. Our campground, filled with tiny four-person cabins nestled near a mountain stream, added to the tranquil autumn atmosphere. Forty-seven women and eight men had assembled at this church youth camp for a five-day workshop called Empowering the Authentic Self.

The attendees, from affiliate churches throughout California and Nevada, seemed relaxed and friendly. Everyone was eager to begin their search for "the purpose of their soul," for their true mission in life and for the tools to carry out that mission. Our spiritual leader, Reverend David, and his wife, Carolyn, traveled from Oklahoma City to guide our journey.

We began each day with an early morning meditation in a warm, fire-lit room adjacent to our meeting hall. This special sanctuary was reserved for quiet time and reflection. The fire, tended by our camp hosts, would remain lit during our entire visit, signifying an eternal flame of peace and spiritual healing. It wasn't unusual to find an individual sitting by the fire at two or three in the morning, meditating in search of God's plan for them. The workshop was a time to explore unanswered questions and new possibilities in a place of worship and peacefulness.

At the beginning of every workshop session, we spent time sharing dreams, expectations, disappointments and lessons learned from the previous days activities. For some, standing in front of total strangers and divulging personal stories was painfully difficult and often tearful. In fact, many participants weren't able to do this, and they were never made to feel that they had to share an experience with the group. Their presence alone helped create a safe haven where sharing was welcome and accepted without judgment.

We often, in groups of three or four, shared intimate details of our lives. For twelve to fourteen hours a day, we dug into our pasts and struggled to find a connection between our adult selves and our inner child. Every night we were asked to describe in our daily journals what we had experienced in the day's workshop.

The second evening of the workshop, during a group session focusing on traumatic events that had affected our lives, Jan spoke for the first time. She was quite shy and had trouble beginning her story, but with Reverend David's compassionate encouragement she began. Emotionally distraught and tearful, Jan told us about how she had recently attended a class reunion. Many years had passed since her graduation and this was her first reunion. Coincidentally, she was now a teacher and loved her work with children, though she often wondered if she was truly inspiring them.

Jan was approaching middle age and her body had changed. As her weight increased, her self-esteem decreased. Nevertheless, before the reunion, she decided to do her best to lose some weight, have her hair styled and her nails manicured, and buy a new dress. When the big day arrived Jan was excited. She had transformed herself and felt beautiful. Her enthusiasm carried her right into the reunion where she mixed with the crowd.

As the night progressed, the band started playing wonderful music. The songs brought back many glorious memories of Jan's childhood, and she remembered how she loved to dance. She found a seat near the dance floor to be available when another single partner asked her to dance. Too shy to ask anyone herself, she sat alone, silently listening to the music. Her soul danced every dance, but as the night wore on and no one asked her to dance, sadness overwhelmed her. Devastated and feeling rejected, Jan went home, her spirit broken. She wasn't pretty enough, petite enough or charming enough to be asked to dance.

The room was silent as Jan finished her story. Our hearts were wounded, too. We wept with her, gave her comfort and held her hands.

The next morning, as we assembled for our early session, the room was unusually dark. As we took our seats, Reverend David's first request was that we hold hands and pray together. He prayed that our lessons would bring God's word to us abundantly and open our hearts to his offerings. We sat in prayerful silence, then we heard the song—"I Hope You Dance," by Lee Ann Womack—softly begin to echo through the room. Reginald, a male singer from the group, stood up and walked across the room toward Jan. As he approached her, he gently held his outstretched hand for hers. "May I have this dance?" he asked.

They danced gracefully around the room, holding each other closely as Jan cried. I stood, made my way to the dance floor and asked Reginald for Jan's hand. As we began dancing, all the males in the room gathered and waited in line to dance with Jan, too. Reverend David was the last to dance with her. When the music stopped, the men all gathered around Jan. We hugged her and escorted her back to her seat.

Reverend David, fighting back emotion, said he hadn't planned on bringing that CD to the workshop. While driving to the camp, however, he had stopped at a music store, saw the CD and sensed he was supposed to buy it. He didn't know why. When Jan told her story the day before, he knew why. It had been God's plan that he purchase the music and be a "messenger."

Jan changed that day. She talked a few more times before we completed our five-day workshop, and on the last day she told us how the dance had healed her heart and made her feel accepted. Before she left for home she said, "Now I will inspire students—and teach them not to be judgmental or form opinions based on appearance."

Jan had found the purpose of her soul.

Duane Shaw
Dedicated to David and Carolyn Jones

4

FRIENDSHIP

A true friend is a gift of God, and only He who made hearts can unite them.

Robert South

That's What Friends Do

Jack tossed the papers on my desk, his eyebrows knit into a straight line as he glared at me.

"What's wrong?" I asked.

He jabbed a finger at the proposal. "Next time you want to change anything, ask me first," he said, turning on his heels, leaving me stewing in anger.

How dare he treat me like that, I thought. I had changed one long sentence and corrected grammar, something I thought I was paid to do.

It's not that I hadn't been warned. Other women who had worked my job before me called Jack names I couldn't repeat. One coworker took me aside the first day. "He's personally responsible for two different secretaries leaving the firm," she whispered.

As the weeks went by, I grew to despise Jack. His actions made me question much that I believed in, such as turning the other cheek and loving your enemies. Jack quickly slapped a verbal insult on any cheek turned his way. I prayed about the situation, but to be honest, I wanted to put Jack in his place, not love him.

One day another of his episodes left me in tears. I

stormed into his office, prepared to lose my job if needed, but not before I let the man know how I felt. I opened the door and Jack glanced up. "What?" he asked abruptly.

Suddenly I knew what I had to do. After all, he deserved it.

I sat across from him and said calmly, "Jack, the way you've been treating me is wrong. I've never had anyone speak to me that way. As a professional, it's wrong, and I can't allow it to continue."

Jack snickered nervously and leaned back in his chair. I closed my eyes briefly. *God help me,* I prayed.

"I want to make you a promise. I will be a friend," I said. "I will treat you as you deserve to be treated, with respect and kindness. You deserve that. Everybody does." I slipped out of the chair and closed the door behind me.

Jack avoided me the rest of the week. Proposals, specs and letters appeared on my desk while I was at lunch, and my corrected versions were not seen again. I brought cookies to the office one day and left a batch on his desk. Another day I left a note. "Hope your day is going great," it read.

Over the next few weeks, Jack reappeared. He was reserved, but there were no other episodes. Coworkers cornered me in the break room. "Guess you got to Jack," they said. "You must have told him off good."

I shook my head. "Jack and I are becoming friends," I said in faith. I refused to talk about him. Every time I saw Jack in the hall, I smiled at him. After all, that's what friends do.

One year after our "talk," I discovered I had breast cancer. I was thirty-two, the mother of three beautiful young children, and scared. The cancer had metastasized to my lymph nodes and the statistics were not great for long-term survival. After my surgery, friends and loved ones visited and tried to find the right words. No one knew what to say, and many said the wrong things.

Others wept, and I tried to encourage them. I clung to hope myself.

One day, Jack stood awkwardly in the doorway of my small, darkened hospital room. I waved him in with a smile. He walked over to my bed and without a word placed a bundle beside me. Inside the package lay several bulbs.

"Tulips," he said.

I grinned, not understanding.

He shuffled his feet, then cleared his throat. "If you plant them when you get home, they'll come up next spring. I just wanted you to know that I think you'll be there to see them when they come up."

Tears clouded my eyes, and I reached out my hand. "Thank you," I whispered.

Jack grasped my hand and gruffly replied, "You're welcome. You can't see them now, but next spring you'll see the colors I picked out for you. I think you'll like them." He turned and left without another word.

For ten years, I have watched those red-and-white striped tulips push their way through the soil every spring.

In a moment when I prayed for just the right word, a man with very few words said all the right things.

After all, that's what friends do.

T. Suzanne Eller

THE FAMILY CIRCUS® **By Bil Keane**

"Real friends don't hafta keep talking all the time."

Prayer Pals

God dwells far off from us, but prayer brings Him down to our Earth, and links His power with our efforts.

Madam deGastarin

"What in the world are prayer pals for?" I asked, when my principal gave me Mrs. Grabol's name during teacher orientation in August. He explained that they were usually older women in the church community who'd committed to pray for our classes. "You'll enjoy Mrs. Grabol," he said. "She's quite a gal."

In public school where I had taught previously, I'd had reading helpers who had volunteered to come work with my first-graders. I'd also had fifth-grade friends who drilled math facts into my students and helped during writing time. Their help was practical. Prayer pals seemed a very strange use of people power.

Many things seemed strange at St. Theresa's. I wondered if I'd made the wrong decision in coming to teach there. Maybe I'd been hasty, but after my dad's death the year before, I thought just being there would help me through the grieving process. I missed him so much.

I told Mrs. Grabol of my dad's death when I called to introduce myself. She consoled me and explained that it was after her husband of forty-seven years had passed away that she'd decided to be a prayer pal. In talking, we discovered that her husband and my dad had something in common—they'd both been bird carvers. Mrs. Grabol assured me that coming to St. Theresa's had been a good decision.

Earlier in the summer, when I'd mentioned teaching in Catholic school, my husband had encouraged me to make the change. "Heck, honey," he said, "getting by on only half as much money will make the transition easier when we start a family. Besides," he added, "your dad would have liked it."

Dad would have. He'd gone to Catholic school all the way through high school, and I supposed that if he hadn't been a coach in public schools, my brothers, sister and I would have gone to Catholic school, too.

Dad would have chuckled at all the lessons I learned in the next few months. In September, when the pastor told us we had to display a Bible in our classrooms, I put out a Protestant one with the seven extra Catholic books missing. Somehow, Mrs. Grabol learned of my mistake. She had her daughter bring me a Catholic Bible and sent a little note saying she wished she could help out more but that it was too hard to get over to school in her wheelchair. She hoped that her prayers were helping; not just her prayers for the kids, but her prayers for me, too.

In October I didn't know what to teach about All Soul's Day, but Mrs. Grabol mailed me an article about how families in Mexico celebrate the Day of the Dead. The kids thought it was neat. We made some little sugar skeleton heads like those we saw in the pictures. I took one over to the assisted living center for her. She thanked me, but explained she couldn't eat sweets because she was diabetic. I felt grateful that my dad died without having many illnesses. He'd have hated losing his feet like Mrs. Grabol had lost hers.

In November, when it was time to make Advent wreaths, I couldn't remember whether you needed three purple candles and one pink candle, or three pinks and one purple. Mrs. Grabol sent a big class wreath for us to copy so I didn't even have to admit my ignorance to any of the other teachers. She also sent some old green garland so we could make little wreaths. "I just don't decorate much anymore," she wrote. "But I'll be praying with you when you say the Advent prayers."

December came, and with it, depression. How could we celebrate Christmas without my dad? He wouldn't be there to put the lights on the tree. He wouldn't be there to beg me to wrap his presents so he wouldn't have to do it. He wouldn't be there to tease my mom about putting enough vanilla in the traditional cream puffs. I was so busy feeling sorry for myself that I hadn't realized I'd not heard from Mrs. Grabol for a few weeks.

The week before Christmas vacation, she called. She'd been in the hospital, she explained, but was back home now and was sending a treat for the children. That afternoon her daughter arrived with a huge box. On the card addressed to me was a beautiful cardinal, just like the ones Dad used to carve. Mrs. Grabol wrote that she'd been praying for me. She hoped this first Christmas without Dad wouldn't be too hard.

I opened the box. It was filled with cream puffs!

When I called Mrs. Grabol to thank her and explain the significance of the cream puffs, and how much her prayers had meant to me, she answered in her sweet soft voice, "That's what prayer pals are for."

Ellen Javernick

"My cooking has improved, Mom. Now we pray before we eat, rather than before I cook."

Reprinted by permission of Dave Carpenter.

Tammy and the Diamond Dress

Sitting on the flowered print couch, I paged through the Kissees' family album: there was nine-year-old Tammy, ten-year-old Tammy, eleven-year-old Tammy. Then I looked across the room at twelve-year-old Tammy playing checkers with her father. Her long blonde hair was gone; the radiation had left only a wisp of fuzz on her head. Her fair complexion was now a chalky gray. The skeleton-like limbs made her appear weak and breakable.

Tammy caught a side glimpse of me staring, and she figured out pretty quickly that I had to be comparing her to the robust girl sitting astride the black horse in the picture. She smiled at me as if to say, "It's okay. I'll be that girl again someday."

My four-year-old daughter Kimberly leaned over Tammy's shoulder to watch her next move on the game board. "I think you should jump the black checker with the red one, Tammy." Tammy laughed, touching her dark curls with envy. "I *am* the black checker."

We met the Kissee family a year earlier when they began attending our small country church, soon after Tammy had been diagnosed with liver cancer. They joined the congregation, and we all began to pray daily for a healing miracle.

There was something so ethereal about Tammy. Kimberly couldn't resist her and became her shadow. Often Tammy felt weary from treatment, but she somehow managed to add strength to her patience in dealing with this admiring fan. Tammy had two older brothers, so she treated Kimberly as a welcomed younger sister. With their heads together, one nearly bald and the other thick with lustrous curls, they paged through the children's Bible.

One day as I sewed, Kimberly said, "I need a diamond dress to wear for special occasions, like to parties and weddings and funerals." I flinched at her last word. Tammy laughed and seemed to understand something I could not grasp.

"Why funerals?" I could not meet Tammy's eyes.

"Because when people die they go home to heaven. I really need a dress for that celebration!"

Monday morning, Kimberly and I sorted through stacks and rows of fabric in the basement of an old Ben Franklin store.

"Here it is!" she exclaimed, holding up some purple cloth with a colorful jelly-bean print on it. "Diamonds!"

"Honey, those are jelly beans."

"No, they are diamonds, beautiful colored diamonds."

I looked at the material for a long time, trying to see what Kimberly saw, but finally gave up. I asked for two yards to be cut, picked out matching thread and paid my money. All week I struggled with making my daughter's diamond dress. To make it fancier I sewed on a lace collar and dotted it with rhinestones. Kimberly was happy with the result; she saw diamonds, I saw jelly beans.

Christmas was festive at church with a wonderful program and platters of carefully prepared food. Tammy admitted she felt awkward around girls her own age, as they didn't quite know how to act toward the girl who looked so different from them. So she remained by her little four-year-old friend and was a wonderful help in serving the food.

I thought I detected a little color crawling back into Tammy's wan cheeks. *Surely she will recover and be just fine.* I said another silent prayer for the hundredth, the thousandth, the millionth time.

I watched Tammy out of the corner of my eye all evening. She checked plates and cups, making sure everyone had enough to eat and drink, and served more when needed. She seated the elderly in the most comfortable chairs. I saw her push back the constant fatigue she experienced in order to help turn the pages for the pianist's music. At last, she sat with the children gathered about her feet, leading them in Christmas songs, listening intently to their stories. She was a young girl who was not self-absorbed in makeup and boyfriends. She was a young girl absorbed in helping others.

Two days after Christmas, we received a call from Tammy's parents. She had been rushed to the hospital. Walking into her room, I noticed how small she looked among the bed sheets. Her mother rubbed her forehead and smiled into the blue eyes that were heavy with sleep. My husband and I stood by her bed, along with her parents and brothers. Although we had prayed for healing, God performed His own miracle and just before midnight took Tammy home to live with Him in heaven.

The members of the church dreaded the funeral of one so young. We seem to understand and accept better the death of someone elderly who has lived a long and full life. This young life slipping away from us, however, made our own mortality seem more brittle. And there were the nagging questions: Had we failed Tammy in not believing hard enough, in not praying long enough?

I held my four-year-old daughter's hand as we walked up to the old oak casket. Tammy appeared as if she had gotten ready for church and then simply laid down for a quick rest among her favorite toys. I squeezed Kimberly's hand tighter. If she got too close to the casket, would death snatch her too? Sensing my fears, Mr. Kissee picked Kimberly up into his arms so she could clearly see Tammy's face.

"She is at peace now. See, no more pain on her face," he told her.

Kimberly looked into the pain-filled father's eyes and then nodded seriously, turning her attention back to her friend.

"Thanks for helping me be quiet in church," my daughter whispered to her. "See, I wore my diamond dress for you today. You knew how important it was. I am so happy that you can see heaven. Save me a seat next to you."

During the service, Tammy's parents sat close together holding hands, their grieving sons on either side. The pastor spoke, "This is not the end but the beginning for Tammy. Let her beginning be a new beginning for us as well. Let's finish what she has started, and may it be a work in progress."

It was true. Tammy left us with so much. She set her own needs aside to help others. She cheerfully illustrated to my impressionable daughter, to children yet to be shaped, and to adults set in their ways, how to be of service to others when pain and tiredness are your greatest enemies.

That night I tucked my own little daughter into her bed, thinking that Tammy would never be tucked into hers again. Kim looked at me with concern. Her tiny finger brushed away one of my tears.

"Mommy, when I close my eyes I can see Tammy. She

has her long blonde hair back and wears a beautiful dress with stones all over it. I think her diamond dress is even prettier than mine," Kimberly whispered while pointing to her jelly-bean dress hanging in the closet.

I closed my eyes too. Yes, I can imagine Tammy with her long hair and pink, glowing complexion. I think she is probably wearing her own diamond dress as she gallops through the streets of heaven.

Robin Lee Shope

Strengthened by Angels

The Lord, before whom I have walked, will send His angel with you and make your journey a success . . .

Genesis 24:40

"Mom, where's my black jacket?" my teenage daughter asked as she joined me in the kitchen while I prepared school lunches.

"I don't know, Jennifer. Wherever you left it," I snapped abruptly, finding it difficult to think about anything but cancer.

Tomorrow! My mastectomy is tomorrow. The thought consumed me as the fear and helplessness that came with this disease roared like a ferocious lion inside me.

My thoughts were interrupted again as my other daughter Melissa exclaimed, "Look at my hair, Mom. My bangs need cutting. I can't go to school looking like this."

She held a pair of scissors in her hand.

"Sit down, Melissa, and give me the scissors," I said halfheartedly.

While trying to focus on cutting her soft blonde hair, the

thought occurred to me that some day I might not be alive to do this. Tears filled my eyes.

"Are you crying?" she asked. "What's the matter, Mom?"

"It's just that I'm glad to be your mother," I spoke softly. I finished cutting her bangs and took my daughters to school.

When they left the car, I kept thinking about my husband of twenty-three years and our girls. Returning home, I joined my husband for a cup of coffee on the patio before he left for work. "You're going to be all right, honey," he reassured me as his tender arms embraced me like a comforter. "We can bear this. After all, we have the Great Physician with us."

Finally alone, I kept wondering: *If I die, who will take our daughters shopping for just the right outfit for their first date? Who will help them learn the importance of friendship, if I am not able to be their friend? Who will support my husband during the tough times, like when he loses a job? And who will help him find the simple things, like mayonnaise in the refrigerator?*

Many thoughts paraded through my mind. I had supported friends when cancer had invaded their lives, but now I had to accept the fact that this was not someone else's nightmare—it was mine! For years God has been my companion, but I'd never been terrified enough to fully "trust in the Lord and be of good courage."

The silence of our home was not a welcomed relief from the demands of my children. I was alone—alone with my thoughts, which kept overflowing like a broken faucet. I curled up in my favorite chair and reached for my King James Bible. I desperately needed solace.

My fingers slowly turned the pages, groping for words of strength and peace. I stopped in Luke and began reading the passage about Christ praying in the garden of Gethsemane: "Father, if You are willing, take this cup from me; yet not my will, but Yours be done." An angel from Heaven appeared to Him and strengthened Him. (Luke 22:42–43) I had read these verses many times but never realized God sent an angel to comfort His son.

"This is what I need," I spoke aloud. "You sent an angel to strengthen Your son. Please give me something to hold on to today. I need an angel."

Routine household chores failed to free my mind from fearful thoughts. I needed a diversion and decided a trip to the market would help. At the store, my grocery list helped me focus. What a relief to think of practical needs like milk, bread and butter. I headed for the cookie aisle to stock up on our daughters' favorite cookies so they would have them while I was in the hospital.

Reaching for the package, I recognized a friend and fellow teacher from years ago.

"Hi, Pat," I tried to sound cheerful.

"Sharon, how are you?" she asked as she steered her cart closer to mine. It was strange how the depth of the question, "How are you?" had changed. It was no longer just a lighthearted social greeting.

"Do you really want to know?" I asked as the knot in the pit of my stomach tightened.

"Of course I do," she replied sincerely.

"They found cancer in my left breast, and I'm going to have a radical mastectomy tomorrow morning. I'm not sure how far the cancer has spread." I fought back tears.

Pat listened intently as I shared my diagnosis and biopsy experience.

"Do you remember Bert Seacat?" she asked while softly touching my shoulder. "She's a teacher, too."

"Yes, I do," I answered. "We taught at the same elementary school. I haven't seen her in twenty years."

"Well," Pat continued, "she had a double mastectomy ten years ago, and she's just as feisty as ever."

I pushed my cart closer to Pat. "She is?" Hope began to flicker within me.

We reminisced for awhile and then we both continued shopping. I quietly thanked God for the encouraging news Pat shared about our mutual friend. My heavy burden of anxiety began to lift. I no longer felt limited to my shopping list and began to feel a sense of freedom.

A few minutes later, I made my way to the front of the store and looked down the row of fifteen checkout aisles. I saw Pat again, ready to unload her groceries. I steered my cart behind her.

We started to talk, but my eyes looked beyond her to the woman paying for her groceries. A strange feeling came over me. I looked closer. *No, it can't be,* I thought, as the woman turned, looked at me and smiled.

"Hi Sharon," she said sympathetically. "Pat was just telling me what's going to happen to you tomorrow morning."

"Bert Seacat," I replied, almost breathless, as tears filled my eyes.

"I'll unpack your groceries, Sharon," Pat offered. "Go and talk with Bert."

Bert put her loving arms around me and my fear began to melt away. "You can do it, Sharon," she encouraged. "You can do it!"

I dried my eyes while she began sharing her experience. "I thought I was going to die. I wondered how my husband and I would be able to accept the loss of part of my body. Many times, I thought my children might be left without a mother to love them. But look at me now!" she exclaimed. "I had both breasts removed. Do you like the ones I had reconstructed?" she chuckled, pulling her shoulders back.

"Your groceries are ready now," Pat interrupted.

"Remember, Sharon," Bert insisted, "you can do it! Call me anytime. I want to help."

After paying my bill, I walked out of the grocery store a much different person than when I had entered. Never before had I ever felt so loved by God. My body was filled with His peace.

Standing by my car, I looked up at the clouds. "Thank you, God, for two special angels. I know I can do it! I can face tomorrow."

Sharon Wilkins

Wigged Out!

When a person is down in the world, an ounce of help is better than a pound of preaching.

Edward George Bulwer-Lytton

"So," my oncologist's nurse continued, handing me a list of names and addresses, "you may want to check one of these out."

Glancing at the sheet, I caught my breath: "Stores Specializing in Wigs for Chemo Patients."

Chemo. I still could hardly bring myself to accept the word. Numbly, I headed for one of the wig stores on the list. Inwardly I seethed. *Not fair, God. You know I hate wigs. Last time I wore one was in the seventies. Loathed it. I looked like something in a B-movie. No, make that a D-one. Surely You don't want me to look like that!*

Stepping into the little shop, I felt even worse. Almost every inch was filled with row upon row of artificial heads with artificial smiles topped with artificial hair.

The shop owner's smile, though, was warm and real. An older Asian woman, she tried to put me at ease. She picked out a few of her treasures that seemed closest in style, length and color to mine, then tried them on me. She expertly flipped the shiny locks this way and that, showing me how easy they could be arranged and cared for.

I had to admit that things had improved since the seventies. But I still rebelled. I liked to be natural, real, unpretentious. Wigs were so not me. Period.

Just then, an older gentleman came in, wearing a smile, golf togs and a glowing head of white hair. What in the world was he doing here?

"Hi, again," he greeted the shop owner. "I'm ready for a new wig. This one's fine, but I'd like an extra on hand. What have you got in stock?"

Smiling at me, he said, "These little things sure are a bother, but for us chemo patients, they're worth their weight in gold." *Chemo patient? Him?*

He gave me a thumbs-up. "Don't let it get you down, dear. We're all in this together."

Just then a tall, well-built younger woman breezed in. Her cap of glowing red curls caught my eye, but what really lit up that little shop was her vibrant smile. Perfect picture of health!

"I'm back!" she announced. "I really liked the one I had last year. Got any more in red?" Then to me, "You'll like shopping here. Started chemo already?"

"No, uh, will you be having it too?"

She laughed. "Oh, I'm an old-timer at this. Went through the whole business, lost all my hair. Took a year to grow it back. I was so thrilled to see it again." She wistfully touched one of her curls. "But now they've found a tumor somewhere else. So I'm going on Taxol. Hello, chemo, bye-bye, hair." Laughing, she continued. "Oh, but it is just hair, isn't it? After all, hair can always come back. Life can't."

Tears stung my eyes. "You are so right," I said. "Here, let me help you find what you need." And suddenly we were sisters, laughing and chatting together as I picked a wig out and tried it on her. Perfect!

The storekeeper wrote all three of our names down in a simple spiral-bound notebook, following hundreds of others. "This is my prayer book," she said simply. "I pray for all my customers, in chemo and out. I'll pray for all of you, too, that God will be with you and help you."

That little shop was still crowded, shabby and dark. But suddenly it was filled with light and joy as we all hugged each other. Yes, our newly purchased hairpieces were artificial. But our newfound hope and love as instant friends and supporters was real.

Bonnie Compton Hanson

Rhythms of Grace

My deacon-husband left for church early, leaving me to follow with our three children. My incessant nausea, sprints to the bathroom and overwhelming urge to sleep threatened that plan. I changed the baby's diapers, mopped up spilled cereal and finally got everyone strapped into the van and on the way to church.

After a scramble in the nursery, I filed into the sanctuary. There was one seat left. I slid into the row and smiled at the stunning woman beside me. *She didn't change any diapers this morning,* I thought. A young girl beside the woman flashed an awkward smile.

The music ended and we all turned to greet our neighbors. The stunning woman was named Gail. I chatted with her then extended a hand past my bulging belly to her daughter.

"I'm Kelly," she said, exposing her own curved stomach. Kelly lifted her eyes, pleading for acceptance.

"I'm Mary. It's so nice to have you," I said with a reassuring smile. Gail squeezed my elbow as we reclaimed our seats.

The pastor's words sounded distant as I remembered

my own confusion and fear as a young girl—and my own growing belly then. Shame from my teenage pregnancy resurged, raw and fresh. Realization swept over me. Through Kelly, my own wounds, long crusted over, would receive God's healing love.

"And so I challenge you," the pastor's voice echoed, "to give God's comfort to someone else. Stop watching people bleed to death because you are ashamed."

My heart melted, but my muscles tightened. *Tell her?* I asked, already knowing the answer. *Yes. Tell her,* my heart replied.

We were dismissed and I stepped back to let Kelly pass. As she did, I took her hand.

"Can I tell you something?" I said, hoping no one would hear.

"Sure. Go ahead."

"When I was about your age, I had a baby. A girl. I gave her up for adoption. God reminded me today how hard it was. How mean people were. If you ever need to talk, here's my number." Half-blinded by tears, I scribbled the numerals on a bulletin and shoved it toward her.

Gail, now at my side, stroked my back. She was crying too. "Thank you," she said. "This is the hardest thing we've ever been through."

Kelly was nearer to delivery than I was. Each week at church, stares focused on her belly as if it was a scarlet letter. She looked at me for anchoring. I sent tired smiles back to her, hoping to be a beacon in a forest of darkness.

Kelly came and went to church, cold and distant. I left goofy phone messages for her out of concern. She never called back.

One Wednesday, while I assembled "church night" sandwiches, the phone rang. It was Gail. She gave a breathless account of Kelly's active labor. Her voice held a hint of fear. "I'm sorry for calling you, but Kelly insisted. Can you come? It would mean a lot to her."

Gail gave me the room number and I started to hang up. "Wait," I said, a question on my mind. "Did she have my number with her?"

There was a pause. "No. She knew it by heart."

I gave the details to my husband, who nodded and threw me the keys.

I was at the hospital all night. When the midwife was called away, Gail and I coached Kelly through her contractions. Her sixteen-year-old boyfriend looked on, torn with emotions. A tear traced my face as the baby, Emily Grace, was placed in my arms, wrapped in her father's flannel shirt. "Best baby blanket in the world," the midwife said. "She'll always know her dad was here." I smiled. My Father, my God, was there too.

I gave Kelly a devotional book for new mothers and Gail compliments for her courage and faith.

They gave me the joy of giving the love and support that I had needed so long ago.

Marilynn Griffith

God's Timing

Of course, this side of heaven we'll never know for sure. More than ever, though, I realize that truly, our times are in His hands.

Psalm 32:15

One of my favorite things to do in colonial Williamsburg is spend an evening at Chownings' Tavern in the historic area where they do "gambols" every night at nine. Complete strangers sit in the colonial restaurant playing energetically at board games like "Goose," and singing rousing folk songs with costumed troubadours. My husband Scott and I went there one night just after Labor Day and a sudden change in vacation plans. We were supposed to spend two nights at the beach, but when our hotel turned out to be something from a horror movie, we endured but one night and decided to go to Williamsburg a day earlier than expected. Although we had the rest of the week to do gambols, I really wanted to go on our first night.

As we waited in a line outside Chownings' in the warm dusk, we struck up a friendly conversation with a couple from Buffalo. When the hostess appeared at nine, the four of us decided to sit together. She led us to a back booth, causing us to hesitate. Gambols are a lot more fun with a larger group in the center of the action. When I spotted a husband, wife and a young girl at a table in the middle of the room surrounded by empty seats, I said, "We'd like to sit there instead." The hostess seated us there and placed menus before us on the rustic table.

We introduced ourselves, then waited for what seemed an inordinate amount of time for our food to arrive and the colonial entertainment to begin. We did, however, get to know each other better, and the seven of us quickly hit it off. When I learned that the girl, Jenny, loved to read, I revealed that I was an author and promised that if she would give me her address, I'd send a copy of one of my kids' books. Her starry-eyed gaze returned any thanks necessary as she carefully printed her address on a napkin. We shared other information—where we lived, our favorite baseball teams and where we worked. Everyone was impressed that Jenny's dad, Rich, worked for a respected financial services company in New York. By the time the strolling musicians came along, we felt like friends.

Our enjoyment reached a more serious level when we started playing a game called "Buck." Each time one of us scored a point, he or she was to yell, "Buck!" If we got two points, we were to say "Buck! Buck!" and flap like a chicken. Scott and Rich really got into this. Every time someone said "Buck" too quietly, they would act like drill sergeants and say, "I can't hear you!"

That night ended a lot faster than we wished, and we reluctantly said goodnight to our new friends. As we drove back to our hotel, we spotted Rich and his family crossing a street. Realizing that I had some books in the car, I asked Scott to stop. They were pleasantly surprised to bump into us like that, and I signed a book for Jenny. When we finally left, Scott and I exclaimed, "What timing!"

"You know, in all the years we've been coming here, we've never run into people twice like that before."

He nodded. "I know what you mean."

"I have a feeling we should pray for them."

Scott glanced at me in the darkness.

"The book I gave Jenny is the most evangelistic of my children's mysteries," I continued. "I think God may be working in their lives."

As we drove along the quiet roads, we prayed for this family's well-being and that God would draw them close to him.

Three days later, on our last full day in Williamsburg, we debated about our dinner plans, finally settling on reservations at a seafood buffet at 7:30. Around 8:15, as we ate in a romantic candlelit alcove, a man approached our table, leaned over Scott, and said, "Buck! Buck!" It was our friend Rich and his family. None of us could believe that we had run into each other a third time and that we were at adjoining tables. We spent a delightful evening together. I wondered if Jenny had read my book and what she had thought of it, especially the faith part, but she said that she hadn't got around to it yet. *All in good time,* I thought.

Before we left, we exchanged e-mail addresses, and Scott gave Rich his business card. Rich didn't have one on him, but it didn't seem important because we had their home address on the napkin, knew Rich's e-mail address and had been told that he worked at the World Trade Center.

"That was so strange," we said outside the restaurant. "What are the chances of that happening?"

We had an even stronger sense that God had brought

them into our lives for some reason. We continued to pray for them and vowed to stay in touch.

The following Tuesday morning, September 11th, I was in the car listening to a classical station when an announcer came on to report that two planes had struck the World Trade Center. *Dear God—Rich works there!* I thought. I started shaking as I recalled the look on his face when he stood over Scott saying, "Buck! Buck!" That little family had been so happy together the week before. *Was that their last vacation together, and were we witnesses to it?* As the tears flowed, I prayed for them again.

Back home I searched for the napkin with their address, hoping that Jenny had included her phone number. She had not. I called directory assistance and discovered their number was unlisted. We had no success getting through via e-mail. There was nothing to do but wait and pray that Rich wasn't one of thousands of casualties. The next morning I mailed them a brief note, asking them to please let us know how they were.

That Saturday, as we prepared to leave the house, the phone rang. Scott looked at the caller ID, which registered simply "New York." We braced ourselves for the news. A moment later I heard Scott exclaim, "Rich!" Our new friend was saved because he was late for work on the morning of the eleventh.

I don't know if our prayers spared Rich's life, but I do know that God's timing is everything.

Rebecca Price Janney

5

MAKING A DIFFERENCE

It was with people like ourselves that Jesus set out to change the world—and did it.

Carolyn Lynn

Ivy's Cookies

Blessed are those who can give without remembering and take without forgetting.

Elizabeth Bibesco

The clank of the metal door and the echo of their footsteps rang in the ears of Ivy and Joanne as they walked down the dingy corridor behind the prison guard toward the "big room." The aroma of Ivy's homemade chocolate chip cookies wasn't enough to override the stench of ammonia from the recently mopped floor, or the bitterness and anger that hung in the air. Women's Correctional Institute was not the kind of place where most seventeen-year-olds go for an outing, but Ivy had a mission.

She didn't know what she was getting into, but she had to try. With trembling fingers, she had dialed the number for an appointment at the prison. Warden Baylor was receptive to Ivy's desire to visit and referred her to Joanne, another teen who had also expressed interest.

"How do we do this?" Ivy asked.

"Who knows? Maybe homemade cookies would break the ice," Joanne suggested.

So they baked their cookies and came bearing gifts to strangers.

"I put almonds in these," Ivy rambled nervously as they moved along. "The dough was gummier than usual . . ."

"Don't chatter," the guard snapped. "It gets the prisoners riled."

The harsh words made Ivy jump and her heart pound. She walked the rest of the distance in silence.

"Okay. Here we are," the guard grunted, keys rattling. "You go in. I'll lock the door behind you. Be careful what you say. They have a way of using your words against you. You have fifteen minutes. Holler if you have any trouble." Ivy noted the prisoners' orange jumpsuits and felt overdressed. *Maybe we shouldn't have worn heels,* she thought. *They probably think we're snobs.*

Remembering the guard's admonition, the girls put the cookies on the table next to plastic cups of juice, without saying a word. Some prisoners leaned against the wall; others stood around watching, studying, thinking, staring. Nobody talked. Ivy smiled at one of the women, who scowled back. From then on, Ivy avoided eye contact with the inmates. After five minutes of strained silence, Joanne whispered, "Let's move away from the table. Maybe they'll come over."

As they stepped back, one of the prisoners blurted out, "I'm gettin' a cookie." The others followed and began helping themselves. Soon they heard the rattle of keys. Time was up.

"What a relief to get out of there," Joanne sighed as a gust of fresh air caressed their perspiring faces.

"Yeah," Ivy agreed. "But I have a strong feeling that we're not done. Would you be willing to go back?"

Joanne nodded with a half-smile. "How about Thursday after school?"

Week after week they came. And week after week the

prisoners ate the cookies, drank the juice and stood around in silence. Gradually, antagonistic looks were replaced by an occasional smile. Still, Ivy couldn't bring herself to speak—not a word.

Then one Thursday, an evangelist walked in. Her step was sure, her chin was high and she glowed with the love of God. But she meant business. "I've come to pray with you," she announced to the inmates. "Let's make a circle."

Ivy was awed by the women's compliance. Only a few resisted. The others, although murmuring, inched their way toward the middle of the room and formed a lopsided circle, looking suspiciously at one another.

"Join hands," the evangelist instructed. "It's not gonna hurt you, and it'll mean more if you do." Slowly, some women clasped hands, others barely touched. "Now, bow your heads."

Except for the orange outfits, it could have been a church meeting.

"Okay. We're gonna pray," the evangelist continued, "and prayer is just like talking, only to God. I want to hear you tell the Lord one thing you're thankful for. Just speak it out. Don't hold back."

Ivy's palms were sweaty. *I can't pray aloud, Lord. I can't even talk to these women. I guess I should set an example, but they probably don't even like me—they probably think I'm better than they are because of my clothes.*

The words of an inmate jolted her from her thoughts.

"I'm thankful, God, for Miss Ivy bringing us cookies every week."

Another voice compounded the shock. "God, thanks for bringing a black lady to see us."

Ivy's eyes brimmed with tears as she heard, "Thank you, God, for these two young ladies giving their time every week, even though we can't do anything to pay them back."

One by one, every inmate in the circle thanked God for Ivy and Joanne. Then Joanne managed to utter a prayer of gratitude for the prisoners' words. But when it came Ivy's turn, she was too choked up to speak. Her eyes burned in humble remorse over how wrong she'd been about these women. She wished she could blow her nose, but the inmates were squeezing her hands so tightly, she resorted to loud sniffles and an occasional drip.

The following week, Ivy and Joanne returned, bright eyed, to find the prisoners talkative.

"Why do you bring us cookies every week?" a husky voice inquired from the corner of the room. When Ivy explained, the inmate inched a few steps closer. "Can you get me a Bible?" she asked. Others wanted to know more about the Jesus who inspires teenagers to visit prisoners.

A ministry was born from Ivy's cookies. What started as a silent act of kindness and obedience turned into a weekly Bible study at the prison, which eventually grew so big, it split into several groups that continue to this day. After Joanne married and moved away, Ivy continued to minister to the inmates alone for years. Eventually Prison Fellowship picked up the baton.

Ivy is a grandma now. Her radiance has increased over the years, and she brightens any room she enters. But last Thursday afternoon she indulged herself in a good cry. Curled up on the couch, wrapped in the afghan her daughter had made, she wept on the first anniversary of her daughter's death. "Her kids can live with me," Ivy had said. Now they napped as the doorbell rang.

A young woman, about seventeen, stood there with a plate of homemade cookies.

"Are you Ivy Jones?" she asked.

"Yes," she answered, dabbing her eyes with a wadded tissue.

"These are for you," the girl said as she handed the

cookies to her. With a shy, sad smile, she turned to leave without another word.

"Thank you," Ivy whispered in a daze. The girl was halfway down the sidewalk when Ivy called out, "But why?"

"My grandmother gave me her Bible before she died last week, and her last words were, 'Find Ivy Jones and take her some homemade cookies.'"

Candy Abbott

An Unexpected Moment

Wisdom is to see the miraculous in the common.

Ralph Waldo Emerson

It was hard to watch her fail. Physically she was growing thinner and more stooped. Mentally she was losing her ability to sort out reality. Initially, my grandmother had railed angrily against the symptoms of Alzheimer's disease that were eroding who she had always been. Eventually, the anger gave way to frustration, and then resignation.

My grandmother had always been a strong woman. She had a career before it was common for women to have careers. She was independent. In her eighties, she was still dragging out her stepladder every spring to wash all the windows in her house. She was also a woman with a deep faith in God.

As my grandmother lost her ability to live alone, my father moved her into his home. Grandchildren and great-grandchildren were often in the house. She seemed to enjoy being surrounded by the noise and activity of a large, extended family.

As she slipped further away from us mentally, my grandmother would occasionally have moments of lucidity when she knew where she was and recognized everyone around her. We never knew what prompted those moments, when they would occur or how long they would last.

Toward the end of her life she became convinced that her mother had knit everything she owned. "Mama knit my boots," she would tell strangers, holding up a foot clad in galoshes. "Mama knit my coat," she would say with a vacant smile as she zipped up her raincoat. Soon we were putting on her boots for her and helping her zip up her coat.

During my grandmother's last autumn with us, we decided to take a family outing. We packed up the cars and went to a local fair for a day of caramel apples, craft booths and carnival rides. Grandma loved flowers, so my dad bought her a rose. She carried it proudly through the fair, stopping often to breathe in its fragrance.

Grandma couldn't go on the carnival rides, of course, so she sat on a bench close by and waited while the rest of the family rode. Her moments of lucidity were now a thing of the past—having eluded her for months—but she seemed content to sit and watch as life unfolded around her. While the youngest members of the family ran, laughing to get in line at the next ride, my father took my grandmother to the nearest bench. A sullen-looking young woman already occupied the bench, but said she wouldn't mind sharing the bench. "Mama knit my coat," my grandmother told the young woman as she sat down.

We didn't let my grandmother out of our sight, and when we came back to the bench to get her, the young woman was holding the rose. She looked as though she had been crying. "Thank you for sharing your grandmother with me," she said. Then she told us her story. She had decided that day was to be her last on Earth. In deep despair and feeling she had nothing to live for, she was planning to go home and commit suicide. While she sat on that bench with Grandma, as the carnival noises swirled around them, she found herself pouring out her troubles.

"Your grandmother listened to me," the young woman informed us. "She told me about a time in her own life, during the Depression, when she had lost hope. She told me that God loved me and that He would watch over me and would help me make it through my problems. She gave me this rose. She told me that my life would unfold, just like this rose, and that I would be surprised by its beauty. She told me my life was a gift. She said she would be praying for me."

We stood, dumbfounded, as she hugged my grandmother and thanked her for saving her life. Grandma just smiled a vacant smile and patted her arm. As the young woman turned to leave, she waved good-bye to us. Grandma waved back and then turned to look at us, still standing in amazement. "Mama knit my hat," she said.

Sara Henderson

Miracle on Mercer Street

How little do they see what is, who frame their hasty judgments upon that which seems.

Robert Southey

It was a balmy summer day of sunshine and gentle breezes. Sea gulls screamed and fluttered overhead in the blue skies as a group from our church boarded the ferry bound for Seattle. We were headed for Seattle Center's opera house to see Chico Holiday and a cast of stars perform the musical, *Miracle on Azusa Street.*

After the ferry ride, our party walked to a waterfront restaurant for seafood.

While the rest of our family ordered fish and chips, five-year-old Ryan wanted a hamburger and fries. He was too excited to eat more than a few bites.

After lunch, I grasped Ryan's hand as we trudged up steep hills toward the monorail that would zoom us to Seattle Center. Ryan clutched a doggy bag holding the remains of his lunch. My husband Ted and our teenagers mingled with the group ahead of us.

We heard groans as we approached the monorail. It was

closed for repairs. From there we decided to catch a city bus.

Our gang spread out as we boarded the crowded vehicle. My friend Ann, Ryan and I found seats near the front of the motor coach. Ryan stared at a bedraggled stranger sitting across the aisle from us. The unkempt man eyed Ryan's doggy bag.

"Would you like my hamburger?" Ryan asked.

The stranger nodded and mumbled "Thank you," as he reached for the bag. His intoxicated smile revealed missing teeth. He was unshaven and his clothes were dirty.

Ryan's blue eyes watched intently as the man wolfed down the hamburger and fries. He wiped his mouth on the back of his hand and asked, "What's your name, little boy?"

"Ryan. What's yours?"

"My name's George. Thanks for the burger."

"You're welcome," Ryan said.

George directed his gaze towards me. "Where are you all going this fine day?"

I told him we were on our way to see a play at the opera house.

"Oh," he said, before proudly announcing, "I'm an American Indian."

"Really!" I said. "My friend Ann has Indian blood, too."

Ann engaged him in a discussion of their ancestral ties. George gave his full attention, but his responses didn't make much sense.

We reached our destination and our gang filed off the bus. My husband caught up with us and reached for Ryan's hand. George got off the bus too, and fell into step behind us. His disheveled clothing reeked of body odor and stale urine.

"How much does the play cost?" George asked. Alcohol fumes permeated his breath.

"It's free!" Ted answered.

"Can anyone go?" George asked.

"Sure," Ted said. "Would you like to go with us?"

George nodded.

Ann and I exchanged glances as we joined the throngs of well-dressed people headed for the Mercer Street opera house. The splendor of the posh lobby impressed our guest. George stuck close as we made our way through the crowd and were ushered down thick red carpet to the front of the theater.

Since we were early, we had time to kill before the play started. Ted struggled to ignore the rank odor as he conversed with George. George began confiding in Ted, educating him about the danger of life on the streets. He confessed that he had "a bit of a drinking habit."

He said he'd been burned in a fire when he was a boy and had scars over most of his body. He rolled up his shirtsleeves and showed us disfiguring scars.

Before long the huge opera house was full. We had the best seats in the house! The lights dimmed and the play began. We were soon carried away to Azusa Street as singers and actors portrayed the story.

When the time came for intermission, George left the theater abruptly. Ted went to look for him, but couldn't find him in the crowded lobby. We were saddened to think that George left before the end of the play. Shortly before the lights dimmed, George returned to his seat. He'd washed his hands and face, and combed his hair. He seemed to have sobered up considerably. Somewhere beneath his grimy exterior lived the soul of a ruggedly handsome man.

I overheard George confide to my husband, "You know my mother has been praying for me for years, always begging God to save me."

The curtain opened as the orchestra began playing. As

the story progressed towards the climax, George repeatedly brushed tears from his eyes. When the play ended with an altar call, young and old alike made their way to the front of the theater to dedicate their lives to Christ. George was at the head of the line.

We bid our new "brother in Christ" good-bye as we exited the grand opera house. George held his head a little higher as he slowly made his way down Mercer Street.

Carol Genengels

Eulogy to a Stranger

I long to accomplish a great and noble task, but it is my chief duty to accomplish small tasks as if they were great and noble.

Helen Keller

Several years ago, when my husband was having back surgery, I had a conversation with a lovely nurse about how various patients faced their mortality. I'd done bereavement ministry for several years and was always interested in this subject. She told me about a patient of hers who was dying of lung cancer. Every time he was admitted for treatment, he went around to the other patients on his floor, cheering them up and offering them words of hope. He wasn't expected to live much longer and only hoped to make it to his next wedding anniversary.

I was so moved by the heart of this man, that I decided to write him a letter and tell him that I was truly inspired by his strength and courage. I wanted to thank him for making a difference in my life. I asked the nurse if I could mail the letter to her and have her give it to her patient. She said, "Of course."

I wrote the letter and mailed it off, not giving it another thought. Two months later, my phone rang and a woman said, "You don't know me. But my husband was a patient in the hospital and you were kind enough to write him a letter." She went on to tell me that he had recently died and as they planned his service at their temple, she gathered her children together and asked them each to write a letter about what their father meant to them. From their letters, they would write their father's eulogy.

Meanwhile, she retrieved the letter I'd written which had been tucked inside the family Bible. After reading her children's letters, she shared my letter with them.

"I'm calling you today," she said, "to tell you that the only eulogy delivered at my husband's service was your letter."

I was totally humbled and touched. And I learned a valuable lesson: Whenever we are moved to reach out to someone—even a total stranger—we should take that risk. For we never know when we can truly make a difference in someone's life. We should never hesitate to tell anyone who has touched our life that they have—we may never get the chance again.

Carol Hamblet Adams

Never Too Late

Not everything that is faced can be changed, but nothing can be changed until it is faced.

James Baldwin

The morning dawned sunny and warm; it was a perfect day for a wedding. All of the preparations had gone smoothly. My shining moment was near. My maid of honor had just begun her walk down the aisle, stepping in perfect time to the music. There I stood in a beautiful satin wedding gown my mother had so lovingly made for me. It was my turn. My heart filled with joy and anticipation as I stood ready to walk down the aisle toward my new life.

Then I saw my father, Ralph, stagger drunkenly toward me. I was sickened by the smell of alcohol on his breath. He nearly fell as he hooked his arm through mine. Within seconds, the "Wedding March" started playing—it was time to go.

So I did the same thing I had done so many times before—I faked it—just to keep up appearances. I glued on my best smile, mustered all my strength to hold my dad upright and then walked him down the aisle. Only when my dad was safely seated, and I stood at the altar holding my fiancé's hand, could I concentrate on the ceremony. For me, the most important part of my wedding had been ruined. I was angry, embarrassed and extremely hurt. I decided that day to never forgive my father.

My dad had been an alcoholic since I was a little girl. His drinking just snuck up on our family—starting quietly, but getting slowly worse each year. The escalating problem became very real for me one beautiful October day in 1963 when I was eight years old.

I sat on the back step of our home breathing in the fragrance of the autumn leaves and admiring the perfect blue sky. Then I saw my dad begin to load all of his belongings in the car. I looked up at him in disbelief and asked, "Daddy, where are you going?" With tears in his eyes, he answered, "I'm taking a job downtown and need to live there for a while. But I'll be back soon."

I held out a child's hope that he would return home one day. But his out-of-control drinking led to a divorce. He never moved back.

After that, I spent virtually every Saturday with my dad—all the way through my teen years. I wish I could say that those were happy days, but frequently they were spent waiting in the car while my dad went into the tavern to "make a few phone calls." My resentment toward him grew and continued to increase until that fateful wedding day.

My resolve never to forgive my father lasted for more than three years after my wedding. Then, something happened. On his seventy-first birthday, my dad visited a doctor to have a complete physical. Shocked at my dad's condition, the doctor told him, "Ralph, unless you quit drinking right now, you won't be alive to give your daughter away at her wedding." My sister's wedding was just six months from then.

Those words scared my father, so he checked himself into a thirty-day, inpatient alcoholic treatment center. Relieved he was finally getting the help he needed, my sister and brothers and I rallied around my dad to give him support. We attended family counseling sessions to learn more about the disease. Although I was supporting his attempt to get sober, I still felt a lot of anger toward him and was unable to forgive him for past hurts.

One day the physicians and counselors met with us and said, "Do not expect a miracle. Your dad is retired, lives alone and has been drinking for over forty years. He *will* relapse." So we didn't get our hopes up, but we did continue to pray for a miracle.

Then, one day, the miraculous happened. Dad called me and asked if he could meet with me. When we got together, the first thing he said was, "I'm sorry for all the pain I've caused you and the rest of the family. I know I don't have a lot of years left on this earth, but I want to live them sober." Dad took my hand, looked me in the eyes and asked, "Will you say the Lord's Prayer with me?"

Crying together, we held hands and prayed. As I recited the words of the prayer, I could feel the anger and hurt begin to melt away. The healing had begun. From that day on, Dad never took another drink. He read the Bible daily, joined Alcoholics Anonymous and became involved in a church. He frequently quoted scriptures to me and claimed only one thing was standing between him and alcohol: "Jesus." My own faith grew with each day of my dad's recovery. As my faith strengthened, my ability to forgive strengthened and I was finally able to let go of the past.

Dad remained sober for the next fourteen years and the miracle continued. At age seventy-two he founded an alumni association for recovering alcoholics and typed an inspirational newsletter on an old typewriter, then mailed it out monthly to nearly 100 people.

At age seventy-three, my dad helped organize an annual hospital event where hundreds of recovering alcoholics and their families gathered to celebrate their sobriety.

At seventy-six he became a proud Red-Coat volunteer at a local hospital, delivering newspapers, flowers and encouragement to patients, and pushing the wheelchairs of new mothers holding new babies who were going home. Dad volunteered there until he was seventy-nine, when he became ill with prostate cancer and moved into a nursing home.

Instead of moping about his situation, however, he appointed himself "the ambassador" for the home. My father took newcomers under his wing, giving them tours of the place and showing them humor in every corner. On holidays, he occasionally called to say, "I'm going to be a little late today because some people here have no visitors—and I'm not leaving anyone alone on Christmas."

When my father died at eighty-five, my brothers, sister and I expected only a few people at his funeral, but over 100 people came. Most were strangers to us, yet one by one, they shared their memories of my dad.

"Your dad is the reason my dad is sober today."

"Your dad is the reason my mom survived living in that nursing home."

"Your father is the glue that held our family together during our dad's drinking crisis."

Then seven men—all wearing red coats—quietly walked in to pay tribute to Dad for inspiring them to volunteer at the hospital. Many of them were over eighty years old.

Had I not removed the blinders of anger and resentment—had I not forgiven my dad—I'd never have witnessed the positive ways he had touched the world.

I know now that it's never too late to forgive.

Debra J. Schmidt

The Woman Who Wouldn't Pray

He who bears another, is borne by another.

St. Gregory the Great

The chaplain had tried everything with the woman but prayer—her prayer. Oh, he had prayed, ever since the doctors admitted there was nothing they could do but keep her comfortable. But she was so bitter, so alone and aloof. And, despite drugs, her last days were bound to be difficult.

It was while praying for her and a long list of others that he got the idea. He wondered if there was a chance. It certainly couldn't hurt.

"Sara," he said tentatively, "I know you have a great deal on your mind, but I want to ask a favor. There's a family that needs extra support just now. Their four-year-old daughter is in a coma. She's in the last stages of leukemia. They need strength to get through this."

Sara seemed puzzled. "What has this got to do with me?"

"I need help. Sometimes it's just too much for me. I pray daily for the people of this hospital, but I could use another voice, another heart. I'm asking you to pray for the family of little Carrie, to ask God to put his loving arms around them."

"Chaplain, I don't mean to be rude, but it's been a long time since I prayed. With my diagnosis, if I had any inclination at all, it would be to pray for myself."

"You may certainly do that," he said, "but I'm asking you to pray for others." He took her hand. "Please, Sara, for me. I get so discouraged."

Before she pulled her hand away, she nodded briefly.

Two days later he came back. Little Carrie had slipped peacefully into the next world, and her parents were as strong as any he had ever seen in the loss of a child.

Now he asked another favor, for a teenager on a voluntary drug withdrawal program. The boy said he wanted to stay clean, but he feared he'd lose his nerve when he got back with his friends on the outside. Would she pray for him?

"I'm rusty," Sara said angrily. "Never did have the knack. I hated resorting to prayer only when I was in trouble, and it never occurred to me otherwise. It all seems so hypocritical."

"That's the reason I want you to pray for others," the chaplain said. "Surely you don't think God would question your motives in praying for Carrie's family or this teenager?"

She sighed. "It does give me something to do. When I begin to need a painkiller, I make myself pray for fifteen minutes before putting on the call light. It's silly, though."

On Tuesday he asked her to keep praying for the teenager, and also to add a man who'd suffered a stroke. The chaplain described the old fellow's frustration as he struggled to speak to his son and daughter-in-law. "I told him there were at least two people here praying for him—you and me." He saw Sara wince. "Is the pain getting bad?"

She lifted an eyebrow. "I play a new game with myself now. As the shots get more frequent, I also increase the length of my prayers. When I can't stand it any longer, I give myself a reward. Morphine." She smiled. "A payoff for praying."

The following week Sara's deterioration was obvious. She spoke hardly above a whisper, and the nurses said the end was near. The chaplain described to her the successful laser treatment on the eyes of an artist with detached retinas. The next day he told her about an older woman the doctors suspected of having bone cancer. Her condition turned out to be a fairly mild form of arthritis. The chaplain asked Sara to give thanks for these events and others taking place throughout the hospital and the city.

One day the chaplain persuaded the teenage boy she had prayed for to come with him and visit Sara. At her bedside the streetwise boy groped for words. "I feel stronger now," he said, wonder apparent in his voice. "It's gotta be coming from somewhere. I tried to kick it twice before, and it didn't work. I gotta believe you must have some influence, lady." He paused, struggling. "I been pr-pr-praying for you too." His glance went to the ceiling, then back to the woman in the bed. "Hang in there, lady." He hurried from the room.

Sara motioned the chaplain to come closer. He pulled a chair over so their eyes were level. "I saw through your little scheme almost from the start," she whispered. "But I still have to thank you. You've turned my last days into—into a rather interesting adventure."

"Don't thank me," the chaplain said, his voice husky. "Let's both thank God together." He took her dry hands in his and began, "The Lord is my Shepherd, I shall not want . . ."

Sara joined him and they repeated the words slowly, softly, in unison. By the time they got to "surely goodness and mercy," he was saying the psalm alone. His silent thanks poured forth as he sat holding Sara's hands and watching her quiet, even breathing.

For the first time in weeks, she slept without the help of drugs.

Carol V. Amen

Reprinted by permission of Henry Boye.

Take My Hand

You will not fear the terror of night, nor the arrow that flies by day . . .

Psalm 91:5

Harriett jumped when I touched her arm. Then, seeing who it was, she burst into tears. "Oh, where have you been? I needed you! I needed you! I can't go through this without you!"

Bending over an old metal hospital bed, I reached for her thin, bruised hand. Trapped in a weakened, morphine-laced body, Harriett looked so helpless and fragile, yet alert to my presence in the dimly-lit room. Eighty-seven years old and dying from lung cancer, she surprised me by explaining her distress, "I had a heart attack last night."

Her pleading, fear-filled eyes searched my face. "Where were you when I needed you? Please don't leave me."

During the past months, as her hospice pastoral care volunteer, I'd watched Harriett mature spiritually. Often we talked about heaven and the fun of seeing those who'd gone on ahead. There were, however, a couple of her relatives she wasn't sure would be there because they were such "ornery critters." She'd squint her eyes at me when I told her to be ready for some great surprises.

Between my visits, she'd forget to focus on Jesus during difficult times—like the prior night. Each time I visited, she'd ask me to pray that she wouldn't forget next time.

Harriett's eyes were wild and weepy as she described her panic during the heart pain. "The nurse didn't come. It was the worst pain of my whole life and I was so scared." Though she had accepted the fact that she was dying, it still sometimes terrified her.

"So what did you do?" I asked.

"I just laid here and waited it out—all alone," she wailed.

After hugging her frail shoulders, I told her I needed to leave for a few minutes to get her a surprise. Hurrying to a nearby Burger King, I bought her favorite lunch: a fish sandwich and a strawberry milkshake. While I was waiting at the drive-up window, I asked Jesus to take my hand and walk me through this dilemma with Harriett.

Back at the nursing home, I realized how peaceful my prayer had left me feeling, so I suggested to Harriett that she ask Jesus to take her hand. "When the pain comes," I told her, "when you feel fear or panic, reach up and say, 'Jesus, take my hand.'"

The bony, bruised arm slowly reached into the air while Harriett rehearsed the words repeatedly. "Jesus, take my hand. Jesus, take my hand."

"Harriett," I spoke louder to assure she'd hear me. "He'll take your hand and bring you comfort. He'll hold on until the pain lets up. He'll sit with you in the darkness of the long nights, and one of these times, you'll hear Him say, 'Come on Harriett, let's go home.'"

A peaceful look began to replace the deep lines of fear in Harriett's face. Paraphrasing Psalm 91, and inserting Harriett's name for "you" and "your," I read to her: "Harriet will not fear the terror of night, nor the arrow that flies by day. . . . For Harriet has made the Lord her refuge. He will command His angels to guard her in all her ways; they will lift her up in their hands. . . . Harriet will call upon the Lord and He will answer her. . . ."

While I read, Harriett's frail, bony fingers stroked my hair. I felt her hands move around in my curls. Then she spoke softly, "You have beautiful hair. The sunlight is streaming through your curls and the gray has turned to silver. There is a special glow about you every time you come, and I feel surrounded by your love. You are God's gift to me—to walk beside me on this journey. I love you."

I was overwhelmed by the tremendous love that God allowed us to share for this short time.

Full of lunch and tired, Harriett closed her eyes. I whispered, "Good-bye," and told her I'd be back soon.

I stood in the doorway, looking back at my short-term friend, missing her already. Then a thin arm came slowly out from under the blanket and reached into the air. Her mouth formed the words, "Take my hand."

Barbara Baumgardner

The Ministry of Life

Working in the surgery department of a small rural hospital, I was startled to learn we were going to work with a transplant team to remove organs from an accident victim. Organ transplants were something I had only read about in nursing school or seen on television. It wasn't the kind of thing we experienced in this quiet little community. The entire surgery department was excited about this learning experience, yet at the same time, we felt a sense of loss for the donor and her family.

The transplant team came in and explained all the technical details of the organ harvest—the equipment needed, the forms, the timing of the event. So much information, so many strangers to our department—it gave a surreal feeling to the whole event.

Reality kicked in, however, when the donor was wheeled into the operating room. She was an actual person: thirty-four years old and married with two young kids. She looked perfect. The accident that had caused a blood clot in her brain had left no visible marks. As we lifted her limp, warm body onto the operating table, I noticed her toenails were painted red. I stopped and stared. Never in her wildest dreams would she have thought that someone would be gazing at her toes in surgery. We are never really prepared for that final moment of death. And yet, this woman had been prepared enough to mention to her family that, should the unthinkable happen, she wanted to help others live by donating her organs.

This simple act of signing a Uniform Donor Card, which allows the donation of an organ, is an act of stewardship, ministry and serving God toward the greater good. *Anyone* can do it. And yet, even among professionals, organ donation is frequently forgotten or misunderstood. My senior year in nursing school, a spokesperson for organ donation came to speak to our class. At the conclusion of her presentation, she handed out Uniform Donor Cards. My friend Lynn leaned over to me and whispered, "Why would anyone want to donate their uniform?"

In 1 Timothy, Paul instructs that even if we don't have material wealth, we can be rich in good works toward others. No matter how poor we are, we have something we can share with someone. True ministry happens every day, not just on Sundays, and with planning and forethought, it can continue even after our physical death.

The machinery was pulled around, and the patient was draped for the surgery that went on for hours. Heaviness weighed on my heart as I thought about her husband, her children, her parents and her friends. How could life be so unfair?

Then, within twenty-four hours, we began receiving reports: a fifty-three-year-old man was producing urine on his own with his new kidney; a forty-five-year-old woman had also successfully received the other kidney. The recipients of the lung and heart were reported to be in stable condition. News continued to trickle in over the next couple of days about people whose lives had been saved or enhanced by the unselfish act of this remarkable woman.

Her ministry continues!

Karyn Buxman

[EDITORS' NOTE: *To continue her ministry and be a donor, too, see* www.organdonor.gov. *An Organ/Tissue Donor Card is available there, or if you prefer to have a card sent to you, contact the HRSA Information Center (HIC) at 1-888-ASK-HRSA. Fill out the card and carry it with you at all times. Please share your decision to donate with your family and give them a copy of the card.*]

Flying a Kite

In death is always a new life.

Amar Jyoti

Her skin was the color of rich, hot chocolate and her brown eyes twinkled with intelligence and humor. Her name was Michelle and she spent her days in a purple wheelchair because she had been born with cerebral palsy. She rolled into my classroom—and my heart—when she was just three years old. Her courage was an inspiration to me and her spirit touched my heart.

Michelle and her mother once gave me a figurine of a beautiful black child sitting in a wheelchair. I displayed the cherished gift on a shelf in my den at home. It always reminded me of the little girl I loved so much.

When Michelle was seven, she was to undergo open-heart surgery for the third time. The night before surgery, I sat in the chair beside her bed and held her hand.

"I'm tired, Bicki," she said weakly.

"Why don't you close your eyes and try to get some sleep?"

"No, not sleepy. *Tired.*"

I thought of the tiny, imperfect heart that had to work so hard, the grand mal seizures, terrible headaches and tight, spastic muscles that made her every move difficult and painful. I was heartbroken at the wisdom of the little soul who understood the difference between sleepy and tired at such a young age.

"Will I go to heaven soon?"

I placed my hand on her forehead. "I don't know—that's up to God."

She glanced at the stars through the window of her room. "How will I get all the way up there? An airplane?"

"No, God will send a special angel to show you the way. You won't have to take your wheelchair or your leg braces or any of your medicine because you won't need any of that in heaven. You'll be able to run and play just like your brother."

Her eyes filled with hope. "Do you think I could fly a kite?"

I swallowed a tear and smiled, "I'm sure if you ask God for a kite, he would find one for you."

"Oh, I hope so, Bicki."

It was very early in the morning while I was doing my prayer time when the figurine of Michelle, for no apparent reason, fell from my bookshelf to the floor. The impact of the fall separated the figure of the girl from the wheelchair. I was devastated and vowed to have it repaired. Later that same day, Michelle's mother called to tell me that her daughter's heart had simply stopped beating and she had peacefully slipped away in the early hours before dawn.

I have since thrown the ceramic wheelchair away, and the little girl sits on the edge of the shelf with her legs dangling over the side. She's smiling toward the sky. I always think of Michelle on warm, windy days. I imagine her running through the clouds with a kite dancing above her!

Vicki L. Kitchner

All God's Children

Accept others without condition. It's the very essence of love.

Linda Allison-Lewis

The night receptionist handed me a slip of paper. "The volunteer chaplain would like to meet with you. This is her extension number."

Her? The hospital chaplain was a woman? I was tired, exhausted really, after a full ten hours supervising my son's third day of intensive therapy at Craig Rehabilitation Hospital. I was certainly not in the mood to explain—for what seemed like the thousandth time—the accident that brought us here.

"Maybe tomorrow," I muttered, ducking into the crisp night air. Street lamps lit my path across the pedestrian walkway, but cast deep shadows as thick as those weighing down my heart. At the guest apartment door, I fumbled with unfamiliar locks and tumbled into bed without even washing my face or brushing my teeth.

The next morning a different receptionist handed me another slip of paper. "The hospital chaplain wants to . . ."

"I know," I sighed, "I know. Is she in now?" She opened her mouth to answer but nodded and pointed instead. Peering over my shoulder, I was startled by the middle-aged woman lumbering toward me. Her walk was lopsided, like a gate swinging on one hinge, her eyes were skewed and even her arms seemed twisted, out of her control. She looked like she could be one of the patients. But her smile radiated warmth as she greeted me.

"Are you Kyle's mother? What a wonderful, charming son you have! I could hardly wait to meet the person who brought him into the world." Although her stumbling words slurred, I understood the message, and it melted the icy knot that had been lodged in my stomach for weeks. Here was someone who only knew my son after his head injury—and liked what she saw.

"Let's sit," she invited. We sat. And talked. And talked.

So began my brief relationship with Patty Cooper, lay chaplain, confidante, teacher and friend. Her regular visits to Kyle cheered him. Her regular visits to me gave me hope—a hope she spread as generously as her encouragement in a facility that treated only the worst of spinal cord and brain injuries.

Like many others at Craig Hospital, as I dealt with my son's infirmities and my own doubts, I came to rely on her unique mixture of relentless optimism and calm acceptance. I needed both in my grief over the losses and my adjustment to the changes.

Patty complimented Kyle's attitude and each small success as he worked hard to rebuild his body and to walk again. She encouraged my involvement and soothed my mother-fears. And she shared her personal story when I asked her how she found herself volunteering here, in this place, where heartache reigned supreme.

"I wanted to have a baby," she said simply.

Twenty-five years earlier during a straightforward,

exploratory surgery of her fallopian tubes, a lethal dose of nitrous oxide gas was administered. It started Patty's life down an unexpected path. Her resulting complications and permanent disabilities read like an index of medical terms: cardiac arrest, anoxia, hypoxic brain surgery, forty-day coma, paralysis, peripheral blindness, impaired speech, cognitive lapses.

Patty awoke from the initial surgery months later to discover herself a patient at this very facility. Over a long period of months, she relearned the basics—how to walk and talk, how to feed and dress herself, how to brush her hair and teeth, and even how to tend her most personal needs. Meanwhile, Patty's husband chose a different path—and a different woman—for himself.

"But you don't seem bitter," I pointed out. "And you've ended up here. By choice." After a month, I still struggled with the heart-wrench of each patient's pain and each family's problems, which I witnessed on a daily basis. How could she do it, night and day, year after year?

The crooked smile I had come to love lifted a corner of her mouth and crinkled her tender eyes. "I'm here because once I entered a hospital to conceive one perfect child of my own to love. But God taught me that love doesn't seek perfection." She paused to brush at a single tear.

"And now—now I voluntarily walk through these doors each day for a more important reason." Patty nodded toward the row of wheelchairs, walkers and weights lining the corridor. "To share my love with *all* of His children."

Carol McAdoo Rehme

Leadership Material

Generosity lies less in giving much than in giving at the right moment.

Jean La Bruyere

I was new to the church the first time I went to a women's fellowship meeting. Had I known it was their night to reorganize their committees, I would have stayed home. Since then I read my church bulletin very carefully.

After explaining what the various guilds did, they asked everyone to choose which one they would be part of. I chose the Parish Guild. That committee sent out cards to new parents, the sick and the bereaved. They also provided food for the funeral suppers. I could do the cards. The food, if I had to cook it, would be a problem. I wondered how they felt about store-bought desserts.

I was about to raise that question when Lori asked if I wouldn't mind being chair. I stared at her like she had spoken Swahili. Then I told her I really was not leadership material. She smiled. It was a "pat-on-the-head-and-don't-worry-about-a-thing-dear" smile. Lori said,

"Everyone will help. You only have to make the calls."

"Okay," I relented.

"It'll be fine," she reassured me.

And the first months were. I selected cards and sent them out. It was easy. It was a joy. Then someone died.

Helen, my pastor's wife, called me and told me. She said I was to call the family and ask if they wanted the guild to provide food for the gathering after the service. I practically dropped the phone. Nobody had told me I had to call the family. Nobody had told me that was part of my job.

I called. I was awful at it. I hemmed and hawed my way through the whole conversation, although I wanted to be so sensitive.

The day of the memorial service I stopped by church to check on the food. The guild women, as promised, had come through—three entrees, three salads, three desserts so far. I hoped that other people would bring food to the house. I left with my small daughter to do errands.

On my way home, I stopped by church to make sure that all the food had been picked up and taken to the house. The organ was playing as I passed the sanctuary. I looked at my watch. *This sure is a long service,* I thought as I rounded a corner. I nearly knocked Helen over. She was wearing her best black dress and practically running, her hands loaded with a huge silver platter.

I recognized the meatloaf entree on it. "They think the meal is here at the church," she whispered. "Pastor is stalling for time while we set up." The sound of a metal tray crashing to the floor echoed from the parish hall. Helen flinched.

Then she straightened. "I've started the coffee," she continued bravely. "The oven in the kitchen is on the fritz. I'm taking the meat home to warm it. I'll be back as soon as I can."

I nodded like a person caught in a whirlwind—which I was.

"Nancy, did you tell them the meal was to be at their home?"

"I, I just assumed that . . ."

"Never mind," said that saintly woman, "it'll be all right." She dashed toward the parking lot.

I sighed and watched her departing figure. Holding my daughter's hand, I trudged across the patio to the kitchen. On the island counter were the three salads, the three desserts and the two entrees minus the meatloaf. I glanced over my shoulder, out the door. The church parking lot was nearly full.

God, what are we going to do? There must be over 100 people at the service. This is going to be a fiasco. I closed my eyes as if to shut out the future. The giant coffeepot perked away merrily. *How dare it?*

I set out the napkins and brought up plates from the cupboards. I removed the plastic wrap from the food containers and put serving spoons in them. The organ stopped playing. My stomach fluttered as footsteps and voices approached the kitchen.

People began streaming in. In their hands they carried green salads and macaroni salads and Jell-O salads, casseroles and sandwiches, bread and cold cuts, pies and cakes, plates of cookies and brownies. For a moment it was happy chaos as we found places for all the food. Then people lined up. Smiling graciously I stepped behind the counter and handed out coffee. I hoped that the tall people wouldn't notice that I was wearing blue jeans.

Later, as one of the daughters of the deceased was gathering up the remains of the leftover food she smiled. "It was great having this at the church," she said. "Mother was worrying and making herself sick over how she would ever get the house ready."

Her words filled me with awe. *God,* I thought, *You sure do move in mysterious ways.*

I managed the next funeral okay. Helen said pointedly, "Tell them, Nancy, that the meal is to be at their house." I did.

However, the funeral after that one found me dog-paddling in disaster again. While loading the food into my car, I broke a salad bowl and chipped a crockpot lid.

At the end of my one-year tenure as Parish Guild chair, I heaved a sigh of relief. I hadn't gotten through unscathed, but it had all worked out. God had made it work out. I congratulated myself that I had done my bit as a leader and now could retreat into being a committee member.

Then the women's fellowship elected me president.

Nancy Ellen Hird

"Does our daily bread mean crust, too?"

Miracle of the Stray E-Mail

If the world is really the medium of God's personal action, a miracle is wholly normal.

D. E. Trueblood

September 11, 2001. I watched in horror as the World Trade Center towers were erased from the skyline of New York City. Glued to the television, I felt deep sorrow for the families of thousands who would be grieving intensely. There was no warning, no good-byes and for most, no bodies to bury. There was only stark horror and lives forever changed.

I so regretted that my book, *A Passage Through Grief,* had gone out of print in December. It could have helped in this desperate time of need. As a hospice and church volunteer, that book had been my text and guide in leading grief support groups. It offered encouragement and hope. Now, the people of New York City needed both.

Before the sun went down on that horrible day, God began laying a burden on my heart too big to ignore. I felt he wanted me to send 10,000 copies of my out-of-print book to the grieving survivors. Incredibly, in place of any doubts, I felt excited and empowered by the task.

I told no one until the following Sunday, when I shared my plan with Pastor Syd. He was supportive but questioned how I would distribute the books once they were delivered to New York. All I could answer was, "If God gets them there, He'll also get them distributed to the right places."

The next morning I called the publisher inquiring about the process of printing and donating 10,000 books. And then I waited. God seemed to be saying, *Trust me.*

Two days later, I was excited to get an e-mail from the publisher saying they were checking prices on printing the books in paperback instead of the original hard cover. While waiting, I talked to several writers about printing costs and heard prices from $2.80 to $4.00 each. Suddenly my mission became raising thirty to forty thousand dollars. Yet God was still saying, *Trust Me.*

I spent hours at my computer sending e-mails to everyone I knew, asking them to send e-mails to their friends. I told them there would be no profit or royalties paid to anyone for this project. "I can't do this alone. I need your help," was my plea. I gave them the address of my home church as a fund-receiving center.

I'll have to admit I was counting up any of my own personal resources that could be liquidated to pay for the books if I didn't get donations. I had a small inheritance from my mom who'd died in June. And I could sell my motor home. It surprised me to have such perfect peace about doing that as I continued to pray, "Please God, send the rest of the money."

Meanwhile, Pastor Syd, still concerned about distribution, wrote an e-mail to two men he knew who would be involved in counseling in New York City. He hit the "send" button and went home. When he returned to work the next morning, messages of willingness to help were waiting, but not from the recipients of his e-mail. Upon investigation, he found that he had apparently hit a wrong button and mistakenly sent his message to every Conservative Baptist church in the United States. Messages came all day: *We just received your e-mail . . . We would like to get the word out to our congregation . . . Please let us know where we can send contributions . . . We would like to include the address in this week's bulletin . . .*

Other messages came: *I'm not sure why I got this e-mail but I can share some input with you. I am currently in New York City working as a part of the NW Medical Trauma Counseling Team. I can see that in the coming months there is going to be a need for material such as you are suggesting. I would suggest you look for a release date about a month from now . . . I am praying for you . . . We are planning to take up a special collection for you next Sunday.*

Later that day, Pastor Syd sent me an e-mail that said, "Now I seldom get too excited, but today I laughed out loud. God doesn't make a mistake, but He uses human mistakes!"

As the days went by, we saw more and more of God's perfect plan for this project. My publisher generously decided to get involved, pricing the books below their cost. However, I would have to prepay the order before the printing could begin. In faith, I charged it all on my two credit cards. I felt certain that the money would come to pay for them—and it did. Money came from all over America—it came from other writers, friends, my family, churches and strangers who I probably will never meet.

God's inconceivable plan even included a distributor. The day I ordered the books, I received an e-mail from a Baptist church in New Jersey that had received my pastor's stray e-mail. They wrote: "We have a 'Heart for the Nation' fund that may be able to help. Is it possible that we could have books sent directly here . . .? We are fifteen miles from the World Trade Center and have a great need to meet in this area. Thanks."

The books were paid for and shipped on October 29th. The Conservative Baptist church in New Jersey went to work distributing 5,000 copies all over the area. Books were given to churches for use in grief support groups and chaplains gave hundreds of them to firefighters and police officers at Ground Zero. The Metro Baptist Association of the Southern Baptist Convention distributed 2,000 books, many of those in Christmas packages given to families of those who died. And the Salvation Army took the remaining 3,000, and used my newly revised leader's guide for training at a weekend conference for grief counselors. I was amazed at God's plan.

Pastor Syd never did get an answer from either of the two men he sent the original e-mail to. But the misrouted e-mail did the job God intended it to do.

Barbara Baumgardner

Love's Power

Too often we underestimate the power of a touch, a smile, a kind word, a listening ear, an honest compliment, or the smallest act of caring, all of which have the potential to turn a life around.

Leo Buscaglia

Does Mom hear that train whistle? Pam wondered. Her mother and grandmother were having a loud argument as they rode in the front seat of the car. Pam's mom had been cross all morning. *I'd better not say anything,* Pam thought.

As the noise got louder, Pam could see the locomotive fast approaching the crossing. Her mother was oblivious to the danger and hadn't even slowed. "Mom!" she cried, trying not to scream.

"In a minute," her mother snapped.

And then Pam did scream, "Mom, look!"

It was too late. The train careened into the car, cleanly shearing off the front seat. Pam and her sister were left unhurt in the backseat as mother and grandmother were dragged beneath the train for a full quarter of a mile down the track.

The tragedy occurred in the summer between Pam's seventh- and eighth-grade years. The eighth-grader who returned to school that fall was not the same girl who had left. In the seventh grade, Pam had been a student that teachers enjoyed having in their classes. Bright and eager to learn, she'd never been a discipline problem and had always seemed to enjoy school. That Pam had ceased to exist. The Pam that came back to school in September was a sullen, angry and inattentive person who was very difficult to have around. It became commonplace for her to be disciplined for her rudeness and disrespectful behavior. She was obviously a very troubled young girl.

As a guidance counselor, Rose was worried about Pam. Rose was usually successful at reaching troubled kids, but so far she hadn't been able to help Pam. Week after week went by, and Rose's frustration grew. No less frustrated was Ken, Pam's science teacher. Great with kids of almost any age, Ken was disturbed by the fact that he couldn't get through Pam's shell. The three of us met frequently to discuss Pam. By November her behavior had worsened. All of us were worried, but we felt like our hands were tied. It's difficult in this day and age to reach out to a student without being accused of some indiscretion or outright perversion.

The week after Thanksgiving, Ken showed me a newspaper article and picture of his high school science teacher who was retiring. It was a long article which traced the life experiences of this man who had been Ken's mentor. Ken had enjoyed a very special relationship with this man who, long ago, had served as Ken's inspiration. In reading the article, Ken became determined to meet with Pam and discuss some personal feelings with her, regardless of the political incorrectness of doing so.

"I can't help but think about where I would be today if Mr. Smith hadn't reached out to me," Ken fumed. "I am so sick of this walking on eggshells when kids need help!" We talked about it for a bit. Ultimately, Ken took Pam's school picture from her student file and decided to go ahead and hang the consequences of overstepping "politically correct" boundaries.

At the end of science class, Ken gave Pam a note for her study hall teacher requesting that Pam come to see him that afternoon. Pam came in with a big chip securely fastened on her shoulder, expecting to be reprimanded for some new transgression. She slumped down in a seat in the first row with a sullen face. Ken moved a chair over next to her and opened his folder on the desk that they now shared.

The folder contained pictures. Pam said nothing and looked suspiciously at the desktop. "This," he said, "is my mother. I love her. She's always been there for me. I can't even imagine my life without her. It must be hard for you." When Pam just looked away, he moved on to the next picture, his mentor. He explained his affection for that man and told her how without that person in his life, he would not be who or what he was today. "He was a great teacher," Ken said. "He inspired me. I loved him, too. But it was a different kind of love than I have for my mom."

There were more pictures in the folder. One was of Ken's two little girls and his wife; another one was of Christ. The love he had for his family was easily expressed as he talked with Pam. The picture of Jesus prompted him to explain how he loved the Lord and how that love differed from any earthly love. Pointing to the pictures, Ken said, "All of these are people that I love."

The final picture in the file was of Pam herself. Holding her picture, he said very gently, "This is someone else I love. I haven't told you until now. I know it's awkward for a teacher to tell a student something like this. But I think you need to know. What happened last summer convinced me that you should know." Tears sparkled on Pam's lashes. "You're a terrific person. I love you for that. And I love you for your love of learning and many, many other things. And I love you unconditionally." The sullen look had been replaced by an expression of pain and hurt as tears streamed down Pam's cheeks. It was the first time Ken had seen anything but anger from her in a long time. Ken retrieved a box of Kleenex from the front of the room and slid the box across to her. They just sat quietly until she seemed ready to leave.

The change in Pam began that afternoon. Day by day, week by week, she began to gain ground again. Rose, Ken and I watched with delight as she progressed. By Easter she was doing very well. She was nearly the delightful girl she had been before that traumatic accident. I congratulated Ken on his success. I was convinced it was the power of Ken's love that had inspired Pam's journey back to her former self.

Rose didn't agree with me. She believed it was the power of the Holy Spirit moving through Ken that inspired him to share his feelings with Pam and thus heal her. Only God knows for sure, as He smiles down on a living photo album of the children He loves.

Harry Randles

Happy Heart Day

A happy heart is the best service we can give God.

Maria Chapian

Wednesday was Valentine's Day—the day of the girls' Bible club meeting. As the club's sponsor, I planned to make "heart day" special. I baked chocolate cupcakes and decorated them with candy hearts. The girls would trade homemade valentines. During craft time, we'd sew calico hearts on pink cloth to make a wall hanging.

I wanted to do more, however. Preteen girls can be critical of their friends. Valentine's Day was my chance to help them see the good in each other. I decided the girls would trade valentines of a different sort. Not lacy cards with printed verses, but spoken valentines—words of appreciation from their hearts.

When I got to class I had second thoughts. While the regular girls chatted and laughed together, a new girl, Julie, sat hunched at the end of the table. Should I scrap my Valentine idea? What positive words could Julie say to girls she didn't know?

I had further doubts when I noticed Brandy in class. Three months earlier a dog had attacked her and tore her left cheek, leaving a large, jagged, red scar on her flawless complexion. The wound had healed, but the scar ate at Brandy's confidence. She often covered her left cheek with her hand. She tended to turn her face and look sideways when speaking to people. Usually a confident girl, I now saw confusion in her eyes at times. Should I risk someone making a thoughtless remark about Brandy's scar?

Despite my doubts, I decided to go ahead.

"Valentine's Day is a time to show love and appreciation for our friends," I told the girls. "I want you to think of something you appreciate about the girl next to you and tell her. It will be a spoken valentine. I'll begin."

I turned to Brenda. "I appreciate your faithful attendance in Girls' Club, Brenda. You work to memorize the Bible verses and you have a great attitude."

Brenda thought a moment. She looked at the girl next to her. "You are real friendly and have a nice smile."

Without hesitation, Justine turned to Julie, the new girl. "You seem like a nice person, someone I'd like to have for my friend."

The girls' remarks were sincere. The valentine idea was working.

It was Julie's turn. What will she say to Brandy, a girl she hadn't met until today?

Julie turned to Brandy with a glowing smile and said, "You're so pretty!"

"Oh!" Brandy gasped. She began to raise her hand to cover her scarred cheek. Instead, she dropped her hand to her side. Brandy's eyes shone. She straightened in her chair. Smiling, she turned to give the girl beside her a valentine.

Did Julie see the scar? No doubt she did. But God allowed her to see more. Her valentine assured Brandy that true friends see beyond scars and flaws. With the heart, they see the heart.

Jewell Johnson

Apron Time

A women who creates and sustains a home, and under whose hands children grow up to be strong and pure men and women, is a creator second only to God.

Helen Hunt Jackson

My daughter walked into the kitchen and asked, "Mom, what are you doing?"

"Having my quiet time," I calmly replied, as I stood there, surrounded by dirty dishes, with an apron over my head. Crazy as it sounds, I had gotten the idea from a very reliable source.

At the turn of the eighteenth century, an Englishwoman named Susanna Wesley gave birth to nineteen children, ten of whom survived infancy. It is said that when she needed time alone with God, she simply stood in her kitchen and pulled her apron over her head!

In addition to finding time for God, she also spent thirty minutes of one-on-one time with each of her ten children, every week. She taught all of them to read using the Bible as her only textbook. Two of her sons, Charles and John

Wesley, were key leaders in the great spiritual awakening of the eighteenth century. We still sing hymns today that they wrote: "O for a Thousand Tongues to Sing," "Hark! The Herald Angels Sing," and many more.

Many historians believe that this great spiritual awakening was the primary reason England was spared a bloody revolution like the one that occurred in France. Susanna Wesley's children literally changed the course of a nation and influenced the destiny of countless thousands.

A man named John Taylor was among the men John Wesley led to the Lord. He heard John Wesley preach on the morning he was to be married and was so moved he ended up late for his own wedding! John Taylor became a lay Methodist preacher and raised several sons who also became lay preachers. Those sons had several sons who became—you guessed it—lay Methodist preachers.

One of those men had a little boy who listened to his daddy pray every day: "O Lord, please send missionaries to China." When that little boy was six years old, he said, "God, I will go to China." J. Hudson Taylor grew up to become the founder of the China Inland Mission (CIM) and the father of the modern faith mission movement. In his lifetime, more than eight hundred missionaries served with CIM and it continued to grow in the decades after he died.

So far, there are nine generations of preachers in the Taylor family, one who is currently serving as a missionary in Thailand.

And it all started where? In the kitchen of Susanna Wesley, one woman who had a vision that mothering could make a difference for eternity.

So, if you ever stop by my house and discover me standing in the kitchen with an apron over my head, don't ask me what I'm doing. I'm changing the world!

Donna Partow

6

CHALLENGES

Jesus did not say, "You will never have rough passage, you will never be over-strained, you will never feel uncomfortable," but He did say, "You will never be overcome."

Julian of Norwich

Tough Love

We must take our troubles to the Lord, but more than that, we must leave them there.

Hannah Whittall Smith

The feeling of terror crept back into my life. This time it was my teenage son, not my former husband. However, the same elements were in place—the gun, the ever-present fear. I sat at my kitchen table and stared into my coffee cup. The coffee was cold, and the night wore on my nerves as I waited for my son to come home.

I cupped my hands around the mug painted brightly with yellow daisies. When he was little, my son gave it to me for my birthday. He liked to give me presents—especially flowers. Clenching them in his small fist, showing a toothless grin, he'd say, "These are for you, Mama." I would get down at his eye level and hug him, then place the wilting wildflowers in a jelly jar on my kitchen table.

I poured the cold coffee into the sink. My heart broke as I remembered the last few months—when my son's anger erupted over the smallest things. "This bike is no good," he screamed as he slammed the ten-speed again and again into the ground until it lay in a crumpled heap. He had used his own hard-earned money to buy the bike, but when it wouldn't work properly, he blew up.

I cringed at his foul language, and I feared his hostility. One day in a rage, he rammed his fist through the basement door and shattered the mirror in his bedroom. He had a drinking problem, but I didn't know how to stop him.

The anger was too terribly familiar. His father had the same anger. It seethed for years under a cool exterior until he finally exploded and threatened me with a loaded gun. My former husband's life ended when he committed suicide while in jail for threatening his second wife.

Now my son had stolen a gun from our bedroom closet, and the same wrath boiled inside him.

I watched Jim, my second husband, pace the living room floor. His brow furrowed in worry. "Where is he?"

I glanced at the digital clock on the television and shrugged, exhausted with worry. "It's 1:30 and we still haven't heard from him."

Many times I'd heard the phrase, "Let go and let God." I had worried for months over how to handle my son. I wondered if it was time to turn him over to the Lord. I decided to leave my child in God's hands instead of taking him back into mine.

I sat down at the kitchen table, bowed my head and prayed. A complete peace washed over me. "I am putting him totally and completely in God's hands," I told my husband. I crawled into bed knowing God was in control. Later, I felt my husband slip into bed.

At three A.M. the ringing phone jarred us awake. Sleepily, I answered. The police officer informed me that once again our son was in jail. This time he'd started a fight with a bouncer in a hotel lounge. When the security people found the gun on him, they called in eight police cars. I was relieved to learn the gun wasn't loaded, but it didn't make the charges any less serious.

"I have been praying about this," my husband said after I hung up, "and I feel a real peace about what I'm about to say. I don't think we should bail him out of jail again."

I swallowed past the lump in my throat. I knew, from all the times my son had been jailed for drunk driving, that my husband was right. But it was hard to turn away from my own flesh and blood. I had to put my trust in God. I would not waver.

When my son called the next morning asking us to put up bail, my husband simply said, "We are through bailing you out of jail. This time you'll have to get out on your own." My husband sighed as he hung up. "He's mad."

I often wondered how a parent could not come to a child's rescue. Yet I had to learn the hard way that if I continued to get my child out of trouble, he would never take responsibility for his own actions. And he would continue to get into trouble.

A few days later our son came home. He didn't speak to either of us except to say, "I'm moving out." He and a friend loaded his car with his belongings and left.

Six months went by before we heard from him again. He drove into the driveway with a blonde-haired girl by his side. He was smiling as they walked into the house. The four of us sat down in the living room and talked softly. I was delighted to learn he wanted to get married soon. Although I had some well-founded apprehensions about his past anger, I certainly hoped he and his future wife would be happy.

As the days, weeks and months flew by, I began to see a profound change in my married son. The angry young man who'd left our home seemed to melt away as he became involved with his new family. Eventually, to my great happiness, he turned his life over to God.

At one of our first Christmases together after his marriage, my son drove to the store with my husband. The cab of the truck was almost silent except for the radio playing low. My son broke the quiet with an unexpected question. "Can you ever forgive me for the pain I put you through?" he asked.

My husband smiled and put his arm around him. "I've already forgiven you," he said, welcoming our son home with compassion, just like the father of the biblical prodigal son.

Later, our son brought a gorgeous poinsettia and set it on my kitchen table. Like a small child he said, "These are for you, Mama."

Nanette Thorsen-Snipes

Mother's Day Angel

As a coal is revived by incense, prayer revives the hopes of the heart.

Goethe

Mornings have always been hectic at our house. The boys rush in from doing farm chores, scurry for breakfast and hustle to shower in time to meet the 7:15 school bus. The morning after Mother's Day in 1973 was no exception. Thomas, age fourteen, and Stephen, twelve, begged for a little more time so they could have bacon and eggs instead of cold cereal.

"We'll ride our bikes to school," they said.

Their thirteen-year-old sister, Diane, decided to ride with them instead of taking the bus. As they charged out the door, Diane handed me a card.

"I forgot to give this to you yesterday. It's a spiritual bouquet. In the next few weeks I'll be saying lots of prayers for you." She gave me a quick kiss and was gone.

Minutes later Tommy called me from a neighbor's house, yelling, "Mom, Diane's dead! A car hit her!"

Dead! She couldn't be dead. It must be a mistake. I flew

from the house to the barn and shrieked to my husband, "John, there's been an accident. We've got to go."

He grabbed his truck keys and as we headed down the road, I had an awful pain in my stomach. I knew in my heart that life would never be the same again.

When we arrived at the scene, all we could see was Diane's mangled bike and her shoes lying on the side of the road.

The paramedics were putting a stretcher into the ambulance. I screamed.

John latched onto my arm as the emergency medical technician said, "Follow us to Mercy Hospital."

At the hospital the doctor pronounced our daughter DOA—dead on arrival. I couldn't even cry.

The next few days were a nightmare. We contacted relatives and made the necessary arrangements. During calling hours we greeted relatives, friends and people we didn't even know. They all came to give their condolences and to share our grief. The room filled with the children's classmates and teachers. They knelt in prayer beside Diane, tears streaming down their innocent faces.

I noticed an old man standing by the casket. His skin looked like worn-out shoe leather. His wrinkled hands were raised in prayer. When I approached him, he looked at me and smiled. "God must love you very much," he said. "He gives the hardest task to those He loves the most. He gave you one of His angels to care for and now He needs her back."

I looked around the room at the children praying. A bright circle of light appeared above their heads. I looked back toward the old man, but he was gone.

The parochial school Diane attended closed the day of the funeral to allow her classmates and fellow students to attend the service. They played their guitars and sang Diane's favorite songs.

I said a prayer of thanksgiving that I'd been blessed with faith. Without it, how could one endure the awful pain?

Almost thirty years later, I still feel the pain of losing Diane. But as I read her Mother's Day card one more time, I am at peace, thanks to my angel's prayers:

When the altar bells are tinkling,
And the priest bends down in prayer:
Where the people bow adoring
I'll be praying for you there.

Jeanne Converse

Disaster on the Mountain

You will not fear the terror of night, nor the arrow that flies by day . . .

Psalm 91:5

When Ruth Hagan was seventy-eight years old, she visited her daughter Judy and teenage granddaughter Marcy in California. They headed for their cabin, zigzagging forty miles up and down the mountains in their Bronco, from pavement to gravel to a narrow one-lane road of brittle shale and powdery dirt that wound terrifyingly close to cliffs.

After dinner Marcy announced the water tank was low and that she would take the Bronco down to the pump and get water. Ruth was nervous about her young granddaughter driving down the narrow dirt road by herself, but Judy reminded her that Marcy had been driving vehicles up there on the ranch roads since she was twelve.

"Just be careful, Marcy," her mother warned. "They've had a dry spell up here and the cliff side is pretty shaky. Be sure to hug the mountain side."

Ruth said a quick prayer as she and Judy watched

Marcy from the big window where they could see the road winding down the mountainside. Fifteen minutes later Judy was still watching when suddenly she screamed, "Oh no! God help us! She went over the cliff, Momma! The Bronco and Marcy—they went over! We have to help her! Come on!"

The cabin door slammed and Judy took off running. Ruth ran behind her, but Judy was quickly out of sight after the first turn in the road. Ruth raced down the steep hill, breathing hard. She ran on and on, down the hill, up the next, trying to catch up with her daughter. It was getting harder and harder to see anything at dusk. Ruth stopped cold and looked around.

She screamed into the darkness "Judy, where are you?" Off to her immediate right and down the cliff she heard, "Down here, Mother! Don't come near the edge! I slipped on loose rocks and fell over. I'm down about twenty feet."

"Oh dear God, Judy, what can I do?"

"Just stay back, Momma! The road is giving out all over! I think I can crawl back up. I saw the white roof of the Bronco when I was falling, Momma, and I heard Marcy calling for help. She's alive! But she's way down there in the ravine. You have to go back to the cabin and phone for help. Tell them to send a helicopter. We have to get Marcy out!"

Ruth resisted looking over the edge to make sure Judy was really okay. She turned around and started running back up the hill she'd just stumbled down. Up one hill, down the next. She had one hill left to climb when she stumbled on loose dirt and rocks and fell on her face. Chest pains took her breath away. She started to sob. "Dear God," she prayed, "please help me get back to the cabin so I can call for help!"

At that moment something went through Ruth. It was like a powerful energy and she knew for certain that somebody was there to help her. She heard the words, "I am here." She stood up, completely relaxed and rested. A surge of pain-free energy propelled her forward.

Ruth ran on confidently, faster than she had before, and up that last big hill. She turned into the cabin driveway, pushed through the front door and dialed 911. She sputtered out details of the disaster but unfortunately, she had no idea where she was. The dispatcher was totally confused. Ruth had to get Judy up to the phone so she could give directions. Ruth stepped out of the cabin into total darkness. She grabbed a three-foot-long walking stick propped against the cabin door and started running back down the switchback road.

She continued to run with energy and determination through the darkness. Up the hill, down the hill, up the second hill. Suddenly she stopped, not knowing where she was. "Marcy! Judy!" she shouted.

A faint voice cried from directly below. "I'm here, Grandma."

Another voice. "Momma!" It was Judy.

Ruth dropped to her knees, then lay flat on her belly as she scooted herself closer and closer to the edge of the cliff. She held the walking stick over the edge and asked Judy if she could see it.

"I see it, Momma, I'm almost there."

Ruth heard gravel rolling around where Judy was climbing. Within minutes, Judy grabbed the other end of the stick and Ruth pulled her 140-pound daughter up and over that cliff. Judy crawled into her mother's lap, shaking and sweating and immediately passed out.

Ruth held her close and stroked her wet forehead. "Judy, Judy, wake up. We have to get help for Marcy!" Ruth kept talking and rubbing her daughter's head. Finally, Judy came to. Ruth pulled her to her feet, and the two women started walking. Dazed and bleeding, Judy fell three times as they worked their way back to the cabin in the darkness.

When they reached the cabin they heard the phone ringing. It was the volunteer emergency crew on the other end. Judy sputtered out directions to where Marcy was. As soon as she hung up, she and her mother started down the mountain again to meet and guide the rescuers. They trudged up the hill, down the hill. Still full of energy, calm and confident, Ruth held on to Judy, for Judy's sake, not hers.

An hour later, the fire trucks, ambulance, paramedics and, finally, the Flight for Life helicopter arrived. It took three-and-a-half hours to cut Marcy free from the wreckage at the bottom of the cliff. At last the sheriff pulled her out of the back end of the Bronco and carried her to the waiting ambulance. She was rushed to the hospital for treatment of a crushed ankle and severely broken leg, foot and finger.

The next day, when the sheriff came to visit Marcy in the hospital, he shook his head and said, "That mountain didn't beat you."

Ruth Hagan knew the mountain didn't beat them because God was there that night, protecting her, guiding her, breathing strength into her frail body. Ruth, Judy and Marcy all have their lives to prove it.

Patricia Lorenz

Angel in Black

God to be praised, who, to believing soul, gives light in the darkness, comfort in despair.

William Shakespeare

I had landed a dream job—a summer on Cape Cod as a mother's helper. Days were spent on the beach or the cabin cruiser; nights I was usually free to hang out at the teen center. One night, though, the mother I worked for asked me to stay on duty. Her husband was away on a business trip, and she planned to spend the night at a friend's. I readily agreed; they had been very kind to me. I was especially close to the woman, having worked for her several times a week all year. We often sat in the kitchen chatting after she came home from work. She treated me like a younger sister. Although her husband traveled and rarely saw me, he was always pleasant when he was home.

I tucked the kids in, listened to music until after midnight, then checked the sleeping children and turned in for the night. I don't know how long I slept, but later a presence beside me jolted me into full consciousness, sending a shock down my spine and paralyzing me with fear. The children's father was sitting on my bed, touching me, whispering to me. He smelled of alcohol. I couldn't believe this was the same man who had let me steer the boat a few days ago, asking me about my friends, my interests, my ambitions. Now I wondered if he had been planning this evening for days. The thought sickened me. With uncharacteristic courage, I sat up in bed and told him to get out of my room. To my amazement, he did. I lay frozen while he finished in the bathroom and went to bed. The sound of his snoring did not relieve my panic; the rest of the night stretched endlessly before me, and, in my mind, the rest of the summer after that. How could I pretend it didn't happen? What if he approached me again?

A crucifix hung on the wall opposite me. I had never been a praying person. Though I found God everywhere—in sunsets, on the rocky cliffs I loved to climb, in the cold sea spray—I saw no need to call on Him. But I called on Him now as I gazed at the cross. I prayed my first prayer that was not a "God bless everybody I know" formula. I don't remember my exact words, but I remember His answer distinctly. It was audible, but without vocal tone. And it was compelling: "Get out of the house."

Now this is something I would not ordinarily do. My Puritan work ethic went back many generations and was firmly ingrained. I had this job, I was responsible for the children and I never asked anyone for help. Yet seconds after I heard the command, I leaped out of bed, threw on some clothes and bolted barefoot for the front door. I walked on the beach until dawn. I was scared, hungry, penniless and lost, driven with murderous thoughts. The first person I saw was a fisherman. He nodded and smiled kindly. I narrowed my eyes to mean little slits, thrust both hands in my pockets and took off at a fast clip. "If you're gonna send someone to help me, God, it can't be a man," I muttered. "Not now."

Ten minutes later I came upon an unlikely sight—a nun in full habit, humming to herself, enjoying the morning. I had never spoken to a nun, and the stories I had heard from my friends in parochial school did not encourage me. But there was no one else in sight, and I was really at a loss. I needed some advice. What does one call a nun? I felt awkward with "Sister," since I wasn't Catholic, so I skipped the formalities altogether. "Um, what town am I in?" I figured that was as good a conversation starter as any. She must have assumed I was a runaway. In a sense, I was. My story unfolded as we walked together, and to my surprise I found myself trusting her. "So what do I do now?" I finished.

"You must call your mother."

"I don't want to worry her."

"Your mother is your God-given guide. She will tell you what to do."

I thought of several excuses why this was impossible. There was no phone nearby; I didn't have any money. The nun offered me a ride in her car, gave me some change and waited for me outside the phone booth during the tense conversation. I returned and slumped in the front seat. "Okay, I told my mother. She's really nervous. My father's out of town and she's getting my aunt to drive here with her. She says I have to come home."

"That is good advice. Now there is something else you must do."

"Yeah, sneak into the house and get my stuff while they're at the beach."

"No. You must face them and tell them why you are leaving. The woman is your friend, you said. Friends don't leave without a word. The truth is hard, always, but it must be told."

"I have to tell her what her husband did to me? And break her heart? Some friend!"

"Her heart is broken already. Go and talk to her. Would you like me to drive you?"

I declined. I was in no hurry to face my friend. "Thanks for your help and the change," I said. "Maybe I'll write. What's your name?"

"Sister Fitzgerald," she answered, "just like President Kennedy's middle name. I live at the convent here," she continued. "It's the only one."

We said our good-byes and I dragged my feet during the long walk back down the beach to the house. My friend was waiting for me at the front door—angry, worried, thinking I had taken off and left her children. "Could we go upstairs alone?" I said to her. "We have to talk."

She was incredulous and could not believe me. It must have been some huge mistake. He'd been drinking. He thought I was one of the children. I was compassionate but firm. "No, he didn't think I was someone else, because he called me by name. I'm going home today. My mother is coming."

Saying good-bye to her was the hardest thing I have ever done. She knew the truth; I could sense it. She couldn't accept it. We never saw each other again. I did, however, learn from a friend at home that it had not been the only time her husband had behaved this way.

Several months later my family was vacationing on Cape Cod. While driving through the area where I'd stayed, we stopped at the convent to visit Sister Fitzgerald and thank her for helping me. We inquired for her at the front door.

"Sister Fitzgerald? There's no one by that name here."

"I met her in July. Has she moved to another convent?"

"I've lived here for years. We've never had a sister by that name."

Thirty years later the story still stirs my heart, a reminder of God's love and very real presence for all who call on Him.

Nancy Massand

Where There's a Wheel There's a Way

Not in the achievement, but in the endurance of the human soul, does it show its divine gradeur, and its alliance with the infinite God.

E. H. Chapim

A few years ago, I was asked by the Multiple Sclerosis (MS) Society to plan a bike-a-thon for our county. Newly diagnosed with the disease myself, I was eager to do anything to help, and so were my husband and five children. My older kids recruited friends to ride with them and sponsors to pledge money for each mile they completed. My husband and I spent days plotting out the fifty-mile route, printing maps and looking for people to donate food and prizes for the riders.

I had become good friends with a nun who also had MS. Sister Ephrem, who was confined to a wheelchair, was the first person I had met with the disease after my diagnosis. She called me every night to see how the plans for the bike-a-thon were progressing.

One evening, while Sister and I were talking, she said tearfully, "Oh, if only I could do something, just one little thing, to help with this bike-a-thon. How I wish I could be in your 'Super Wheels!'"

Why not? I thought. *After all, what could be more super than an MS patient riding her wheelchair in the event?* Knowing how much it would mean to her, I promised to talk to her superiors the next day. Talk I did. Mother Superior explained that Sister Ephrem could barely push herself from the bed to the bathroom, and even that short distance exhausted her. Still, I persisted, and after nearly a week, Sister Ephrem was granted permission to "Ride for MS."

The day arrived, and God's sunshine was bright. People of all ages turned out for the event. Six hundred bikers lined up wearing free Coke T-shirts. People with CB radios were stationed along the route to supervise and protect the younger riders. Everyone ate hot dogs and chips while eyeing the two free, ten-speed bikes donated as grand prizes for the two top pledge earners.

While I was watching the bikers line up, a van pulled up to the curb near me. A sliding door opened, a ramp unfolded and several men helped Sister Ephrem, wheelchair and all, to the ground! She smiled and pulled her free T-shirt down over her veil, then gave me a kiss, said "Thank you," and requested help to the starting line. Slowly, she pushed the wheels on her chair, inch by inch, along the gravel road. When she became tired, she stopped briefly, wiped the beads of perspiration from her brow, said a quiet prayer and continued a little farther down the road.

People of all faiths stood cheering her on. Her determination was an inspiration to everyone present. After almost an hour, reaching her self-set, three-quarter-mile goal, Sister Ephrem gave her super wheels a final turn. "I did it!" she cried, "I really and truly did it! Oh, thank you, God!"

At the end of the day she turned in over $300 in pledge

money. Exhausted but triumphant, she was lifted back into the waiting van and returned to the convent, proving that where there is a wheel and a will there is indeed a way!

Barbara Jeanne Fisher

But You Are Beautiful

The best part of beauty is that which a picture cannot express.

Francis Bacon

Candy Wood stood in front of the bathroom mirror of her new apartment, staring at her face. It had been taken apart by the surgeon six times: twice to remove the deeply imbedded malignant tumors; then four times to scrape away the life-threatening infection on the bones. Plastic surgery had smoothed the scar lines, and hairpieces covered the permanent bald spots, but the alignment of her features was slightly off kilter and her skin no longer had its healthy glow.

At the time of the surgeries, Candy had concentrated on survival and was grateful to have been granted more time to be a wife to Lee and to raise their two young children. But now the children were busy teens, and Lee had chosen someone else. The divorce was final yesterday.

As Candy stared into the mirror, she thought back to the Saturday morning the previous year, when she had awakened to find Lee contemplatively staring at the ceiling.

"What are you thinking about?" she had asked as she snuggled closer to his side.

"God's just dealing with my pride," Lee had answered.

She raised her head to look at him. "Oh? In what area?"

Lee hitched his shoulder away from her. "I'm just proud of myself for sticking it out with a grossly disfigured, skinny wife."

Candy denied the dagger in her heart. "Oh, it's good you can verbalize that," she said. Then she kissed his cheek and headed for the shower. But in the bathroom, she had stared at her face.

Grossly disfigured, Lee had said. Candy touched her cheekbones, then her nose. *Lord, I've been so thankful for restored health and for the chance to watch my children grow up, that I didn't worry about my features. Am I really that grossly disfigured?*

His answer had come in a gentle whisper she heard within her spirit: *I think you are still beautiful. True, you don't look like you once did, but you are still beautiful, and I will bring My good out of this.*

The words came back to her each time she was invited to appear on a talk show or speak at a seminar sponsored by her Mayo Clinic medical team. Then Lee filed for divorce.

Now standing in front of a new mirror, she stared at the same face and remembered that long-ago Saturday morning. This time, though, she said aloud, "Well, Lord, here we are; just You and me. I trust You will show me the beauty—and Your goodness in this." And she turned away to begin her first day as a single woman.

That afternoon, a letter arrived from a gentleman who said he had just seen Candy on TV. In the shaky handwriting of the elderly, he wrote, "I want to tell you that I think you are beautiful. I'm sorry you've had to go through such serious surgery, but please keep telling your story." Then he ended with, "I'm seventy-nine, so it's been a long time since I've written a love letter."

Candy hugged the paper to her heart, whispering her thanks to the Lord for His goodness and beauty.

Sandra P. Aldrich

Desires of Your Heart

We trust as we love, and where we love. If we love Christ much, truly we shall trust Him much.

Thomas Brooks

It was late at night in front of my house. The floodlights were on, and worship music was playing. I sat in the dirt beside four flats of flowers waiting to be planted. My tears rolled down my cheeks as I thought back over the past twenty-five years. I had married this man when I was eighteen years old and now he wanted a divorce. He had just moved his belongings out that day, and I was determined to make myself happy by planting my flowers. When I was a child, my aunt had always told me that if you have lots of flowers outside your home it meant you had a happy home. For the first time in my forty-four years I was totally alone. The children were grown and on their own, and now I was, too.

In my early twenties, I realized I needed to be dependent on the Lord instead of my husband. Through the following years of his workaholism and unfaithfulness, I had struggled to make this wonderful provider happy. I doubled my efforts in being the best I could be, and prayed daily for God's guidance and wisdom for our family. I knew the only one I could change was myself, and I prayed daily for my husband to have God's salvation. In Psalms 37:4 it says, "Delight yourself in the Lord and He will give you the desires of your heart." My desires were to have a family and a husband that loved and adored me. It did not seem to be working out that way, but I hung on to that promise.

Times looked bleak as my husband and I, by the grace of God, managed to get through some very difficult years. We lived through our son's battles with attention deficit hyperactivity disorder (ADHD) and drug addiction, our daughter's depression and our own inner battles with each other.

Now, I was sitting in the dirt crying as I remembered back. I knew I would be all right by myself because I was not really alone. I had built a relationship with God and He did love me.

It was a difficult time, but as I started looking forward to what God had planned for me, it became very exciting—and a relief—to have only myself to consider. I still prayed for my husband each day, but soon realized he had to find his own way. The divorce was in place and the time clock was ticking. I joined a Christian singles group and attended a divorce recovery workshop. I had gone on with my life and had just signed up for college when I got the call.

It was my husband. He was on his way over to tell me something. There he stood on the front porch with tears in his eyes, announcing his acceptance of the Lord. He no longer wanted a divorce and wanted to work on our marriage. It had been six months since he had left, and to be truthful, I was in doubt whether I even wanted to be married. Life was good, fun and exciting, and I was more content than I ever remembered being. Did I want to go back to the distrust and deception I had endured for so many years?

My answer to him was, "I need time." I separated myself from the activities I was involved with and took time to be alone and pray. The psalm had said the Lord would give me the desires of my heart. I had prayed for my husband for twenty-five years to come to know the Lord and now he said he had. I did not trust my husband, but I did trust God. If I chose not to work to save this marriage, I would be doubting God's power and grace.

My husband and I set up personal boundaries and had a lot of Christian counseling. We continued to live alone. As the months went by, God did the work of mending a very broken relationship. As I learned to know my husband and trust him, we fell in love, and Christ became the center of our marriage. We renewed our wedding vows in our church on our twenty-sixth wedding anniversary, with many friends and family in attendance. It was the happiest day of my life. Our beautiful daughter sang, "Let's Begin Again"; our drug-free son walked me down the aisle to meet a completely transformed man. All of my childhood dreams had come true, and I did receive the desires of my heart.

Susan Lugli

"My mom has a lot in common with God. They're both single parents."

Reprinted by permission of Martin J. Bucella.

The Gift

But those who hope in the Lord will renew their strength. They will soar on wings like eagles; they will run and not grow weary, they will walk and not be faint.

Isaiah 40:31

I sat in the stillness of my twenty-month-old daughter's hospital room, holding her hand, watching for signs of life. As I studied her, Laura looked as if her dark lashes would flutter open and she would sit up, ending our almost two-month-long nightmare.

How I longed to hear Laura's giggle as she snuggled with her silky hair against my cheek while I read to her from one of her favorite books.

Impulsively, I leaned over and kissed her cherubic face. "Honey, it's Mommy. I love you—I know you're in there. I'm waiting . . ."

The words caught in my throat. I shut my eyes. *If only I could turn back the hand of time and avoid the collision that had saturated our lives with grief.*

I remembered sitting in the emergency waiting room

with my husband, tearfully awaiting the doctor's verdict. Paul and I hugged each other and shouted with joy when the doctor told us, "Laura's going to be all right. Go home and get some rest." But as I lay my head on my pillow that night, my dreams spun out of control. I woke up in a cold sweat, picturing the blood that had trickled out of Laura's ear. *Laura is not okay. The crash was too violent. I have to get back to the hospital!*

I raced my car through the rain-slicked, predawn streets. Once in Laura's ICU room, I found the staff gathered around her body as it quaked with convulsions.

God, where are You? I cried.

Three months later, Laura had been moved to another hospital, yet she still remained unresponsive. I continued to cry, *Lord, when will You answer my call?*

One evening, as I sat by her bed, the mechanical breathing of her respirator jarred my thoughts. A strange mood of uncertainty settled over me. I looked at the child I had fought and prayed so hard to keep. *She's really in there, isn't she?*

I stood up, trying to shake the doubt that had caught me off guard. My watch read 11 P.M., so I decided to get ready for bed. Because my husband, Paul, was still out of town, I wasn't driving home. I would sleep in Laura's room instead.

Flipping off the light, I shut the door. The nurses had already completed their evening rounds. It would be hours before anyone would check on us. I felt alone, too alone. I popped two extra-strength pain relievers and sat the bottle on a nearby tray table beside my glass of water. *What if the doctors are right, and Laura never wakes up?* I thought as I spread a blanket in the window seat.

Fluffing my pillow, I wondered about God. *Maybe He's abandoned us. Maybe He isn't going to answer my prayers.*

This new thought punctured my tired spirit. *Just who am*

I trying to fool? I questioned. *I need to face facts. Laura will never awaken. She'll live the rest of her life as a vegetable, hooked to life support.*

I tried to stifle the emotions that began to boil as Laura's respirator mocked, *no-hope, no-hope, no-hope.* My chest constricted as I gasped for air. Everything seemed so different, so pointless. *Laura,* I thought, *would be better off if she were to die. After all, I could not allow her to live in this suspended state of life, could I?*

A plan rose from my grief. I couldn't bear to ask the doctors to take my child off life support after I had already forbidden it once before. But now, I realized Laura's smile would never return. My dreams for her life were dashed. *And God?* He had been as silent as Laura's stilled voice.

I was truly alone, miles from my husband, miles from Laura's cognizance, and light-years from the God I had trusted.

Perhaps God's silence meant I needed to take matters into my own hands. Perhaps it was up to me to end this horrible suffering.

I can end Laura's life without the doctor's help, I reasoned to myself. *I can turn off the alarms and unplug the vent from the wall. It would be so simple, except—except, if I take my daughter's life, how could I live with myself? How could I face Paul or my parents?*

The moonlight reflected on my bottle of pain relievers. *If I swallowed them—no one would find us until morning—Laura and I could escape this living Hell. Together.*

Just as my plan seemed like the only solution, I found my hand resting on my belly. My hidden child was only two weeks old, but I knew he was there.

My thoughts slowly cleared. *How could I kill myself? How could I kill Laura? A new life was growing inside me. A life that had the right to live!*

My reasoning returned. *Lord, I'm willing to wait—despite*

the pain and the cost. I'm willing to wait on You.

The word "wait" jolted a verse from Isaiah into my consciousness. *But those who hope in the Lord will renew their strength. They will soar on wings like eagles; they will run and not grow weary, they will walk and not be faint.*

I cried myself to sleep—terrified of the future—terrified of the murders I had thought of committing.

Nine months later, my daughter began to emerge from her coma just before her baby brother, Jimmy, was born.

Although her eyes fluttered open, Laura's gaze was fixed, she still remained hooked to life support and she slumped in her wheelchair, totally paralyzed. Although she was diagnosed as blind, Laura began to greet us with a cheerful "Hi," and slowly, her eyes began to focus once again.

I still sometimes weep over the Laura I have lost, but I embrace the Laura who has returned. How glad I am I waited on God instead of going through with my murderous midnight plan.

I still face obstacles. But God enables me. *I run but am weary—I run the race set before me—a race I now know I can finish.*

Linda Evans Shepherd

7

A MATTER OF PERSPECTIVE

It is not the eye that sees the beauty of heaven, nor the ear that hears the sweetness of music or the glad tidings of a prosperous occurrence, but the soul, that perceives all the relishes of sensual and intellectual perfections; and the more noble and excellent the soul is, the greater and more savory are its perceptions.

Jeremy Taylor

In God's Eyes

By the time I was ten, I was totally ashamed of my father. All my friends called him names: Quasimodo, hunchback, monster, little Frankenstein, the crooked little man with the crooked little cane. At first it hurt when they called him those things, but soon I found myself agreeing with them. He was ugly, and I knew it.

My father was born with something called parastremmatic dwarfism. The disease made him stop growing when he was about thirteen and caused his body to twist and turn into a grotesque shape. It wasn't too bad when he was a kid. I saw pictures of him when he was about my age. He was a little short but quite good-looking. Even when he met my mother and married her when he was nineteen, he still looked pretty normal. He was still short and walked with a slight limp, but he was able to do just about anything. Mother said, "He even used to be a great dancer."

Soon after my birth, however, things started getting worse for my father. Another genetic disorder took over, and his left foot started turning out, almost backward. His head and neck shifted over to the right; his neck became rigid and he had to look over his left shoulder a bit. His right arm curled in and up, and his index finger almost touched his elbow. His spine warped to look something like a big, old roller coaster and it caused his torso to lie sideways, instead of straight up and down like a normal person. His walk became slow, awkward and deliberate. He dragged his left foot and used his deformed right arm to balance his gait.

I hated to be seen with him. Everyone stared. They seemed to pity me. I knew he must have done something really bad to have God hate him that much.

By the time I was seventeen, I was blaming all my problems on my father. I didn't have the right boyfriends because of him. I didn't drive the right car because of him. I wasn't pretty enough because of him. I didn't have the right jobs because of him. I wasn't happy because of him.

Anything that was wrong with me or my life was because of him. If my father had been good-looking like Jane's father, or successful like Paul's father, or worldly like Terry's father, I would be perfect! I knew that for sure.

The night of my senior prom came, and my father had to place one more nail in my coffin; he had volunteered to be one of the chaperones at the dance. My heart just sank when he told me. I stormed into my room, slammed the door, threw myself on the bed and cried.

"Three more weeks and I'll be out of here!" I screamed into my pillow. "Three more weeks, and I will have graduated and be moving away to college." I sat up and took a deep breath. "God, please make my father go away and leave me alone. He keeps sticking his big nose in everything I do. Just make him disappear, so that I can have a good time at the dance."

I got dressed, my date picked me up, and we went to the prom. My father followed in his car behind us. When we arrived, he seemed to vanish into the pink chiffon drapes that hung everywhere in the auditorium. I thanked God for answering my prayer. At least now I could have some fun.

Midway through the dance, my father came out from behind the drapes and decided to embarrass me again. He started dancing with my girlfriends. One by one, he took their hand and led them to the dance floor. He then clumsily moved them in circles as the band played. Now I tried to vanish into the drapes.

After Jane had danced with him, she headed my way.

Oh, no! I thought. *She's going to tell me he stomped on her foot or something.*

"Grace," she called, "you have the greatest father."

My face fell. "What?"

She smiled at me and grabbed my shoulders. "Your father's just the best. He's funny, and kind, and he always finds the time to be where you need him. I wish my father was more like that."

For one of the first times in my life, I couldn't talk. Her words confused me.

"What do you mean?" I asked her.

Jane looked at me really strangely. "What do you mean, what do I mean? Your father's wonderful. I remember when we were kids, and I'd sleep over at your house. He'd always come into your room, sit down in the chair between the twin beds, and read us a book. I'm not sure my father can even read," she sighed, and then smiled. "Thanks for sharing him."

Then, Jane ran off to dance with her boyfriend.

I stood there in silence.

A few minutes later, Paul came to stand beside me.

"He's sure having a lot of fun."

"What? Who? Who is having a lot of fun?" I asked.

"Your father. He's having a ball."

"Yeah. I guess." I didn't know what else to say.

"You know, he's always been there," Paul said. "I remember when you and I were on the mixed-double co-ed soccer team. He tried out as the coach, but he couldn't run up and down the field, remember? So they picked Jackie's father instead. That didn't stop him. He showed up for every game and did whatever needed to be done. He was the team's biggest fan. I think he's the reason we won so many games. Without him, it just would have been Jackie's father running up and down the field yelling at us. Your father made it fun. I wish my father had been able to show up to at least one of our games. He was always too busy."

Paul's girlfriend came out of the restroom, and he went to her side, leaving me once again speechless.

My boyfriend came back with two glasses of punch and handed me one.

"Well, what do you think of my father?" I asked out of the blue.

Terry looked surprised. "I like him. I always have."

"Then why did you call him names when we were kids?"

"I don't know. Because he was different, and I was a dumb kid."

"When did you stop calling him names?" I asked, trying to search my own memory.

Terry didn't even have to think about the answer. "The day he sat down with me outside by the pool and held me while I cried about my mother and father's divorce. No one else would let me talk about it. I was hurting inside, and he could feel it. He cried with me that day. I thought you knew."

I looked at Terry and a tear rolled down my cheek as long-forgotten memories started cascading into my consciousness.

When I was three, my puppy got killed by another dog, and my father was there to hold me and teach me what happens when the pets we love die. When I was five, my father took me to my first day of school. I was so scared. So was he. We cried and held each other that first day. The next day he became a teacher's helper. When I was eight, I just couldn't do math. Father sat down with me night after night, and we worked on math problems until math became easy for me. When I was ten, my father bought me a brand-new bike. When it was stolen, because I didn't lock it up like I was taught to do, my father gave me jobs to do around the house so I could make enough money to purchase another one. When I was thirteen, and my first love broke up with me, my father was there to yell at, to blame, and to cry with. When I was fifteen, and I got to be in the honor society, my father was there to see me get the accolades. Now, when I was seventeen, he put up with me no matter how nasty I became or how high my hormones raged.

As I looked at my father dancing gaily with my friends, a big toothy grin on his face, I suddenly saw him differently. The handicaps weren't his, they were mine! I had spent a great deal of my life hating the man who loved me. I had hated the exterior that I saw, and I had ignored the interior that contained his God-given heart. I suddenly felt very ashamed.

I asked Terry to take me home. I was too overcome with feelings to remain.

On graduation day, at my Christian high school, my name was called, and I stood behind the podium as the valedictorian of my class. As I looked out over the people in the audience, my gaze rested on my father, sitting next to my mother in the front row. He sat there in his one and only specially made suit, holding my mother's hand and smiling.

Overcome with emotions, my prepared speech was to become a landmark in my life.

"Today I stand here as an honor student, able to

graduate with a 4.0 average. Yes, I was in the honor society for three years and was elected class president for the last two years. I led our school to a championship in the debate club, and yes, I even won a full scholarship to Kenton State University so that I can continue to study physics and someday become a college professor.

"What I'm here to tell you today, fellow graduates, is that I didn't do it alone. God was there, and I had a whole bunch of friends, teachers and counselors who helped. Up until three weeks ago, I thought they were the only ones I would be thanking this evening. If I had thanked just them, I would have been leaving out the most important person in my life. My father."

I looked down at my father and at the look of complete shock that covered his face.

I stepped out from behind the podium and motioned for my father to join me onstage. He made his way slowly, awkwardly and deliberately. He had to drag his left foot up the stairs as he used his deformed right arm to balance his gait. As he stood next to me at the podium, I took his small, crippled hand in mine and held it tight.

"Sometimes we only see the silhouette of the people around us," I said. "For years I was as shallow as the silhouettes I saw. For almost my entire life, I saw my father as someone to make fun of, someone to blame and someone to be ashamed of. He wasn't perfect, like the fathers my friends had.

"Well, fellow graduates, what I found out three weeks ago is that while I was envying my friends' fathers, my friends were envying mine. That realization hit me hard and made me look at who I was and what I had become. I was brought up to pray to God and hold high principles for others and myself. What I've done most of my life is read between the lines of the 'Good Book' so I could justify my hatred."

Then, I turned to look my father in the face.

"Father, I owe you a big apology. I based my love for you on what I saw and not what I felt. I forgot to look at the one part of you that meant the most, the big, big heart God gave you. As I move out of high school and into life, I want you to know I could not have had a better father. You were always there for me, and no matter how badly I hurt you, you still showed up. Thank you!"

I took off my mortar board and placed it on his head, moving the tassel just so.

"You are the reason I am standing here today. You deserve this honor, not me."

And as the audience applauded and cried with us, I felt God's light shining down upon me as I embraced my father more warmly than I ever had before, tears unashamedly falling down both our faces.

For the first time, I saw my father through God's eyes, and I felt honored to be seen with him.

Candace Carteen

The Blessing Jar

Sacrifice thank offerings to God, fulfill your vows to the Most High, and call upon Me in the day of trouble; I will deliver you, and you will honor Me.

Psalm 50:14–15

Life hadn't been easy. In fact, the list of tragic events and difficulties ran longer than my grocery list. I felt exhausted. Yet my strength was needed to help hold together the pieces of the stress-free life my family once knew.

"Why do I have to take four shots a day?" Jenna Marie, my kindergartener, asked repeatedly. The explanation of being diagnosed with juvenile diabetes didn't seem to satisfy her.

"Just how big is the tank that Uncle Rusty is driving? How far away is the Gulf War? Who is this guy Saddam anyway?" my four-year-old son questioned.

Beep, beep, beep—the steady rhythm of my premature baby's heart monitor echoed in the background. This was our moment-by-moment reminder of how fragile life really is.

Marty, my husband, and I had learned to expect the unexpected. It seemed we anticipated the bad, and braced ourselves for it. We had lost our focus. The challenges of life so overwhelmed us that we weren't seeing the blessings God provided us daily.

As a family, we were reading of God's faithfulness to David, Joseph and Moses.

"Why can't we read about God's faithfulness to us, the Mitchells?" our children asked. At a loss for words, I looked to my husband.

After a long moment of silence he said, "We can and we will. Jenna, you go and get the special note cards out of Daddy's drawer in the study. Jason, you go and get the box of crayons and markers."

The children hurried off, full of excitement. Daddy had an idea, and they couldn't wait to hear it. I sat pondering, wondering what my "non-seminarian" husband might be thinking.

When the children returned we all sat Indian-style on the family-room floor. Everyone sat quietly, all eyes on Daddy as he began to speak:

"There are times in our lives that we don't always see God's blessings right away. Sometimes they are disguised, and the things we once thought of as bad, or scary, turn into a wonderful blessing. Think of a caterpillar. He isn't very pretty. And I wonder if it is a little bit scary for him to seal off the cocoon he entwined around himself. I wonder if it is dark in there. I wonder if Mr. Caterpillar screams, 'Let me out of here! I can't breathe!' But then one day, just at the right time, we see something happening. We see God's plan, the miracle of a beautiful butterfly."

Reaching for the note cards that Jenna clutched tightly in her hands, Marty continued. "Tonight, we're going to think back and remember how God has taken care of us and blessed our family over the few past years. Then we are going to write these blessings on my special note cards."

"But Daddy, we can't write words," Jason said.

"We couldn't read them even if we wrote them!" Jenna chimed in.

"You're right," Daddy replied. "But you can draw."

For the next half-hour our family remembered, drew, laughed and even shed a few tears as we recorded God's faithfulness to the Mitchells. After tucking the children into bed and saying good night to Marty, I went out to the garage, dug around a cluttered shelf and found an old dusty pickle jar. I found an old set of puffy-paint I'd purchased months ago when the children painted T-shirts. On the side of the old pickle jar I painted, "Our Blessing Jar." I gathered the note cards, folded them in half and dropped each one into the jar. Finding a colorful ribbon, I tied it in a bow around the lid as if it were a present, leaving it as the centerpiece on the kitchen table. Before I finally went to bed, I placed another stack of Daddy's special note cards alongside the jar.

The next morning the children found their way to the breakfast table. "What's this?" they said while opening the lid.

"It's our blessings. We have a Blessing Jar."

"Let's see how many blessings we can think of today!" Jenna shouted with excitement.

"You know, Daddy says that God is the one who gives the blessing. We just need to keep track of them," Jason reported.

And for the past ten years we have. Our children now read for themselves stories of God's faithfulness to David, Joseph and Moses. They have learned to trust when they can't see past their cocoons.

Tonight I added another blessing to the Mitchell family's Blessing Jar.

"Lord," I wrote. "Thanks for the nights when all seemed dark, when challenges knocked on our door like a regular visitor. Thanks for the special note cards and crayons. And thanks for giving us a way to read about Your faithfulness to the Mitchells!"

Janet Lynn Mitchell

The Flood

Prayer is and remains always a native and deep impulse of the soul of man.

Thomas Carlyle

My husband Stevie and I woke up early one rainy Saturday morning and noticed that the creek behind our mountain cabin had risen almost to the top of the bank. As it continued to rain I felt a twinge of uneasiness. Just the weekend before, the water in the usually peaceful creek had risen over the bank and flooded our yard. Could it be happening again? The eighty-year-old old-timers on the mountain told us that Paint Creek had never flooded like that in their lifetime.

The radio report called for flash floods in the area. We quickly got dressed and as the water splashed over the bank, Stevie grabbed the keys to our trucks and rushed out to move them to the neighbor's driveway. I ran outside to gather my garden angels and other favorite yard ornaments. Before I could finish collecting them, the water was above my knees. I was afraid it was going to come inside our home. Four years earlier Stevie and I had worked so hard building this cabin ourselves. I couldn't imagine all that work being destroyed.

I waded to the driveway side of the house to check on Stevie. He was trying to save his riding lawnmower, but had to let it go as it washed away downstream. We got back inside the house and began to move some of our most cherished treasures onto beds and the kitchen countertop. Our thirteen-year-old border collie, Reba, was on the front porch shaking with fear. We pulled her inside as the water splashed over the porch. Wilma, our four-year-old Jack Russell terrier, was on the couch watching.

As we grabbed our musical instruments I could see out the bedroom window that our shop was floating away. Everything was happening so fast. We rushed to the front door of the living room just as Stevie's barn hit the back of the house. Water began pouring into the kitchen window, the floor shook and our house began to move. We were being swept away! I cried for God to save us!

The house hit an electric pole. The force knocked us onto the floor as the house spun around, heading down what was now a raging river. All the heavy porch furniture slid up against the front door, keeping us from escaping. We could see our neighbors on the bank watching this nightmare. We rapidly passed them as we were swept over the bridge and across the road toward another neighbor's house. We hit a huge tree and were once again knocked to the floor.

As we scrambled back to our feet we hit the neighbors' barn. During this whole wild ride I was praying as loud as I could for God to help us. We slammed into a tree and the front porch peeled off like the lid on a can of sardines. Stevie, who had just had shoulder surgery three days earlier, had Wilma in his arms and tried to hold my hand when we jumped into the filthy water. The current ripped us apart. There was so much debris in the water, but nothing to grab on to except a little board. I saw Wilma swimming frantically beside me. The board went underwater and so did I. I panicked at first because I can't swim. But then as I prayed for my life I felt peace. I knew that if I drowned, I would be with Jesus. If I lived, I knew that God must have something big planned for my life. Crazy as it sounds, it was a win-win situation.

I stretched my hand high over my head and felt air on my fingertips. I reached for anything that might be above me. Then it was as if God placed that branch in my hand and I pulled my head up above water and took a breath. As I hung onto that little branch, I thanked God for saving my life. I didn't know where I was. Stevie was nowhere in sight. I prayed that God would spare his life, too.

Immediately, I heard Stevie scream my name, and I yelled as loud as I could. I managed to pull myself up out of the water just as Stevie crawled through the brush to get to me. He grabbed my hand and we climbed up the side of the mountain. When we reached a safe place to sit down, we held each other, cried and thanked God.

We had only been sitting there for a minute when a huge tree came crashing down next to us. We climbed higher up through the woods until we found the Appalachian Trail, all the while calling out for Reba and Wilma. The noise of the flood was deafening. We were wet, cold, bruised and cut, but grateful to be alive. We followed the Appalachian Trail to the highway for help.

Our house had landed a quarter-mile down from its original site. Everything was destroyed. Reba was found alive near the house, but we never found Wilma.

We lost a lifetime of possessions, but we were flooded with God's mercy for saving our lives.

Howie Mullis

Judging a Book by Its Cover

Do not judge, or you too will be judged. For in the same way you judge others, you will be judged, and with the measure you use, it will be measured to you.

Matthew 7:1–2

During the mid-1980s I was an American living in the Netherlands at a Christian ministry base, getting familiar with a new culture, new customs and a new language. Common purpose and vision, however, tied me to the people I met, and we newcomers quickly intermingled with the seasoned veterans.

One day our little base in the quiet, conservative countryside hosted a group of visitors from a sister base in the large city of Amsterdam. We were eager to share a time of worship with our guests, and to hear about their specific ministry experiences. But when they walked through the door, I found my personal preparation sorely lacking.

Many of them were dressed from head to toe in black leather with profusions of silver studs and dangling chains. Pierced ears abounded among both the men and the women, and other facial parts sported small barbells and rings. Colorful dyed and bleached hair spiked out in all directions; tattoos decorated arms and necks.

These are Christians? I asked myself. I was certain that Christians should be conventional and traditional, dressed and decorated in a moderate manner like my friends and I. These visitors from Amsterdam strayed far from my narrow guidelines and broke my rules.

But no sooner had I judged these people than I reprimanded myself. *Who was I to say what Christians should look like, how they should dress, what type of jewelry they should wear or where they should wear it?* I definitely had not been assigned by God to act as judge of personal appearances—I'd given myself that job.

Suddenly my eyes were opened and I began to look at our Amsterdam visitors from a new perspective. I saw tenderness in one father's eyes as he cuddled his toddler son on his lap. I witnessed affectionate hugs and firm handshakes as the guests warmly returned their hosts' greetings. I sensed true sincerity from the hearts of these people. Their Bibles were more well-worn and dog-eared than some of ours.

My eyes, my heart, my boundaries of perception opened wider as these visitors shared about their inner-city ministry. In Amsterdam, they found opportunities in bars and pool halls, on the streets where homeless people lived and in the red light district where prostitution abounded. They brought hope to the hopeless by taking Jesus into the murky alleys of the city. They went to places I would never willingly go. And they did it with joy, peace and confidence.

As one young man described sharing friendship evangelism in a bar, I pictured myself, with my conventional dress and conservative appearance, entering that same bar and attempting to strike up conversation around the pool table. I had to laugh.

Now I look at sincerity of heart, not the outer appearances, of the variety of people God created to make Himself known.

Adele Noetzelman

And the Little Child Shall Lead Them

As I sit on the porch watching my children play in the yard, my eyes turn to Jeremy, the youngest of our children, the baby. When we adopted Jeremy, knowing he would be physically and mentally delayed, we planned to teach him so much. However, as I watch him play, I realize God had another plan.

Jeremy climbs onto his older brother's *Star Wars* bike. He does this with such confidence, I'm sure he'd be pedaling down the sidewalk by now if he were just two inches taller. Instead, he straddles the back tire and grips the handlebars, turning them back and forth, willing the bicycle to move.

As I watch him attempt this challenge, I vow to forget my own weaknesses and not let fear of failure stop me when facing a challenge of my own.

Out of the corner of his eye, eyes that are supposedly visually impaired, Jeremy spots the yellow and blue Little Tikes grocery cart on the sidewalk. Sitting on his bottom, he moves easily across the walkway and begins to scoot down the five steps that will lead him to the cart he continues to eye. Stair climbing is not a practiced skill, though he masters the downward descent with ease. His physical therapist would be proud. I am proud.

His determination inspires me. I vow to remember his determination the next time something difficult stands between me and the object of my desires.

He walks with pride across the sidewalk. Though he can't walk on his own, he looks graceful pushing the grocery cart full of wet leaves that helps him balance on two feet. He turns to me and smiles as he takes one careful step after another. When he hits a dip in the sidewalk that stops him from continuing his journey, he attempts to push the cart out of the rut on his own, but finally decides that, without help, he can go no further. He looks over his shoulder, sees his three-year-old brother digging in the rain-softened dirt, and in perfect Jeremy-ese, yells, "OoooohAaaaaaah."

Keyen, who understands Jeremy's language well, walks to the cart, gives it a firm push that releases it from the rut, and Jeremy is happily on his way.

As I watch, I vow to swallow my pride and ask for help the next time life's journey sticks me in a rut I can't get out of on my own.

Jeremy doesn't travel far when the right blue wheel of his grocery cart veers off the edge of the sidewalk. Before I can reach him, he tumbles to the ground. Though at first he is too stunned to respond, seconds later, he is sitting up, rubbing his head and letting the tears fall freely down his cheeks. I pick him up, hold him tightly and whisper, "You're okay, buddy," over and over in his ear. He accepts my comfort for a moment, then pushes himself out of my arms to get back to the challenging journey that awaits him.

As he strolls on, I vow to remember that when life knocks me down, I'll feel sorry for myself for only a moment. I'll heed the encouragement of those who love me, and I'll get right back up and move on.

I stay a few steps behind Jeremy so I can catch him if he falls. As I walk, I'm reminded that there is someone beside me, too. I vow to remember God in my prayers tonight and thank Him for being there to catch me when I fall.

Jeremy has only walked a few feet when something else catches his observant eye and he's on his hands and knees searching for the treasure he knows is there. He picks up a rock. A plain, ordinary rock if you ask me, but Jeremy sees something else. He smiles at the beautiful rock he holds in his hand. He looks at it closely, touches it to his cheek and again shows his pleasure in his familiar language, "Ooooohhhhhuuuuhhhh." He looks at it one more time, then tosses it aside and crawls to the grocery cart that enables him to continue his stroll. As he walks ahead, I pick up the rock he discarded and discover that it's not as plain and ordinary as I'd first thought. Shiny little specks catch the sunlight to make a beautiful sparkle, and when I touch it to my cheek, it's smooth and cool.

As I put the rock in my pocket, I vow to remember to take time to discover the small treasures that may go unnoticed if I travel too quickly on the path of life. I vow to uncover the beauty in what may at first seem plain and ordinary.

By now, Jeremy has walked all the way to the chalk line, three houses from ours, that says, "Stop Here." Although I know he doesn't understand, I explain that we've reached our boundary and turn him and his cart the opposite way. The journey home seems quicker, and with less distractions.

As we near our front steps, I fully expect Jeremy to pass our house and head toward the park across the street. But, as always, he is full of surprises. He stops in front of our house, lets go of his beloved grocery cart and turns to me with arms held high. I lift him over my head. He squeals with delight.

As we walk up the steps and into the yard, I vow to never forget the way home, or that home contains something far more valuable than what may look exciting across the street. As I tell my other children to put their toys away so we can go in for lunch, a neighbor stops to chat. She jokingly mentions that our efforts to grow grass in our front yard are failing. I smile, knowing that as long as there are active children at home, we will never have a beautifully landscaped yard. My neighbor smiles at Jeremy who is already smiling through the drool dripping down his chin. Knowing that Jeremy is adopted, my neighbor says the same thing that we hear so often, "What a lucky boy."

I smile and respond the same way I have a hundred times before, "We're the lucky ones." We say our good-byes and turn to go our separate ways. My neighbor says to no one in particular, but loud enough for me to hear, "What a wonderful family. They'll teach him so much."

And, as my precious children and I walk into our house, I realize that Jeremy has already taught us everything that's important in life.

Dawn Nowakoski

Journey to the Depths of My Purse

I carry the basic essentials of life in my purse: aspirin, lipstick, hand lotion, credit card. You name it, it's in there. If it's not, it will be. I seem to have some sort of purse reflex. I can stuff things in there without even knowing it.

On the positive side, I found a five-dollar bill in a sneaky secret pocket last week. Even better, I found a candy bar. Now that was interesting. It was squished—almost liquified—but it was still inside the wrapper.

Unfortunately, there are other encounters now and then that aren't exactly positive purse experiences. The other day, for example, I was making a return and I had to do an emergency receipt search at the customer service counter. My purse stuff started piling up. I pulled out five loose Life Savers, an old Valentine card, sunscreen, one mitten, six kid-meal toys (including a minitractor with only one wheel), three keys of unknown lock origin, and a dead cricket. But no receipt. There were twelve tissues (none I would actually use), last year's Christmas list, a ticket stub to the Junior High spring concert and the backs from four adhesive name tags.

I also found two Gummy Worms stuck in a hairbrush, a

Denny's coupon that expired in 1997 and a plastic Easter egg. I was pretty sure that the egg was older than the coupon. I shook it to see if it rattled. It did. I think I made it angry.

There was also enough purse fuzz in there to stuff a sofa pillow. How embarrassing. Inside the purse fuzz, something green and squishy caught my eye and it frightened me. I gained courage by tossing the dead cricket and drinking the candy bar.

Just before I dove into the fuzz, I got to the heart of my purse: my mini-Bible. It had all my family pictures tucked inside. That's when I realized that everything important in life could be found in my purse.

Okay, if you want to get technical, I didn't exactly find Jesus in my handbag. But I could pull out the pictures of my husband and my children and see reminders of His gifts to me. And His word was there. Granted, it smelled a little like Juicy Fruit, but it was a great reminder that there's really no place I can go where I won't find the Lord's presence. Not one, fuzz-covered place!

Psalm 139, verses 7 through 10, says it beautifully: "Where can I go from Your Spirit? Where can I flee from Your presence? If I go up to the heavens, You are there; if I make my bed in the depths, You are there. If I rise on the wings of the dawn, if I settle on the far side of the sea, even there Your hand will guide me, Your right hand will hold me fast.

There's no place I can go without Him—not the heavens, not the depths, not the far side of the sea. I climb all the way inside my purse, and He still finds me there.

I'm rejoicing in His love—even though I never found the receipt.

For the record, I think that green squishy thing used to be a jelly bean. I guess we'll never know. One of the kids ate it.

Rhonda Rhea

8

MIRACLES

And Jesus said to her, "Daughter, be of good cheer; your faith has made you well. Go in peace."

Luke 8:48

The Miracle of Medjugorje

Miracles—whether prophetically or of other sorts—always occur in connection with some message from heaven, and are intended by God as a seal, or endorsement of the messenger and His word.

Aloysius McDonough

Mom always had a great devotion to the Virgin Mary. She didn't believe that Mary could answer prayers, but that she was an intercessor to her son, Jesus. While my mom was raising eight kids, she likely thought she needed all the interceding she could get!

Each of us had a rosary, and my mother taught us to say the Hail Mary on each bead. A statue of the Blessed Virgin sat prominently on the buffet, and fresh flowers adorned her, especially in May.

Mom read us stories of how Mary had appeared to a young girl in Lourdes, France, and to children in Guadeloupe, Mexico. Then in the 1980s, Mom told her then-grown children new accounts of Mary appearing to youngsters in Medjugorje, Bosnia. Intrigued by the modern-day miracle, my mom bought books about it, subscribed to the Medjugorje magazine, attended seminars on the topic—and bought a ticket to Bosnia.

I've always said that my mother was eighty going on fifty. In spite of several old fractures, numerous surgeries and a mild heart condition, she taught religious education classes, gave slide show presentations of her safari to Africa and drove "old people" to their doctors' appointments.

"I don't know if I can climb the mountain," my mom said, "but I just want to go. I can't explain it—I just need to go. And I'm not going so I can ask for a miracle," she added emphatically.

But many who went, did. There were hundreds of accounts of miraculous healings and faith conversions at Medjugorje.

Her tour group arrived in Medjugorje late one damp November night. The next morning they learned their scheduled trek had been postponed, due to the rain and slippery slopes. One younger man who had made the trip twice before, said he could wait no longer—he was climbing the mile-long mountain path right then. My mother said, "Me, too."

So with a pin in her ankle, five metal rods in her back and a song in her heart, my mom set off for the climb. She was surprised to see the trail was only jagged rocks. Step by cautious step, she hiked upward—past a woman even older than she, kneeling in prayerful meditation, and past a half-dozen rowdy ten-year-old boys, running and yelping with joy. Soon they raced ahead of her and later she came upon them again, kneeling in quiet prayer.

Within two hours, my mother stood in wonder and awe at the top of the mountain, on the very site the Virgin had appeared. She knelt in the sprinkling rain and did what she always did—she prayed for her children.

The trek down was even more difficult than the ascent.

Each step on the rugged rocks jarred her as she struggled to find stable footing. The rain intensified as they wound their way through the foreign streets. Mom returned to the group, soaking wet but marveling that, not only had she made the climb, she had done so without her usual pain. "Maybe that was the miracle," she mused.

The next day was just another day in war-torn Bosnia, but it was Thanksgiving Day in the States—and the tour guide had a plan to make it a day of thanksgiving in Medjugorje, too. On every tour the staff purchased and distributed groceries and supplies to the most needy in the community. All of the dozen members of my mother's tour group readily offered to contribute to the fund and help with the deliveries.

Their large bus stopped at the grocery store where the ordered bags of goods were loaded into the back. Carefully, the group counted the twenty-four, garbage-sized bags. Local church and government officials had made a list of those in most desperate need, and the bus headed off to share thanksgiving with them.

The first stop was a shanty with the roof partially blown off. Mom and her new friends filed past damaged household furniture sitting on the dirt lawn and entered the one room the family of four occupied. Laughing, smiling and crying, the old couple accepted the food and supplies. Two young boys in clean ragged clothes chattered their gratitude, while their toddler brother clung to his grandma's leg, whining and fussing. Their parents had been tortured and killed by the enemy, the tour guide explained. Yet the family jubilantly hugged my mom and her crew good-bye as they headed off to the next stop.

The bus driver seemed to have the route and stops memorized from the many trips before. At the next rundown house, a wrinkled old woman in a headscarf stood waving from her cluttered front porch. As the group entered, she placed her hands on each of their faces and kissed them, one by one, thanking them in her native tongue. Inside she gathered them in one of the two rooms left standing in her once-three bedroom home. There she prayed, not for herself, but for her guests.

The driver stopped next at a ramshackle house at the end of a lane, and before the tour guide could say, "They aren't on our list this time," a man and two young boys raced toward the bus clapping for joy. At the directive of the tour guide, the bus pulled away.

"Can't we please leave them some food," my mother politely protested as she looked back at the family waving sadly.

"We only had twenty-four bags to start with," the guide explained, her voice thick with sorrow. "We have other families waiting for these—we promised them."

The team sat, despondent, until the driver stopped at yet another war-damaged home. A couple who looked years older than my mom were caring for two grown sons, each suffering from a wasting muscular disease. Yet their faith and joy exceeded even that of the team as they crowded the entire group into their tiny kitchen to pray—then insisted that they all share in the food the old woman had prepared for them.

And so went the day, house after house, family after family, each physically destitute and spiritually wealthy.

"That's twenty-four!" the guide said as she checked the last name off the list after the final stop.

"No, twenty-three," someone corrected. "There is one bag of food left."

Dumbfounded, the group looked in the back of the bus to see one lone bag of food.

"We all counted the bags and the people on the list three times," one member said breathlessly.

"There was no error," the guide said. Then, smiling, she

asked, "Are there loaves and fish in that bag?"

The entire team stared at each other—first in confusion, then in awe, then in elation. They cheered, "Let's go!"

The bus returned to the ramshackle house at the end of the lane, and the man and two boys raced out, as if they were expecting them.

LeAnn Thieman
Dedicated to Mom, Berniece Duello

Casey

This salvation, which was first announced by the Lord, was confirmed to us by those who heard Him. God also testified to it by signs, wonders and various miracles, and gifts of the Holy Spirit distributed according to His will.

Hebrews 2:3–4

His older brother, Justin, was just getting over chicken pox on Casey's second birthday. Poor Justin missed the party while he was quarantined from the other kids. Casey loved his brother and took each gift he opened upstairs to let Justin play with it. After cutting the cake, Casey took the first piece up to his brother. In fact, he spent most of his birthday going up and down the stairs to Justin's room.

Casey had the cutest lisp when he talked, and he stuttered when he was excited. His blond hair lay in wisps across his forehead, and his smile could warm the coldest heart. He was so innocent. No one could have predicted what was about to happen to this precious child.

One week following his birthday, Casey was plastered

with nasty red spots, and then he spiked a fever. He was flat in bed, unable to keep any food or fluids down, becoming more and more dehydrated every minute. It was a Sunday night and I couldn't break his 105-degree fever. I rushed him to the emergency room.

The doctor told me Casey was just going through a normal reaction to chicken pox and sent us home, against my better judgment. The next day, Casey was almost lifeless, and he was admitted to the hospital with severe dehydration and an internal infection from his chicken pox.

I sat by my mother, tears flowing down my face, as she lifted my son and all his tubes into my arms. I felt weak and numb all over. Casey briefly opened his eyes, looked into mine and drifted off again. The doctor told us that Casey's chicken pox had caused a poison in his bloodstream and they were unsure what to do, except continue intravenous (IV) fluids and antibiotics, and try to keep his fever under control. The nurses rolled a bed into his room to enable me to stay with him. I was awake all night holding my precious boy.

In the morning the doctor came in to check Casey again. Four nurses followed and hooked up more wires to my son. Casey was unresponsive, though everyone tried waking him. I kept looking at the heart monitor which would speed up and slow down, then speed up again.

The doctor started making more frequent visits and the nurses were in constantly. Later that evening, the doctor told me Casey was slipping into a coma. I couldn't believe what I was hearing. For the next four days, I never left Casey's side. I didn't even go home to shower and change my clothes. There was just no improvement. Family members drifted in and out. My mother was there most frequently.

Every moment of every day I prayed for my son's life and health. The doctors were baffled. No one had ever heard of chicken pox making anyone this desperately ill. I noticed on Friday that the heart monitor kept elevating and not decreasing at all. The doctor was called in immediately.

I leaned against the wall in the hallway, emotionally exhausted, as the doctor put his hand on my shoulder. "Lisa," he stated, "Casey's on the verge of heart failure and there's nothing more we can do." I felt my whole body go numb. His voice grew farther away and echoed. "Is there any family you would like to call that's not already here?"

The only person I called was my pastor. Then for the next forty-five minutes, I sat in a daze, rocking my son and staring into his blank, pale, yet peaceful face.

Pastor George walked into the room. His face was sober, but reassuring. My mother took Casey from me so I could get up and greet George. He reached out and put his arms around me as I quietly trembled and sobbed. George then went to Casey, kneeled down and kissed his forehead. All of our family gathered in a circle with Casey still in my mother's arms. We joined hands and George prayed for Casey's recovery. We continued to pray fervently, and then sat as George comforted us.

Twenty minutes later, Casey sneezed. His heart monitor went nuts, and then he opened his eyes for the first time in four days. He smiled and reached up to touch his grandmother's tear-streamed face. My mother nearly screamed with joy. "Hello, my sweet boy!"

Casey looked at me. "Mama." He reached his arms out for me.

"Hi, my baby boy!" I whispered between sobs of joy and relief. "You were sleeping for a long time."

Casey sat up and said, "I'm hungry." His voice was raspy from not speaking for so long. He looked around his room and spotted my half-eaten hoagie. "I want that," he pointed.

The doctor stood in the doorway and exclaimed, "Give him whatever he wants. Hey, big guy!" The doctor just shook his head and smiled. "I don't believe this," he said. He stepped over to Casey and listened to his heart. "Perfect! I have never seen anything like this in my entire medical career. His heart rate is perfect. "

It seemed the entire hospital staff was talking about the miracle which happened before their eyes. Nurses kept coming into Casey's room to say hello and kiss him on the cheek.

Two days later, I brought Casey home. Justin was thrilled to see his brother and nearly knocked him down as he came through the door.

Casey has his tenth birthday coming up. He gets straight A's in school, and he and Justin are still extremely close. So if anyone ever doubts that God performs miracles, you tell them to see me.

Kati Dori

"Take two tablets and call you when?"

Reprinted by permission of Chris S. Patterson.

Reconsider the Lilies

Flowers are God's thoughts of beauty taking form to gladden mortal gaze.

William Wilberforce

It was Good Friday, 1957. The woman in the tiny roadside shop assured me the plant I was having airlifted home would arrive, alive and well, the following day. "We have shipped to the States for many years," she said, in that grand British accent that still startled me when I heard it. Around us, the island of Bermuda, famous for its beaches of gleaming white sand and fields of even whiter lilies, rose out of the Atlantic and reached for the sun.

From the field beyond the open-air shop poured a heavenly scent, evoking memories of Easter Saturdays when my father came home from work with a lily plant for my mother.

I filled out the forms needed for overseas shipment, carefully copying the address of the hospital where my dad lay gravely ill and my mother sat by his bedside. Was she remembering, as I was, organdy dresses, knife-pressed pants, her many pre-Easter hours sewing and ironing, and

Dad's gift, centered on the dining room table? Or was she, on this Good Friday, the darkest day of the church year, trying not to dwell on inevitable comparisons?

I wished I could deliver the plant in person and take my mother's place at my dad's bedside, giving her a rest. But a second lieutenant's pay didn't allow for a second trip home this year.

"May I see the plant?" I asked, in spite of the saleswoman's assurance.

"For shipping we harvest plants early and send them to storage," the lady said, "so the blooms will be fresh when the plants are delivered." Her words gave me hope, the very thing I knew the plant would give my mother.

"Consider the lilies," my mother would say each time she inhaled its perfume. She had often quoted that Bible verse to her children, conveniently skipping over the part that they toil not, neither do they spin, lest we interpret it wrong!

"It must arrive on Saturday," I reminded the clerk yet again. She promised that it would, with glorious blossoms.

When I talked with my mother by telephone the next night, she told me my dad had taken a turn for the worse. "His fever went up during the night, and he's still in a lot of pain. He's under heavy medication," she said.

And the plant? Sensing Mother's hesitation, I wormed the truth out of her; she was too weary to put up a front. The plant was dry. It had no scent. Tight buds were brown. "It looks like it didn't survive the trip," my mother said, "but thank you for sending it, dear. That's what matters to your dad and me. You know that."

I did, but I also knew the dread a dead plant must have laid upon her spirit. My mother was a poet. The metaphor would not escape her.

I hung up and reminded myself that God had not promised to grant every wish, only to know every need.

When I called again on Easter Sunday, the lilt in her voice told me before her words did that my father was better, out of danger. Only after telling me that, did she tell me about the lily. She'd considered throwing it out the night before, so that if my dad woke he wouldn't have to see it. But she reconsidered and left it on the windowsill, out of his sight.

When she walked into the hospital room on Easter morning, the first thing she saw was my dad, sitting up, a thin smile spreading his parched lips, and a nurse coaxing a bit of breakfast into him.

"Do you smell that, Mother?" Dad asked her weakly. He didn't mean the breakfast.

A glorious redolence filled the room. On the tray table that straddled my dad's bed, the plant from Bermuda bore five gigantic, fragrant, white lily blossoms.

Consider the lilies. Indeed.

Lee Kochenderfer

"Wow! Look at Jeffy's plant grow.
He is a very good mother."

Reprinted by permission of Bil Keane.

The Birthday Gift

But when all goes well with you, remember me and show me kindness . . .

Genesis 40:14

I was in Churchill, a Lilliputian town on the shores of Hudson's Bay in northern Manitoba. I was a clinical instructor teaching a nurse's aide course to Inuit teenagers. A blizzard raged that Saturday morning in 1969. Wind whistled through the electrical sockets of my room, creating an eerie whine.

Boy, am I glad I don't have to go out today, I said to myself as I scraped the frost from the window. Through a microscopic opening, I could see the snow swirling high in the air in this treeless ice desert. I shivered. I'd set the thermostat up as high as I could to keep toasty warm and just hibernate for the day.

But a strange thing happened. A crazy idea muscled into my mind. *Go to the post office to pick up your mail.* I brushed it aside. No way was I going out today. But the thought persisted. The post office wasn't far—maybe about the length of five city blocks—but it seemed a daunting trip. You couldn't see your hand in front of your face. With the wind chill factor, it was an insane seventy-below-zero: no place for humans, only polar bears, Beluga whales, seals and walruses. People froze to death within fifty feet of their destinations in this type of "white out."

I looked out again. The thought pressed in on me. *Go to the post office.* I sighed, donned knee high mukluks, my red parka with the wolf fur, and my big goose down mittens. I opened the door. The intense cold drove me back. Skin could freeze in one minute in this. I bundled the hood more closely to my face, took a deep breath and slipped outside. I bent forward, almost in half, to knife through the wind pressing against me. My breath hung like a lacy curtain in the frigid air. The fur froze, and little icicles formed on my nose before the drip could fall. After walking for twenty-minutes, I fell into the post office.

"Hey, Arlene, what are you doing out in this weather?" the postmaster smiled. Everyone knows everyone else in these small hamlets. "I think I have something here for you. Let me see." He rummaged around and found a parcel.

Surprised, I grasped it tightly. "Well, hope I make it back!" I laughed as I opened the door to the bitter cold.

When I finally crashed into my room, stamped my feet and blew on my hands, I sat down to look at this mysterious parcel. The box, wrapped in plain brown paper, arrived almost intact—lots of string and a few torn corners. But after a journey of 5,000 miles by railway from Montreal through the vast, empty, icy northern Canadian wilderness, I supposed a few torn corners could be forgiven. The return address was smudged.

Who's sending me a parcel? I wondered, opening it with tremulous hands. White tissue paper crackled open to reveal a beautiful forest green cardigan, my favorite color. A perfect fit, too! I read the note inside from dear, elderly

Marjorie in Montreal, someone I considered a second mother.

> *Dear Arlene, I don't know why I'm sending you this. I just had an urge to send you something, and I found this sweater. Hope you like it.*

I suddenly broke down and wept uncontrollably. A silent inner thought reminded me, *Today is your birthday.*

Even I had forgotten again. It never mattered as a child. I was raised as a sad little girl in a northern Quebec town with all the usual things to keep body intact but never the love and intimacy to warm the soul. Ours was a cold, "earn your living," hard-times kind of upbringing. Lots of rules and no warmth. Lots of criticism but no praise. No hugs. No kisses. And certainly no birthday parties. My birthday arrived and went without affirmation of any kind. It was just another day, so I always forgot my birthday, too. And I never ever told anyone when it was—not even Marge. It was less painful to forget it than to have any expectations.

Suddenly my weeping stopped and the presence of God filled the room. I was overwhelmed that He would remember my birthday when it was such a little thing in the grand scheme of worldly problems.

I suppose if that had been the end of these marvelous coincidences I would have forgotten about it, but a few years later another amazing birthday surprise awaited me in another Northern town in British Columbia. One day, working as a community nurse on the Alaskan Highway, I returned to the office to find a lovely plant, a lavender violet, on my desk. The card read, "To Arlene, because you care so much." It was signed "Mary." I thought about all the Marys I visited as a nurse, but not one would be the kind to send me this. *Who would send this and why?* I wondered. A quiet inner thought reminded me, *Today is your birthday.* I remembered. I wept. I called the flower shop to see if they could enlighten me.

"No, she paid cash so I don't have any check. Sorry," the clerk said.

I asked every Mary I knew if she was the one who sent it. All denied it.

One day, in my church, I asked a Mary whom I didn't think cared for me.

"Yeah. I was downtown that day and couldn't leave until I sent that to you. I don't know why," she answered impatiently.

I told her why. She wept, too.

A year later, I visited a friend in that town and she gave me a lovely crystal candleholder. "Why are you giving me this, Cheryl?" I asked.

"I just had the urge to buy this for you yesterday and didn't see you until today. Hope you like it," she answered shyly.

Again a still small thought said to me, *Yesterday was your birthday.*

He never forgets.

Arlene Centerwall

Do You Believe in God?

Jesus said to the woman, "Your faith has saved you; go in peace."

Luke 7:50

"Mom, I need pictures!" Marie exclaimed. "The bus is going to be here in fifteen minutes, and Mr. Martinez says I need at least ten."

Mr. Martinez says. Well, we surely can't disappoint him.

"Here, look through these," I shoved a box at my youngest daughter and raced off to help find the shoe my older son had "lost."

When I returned my attention to Marie's picture problem, I noticed tears on her cheek. "We'll get enough pictures, honey," I assured her. "Don't worry. If you miss the bus, your dad can drop you off on the way to work."

"It's not that, Mom; it's this." She flipped around the picture she had been staring at. For the first time in a long time, I saw flecks of fear in her ice blue eyes.

Fear doesn't cloud Marie's thoughts very often. She is my adventurous one. "Anything they can do, I can do better," is her motto. She can jump farther, climb higher.

She can fly! She is invincible. Just ask her.

As Marie looked at that picture I knew she remembered the horrible day fear wracked her mind and body. That day, Marie realized she could die.

I sat and soothed my nine-year-old daughter, drawing her trembling body into the lap she had clearly outgrown. I looked at the scene that invoked her tears: a crumpled red station wagon resting atop a flatbed tow truck.

"Mom, how come we didn't get hurt?" she asked, awe thick in her voice. "I don't understand how the windows on my side broke, the roof smashed in and we didn't even get hurt."

Marie wasn't the only one with that question. Everyone had voiced it that day.

It was a typical Wednesday. I was on my way home from a meeting at church with my daughter and three-year-old nephew. I had decided to try a new shortcut and turned off on a dirt road flanked by neat rows of corn. The curve ahead surprised me, as did the sight of the deep canal. Suddenly we hit a patch of gravel and the tires loosened their grip on the road. I had no control.

"Oh God, help us," I prayed out loud, as our car hurled down the ravine, ricocheted off the steep embankment, bounced forcefully in the water and then came to rest. *The children! Oh God, please let the children be all right.* Just then they began to cry. *Thank you.*

I looked back. Both kids appeared to be okay. "Are you two hurt?" They both shook their heads, no.

"My hice, my hice," my little nephew cried.

"What?"

"He spilled his ice," Marie translated for me.

If that's all he's worried about, he can't be injured too badly.

I took stock of the situation. The car was perched on a small shelf of land jutting out into the water. We couldn't stay there. We were hidden from the road above. Even if a car happened along, they wouldn't be able to spot us. And if the water rose just a little bit, we would be in trouble.

"Come on kids, let's get out of here." The driver's side of the car opened into the water, so after I struggled to release the seat belt and car-seat buckles, I herded both children out the passenger door. I gave them the once over. Shards of safety glass tangled their hair and glinted in the sun. But no scratches, no bruises, no broken bones. No sign of injury at all. *Now what?*

I looked at the steep sides of the canal. *Could I climb out?* I doubted it. The muddy walls loomed at least eight feet high. *And how would I get my little nephew out?*

Then I thought about Marie. She could climb anything. I knew it would be a risk but I had no choice.

"Marie, do you think you could climb to the top?"

"Watch!" she dared. Without hesitation she scrambled up the muddy wall, finding footholds on rocks, bits of broken concrete, tufts of grass and roots that jutted out. Triumphantly she heaved herself over the top, turned and stared down at us.

"Climb, Keenan, climb." I cheered my little nephew on. As he grabbed at plants growing on the dirt wall, I shoved his padded bottom upward. "Marie, lie down and grab Keenan's hands. Good. Pull!" I coached. She yanked him up over the side. "Now sit down and hang on to him tightly."

Taking my cues from Marie's assent, I assaulted the slick wall. After losing my footing once, then twice, I finally joined the kids.

I looked down at the car sitting on the only flat surface at the bottom of the ravine. Every other area was covered with huge chunks of concrete. I marveled that we had escaped unharmed, and thanked God again.

We hiked to the nearest house. We knocked. No answer. We went on to the next. As we approached, the door flung open. I told the woman what had happened.

"Oh, sweetie, do come in," she said without hesitation. Before handing me the phone she said, "Can I ask you a personal question?"

"Yes," I said tentatively.

"Do you believe in God? I mean, do you know how many people have died at that same spot? Just six months ago, two teenagers drowned right there. It's just a miracle you all aren't hurt."

Later, the highway patrolman said, "I don't need to ask if those kids were strapped in, Ma'am." Then he added, "They'd be dead for sure if they weren't. It's a wonder you all weren't hurt. Do you believe in God?"

"Do you believe in God, lady?" the tow truck driver echoed as he ruefully considered how to hoist the car out of the canal.

The repairman at the station circled the car assessing the damage. "It's totaled, no doubt about it. You say no one was hurt?" I nodded and he continued. "It's a wonder. I don't know about you, but I believe God had a hand in keeping you and those little ones safe. Do you believe in God?"

"Why Mama, why?" Marie's question brought me back to the present and the gruesome picture. "Why weren't we hurt? Not one little bit?"

"I don't know, dear," I answered honestly. "But I do know that the God we believe in watches out for us."

She smiled. "I need more pictures, Mom. Mr. Martinez says . . ."

Lynn Dean

THE FAMILY CIRCUS® **By Bil Keane**

"I perform miracles, too. Every morning Daddy says, 'If you make the school bus, it'll be a miracle'."

Our Little Pink Blanket

I tell you the truth; unless you change and become like little children, you will never enter the kingdom of heaven. Therefore, whoever humbles himself like this child is the greatest in the kingdom of heaven.

Matthew 18:3–4

I was having a normal conversation with my four-year-old daughter about various things when suddenly she announced, "I saw Jesus, Mommy!"

"Oh you did? Where did you see him, Lauren?" I asked, expecting to hear church or Sunday school as her answer.

"In heaven, when I was sick," she stated matter-of-factly.

My mind drifted back to days I usually try to forget . . .

Lauren, our second daughter, was determined to be born early. My husband Keith and I were expecting twins, and I had miscarried one twin at six weeks. I was then put on bed rest for six weeks to keep Lauren in tow until her May 19th due date. On February 7, 1989, the excitement started—premature labor. We went to the emergency room at the local hospital where the doctor transferred me to a larger hospital with a neonatal unit. As I was being transferred out I overheard him say, "The baby will probably be born dead."

We arrived at the new hospital expecting bad news and were thrilled to hear our chances were fifty-fifty. I was twenty-five weeks along in the pregnancy, and I was hoping to hold out until week thirty-four. I did not like the idea of being confined to bed one hundred miles from home, with a two-and-a-half-year-old daughter and a husband waiting for me there. But I knew I had to do everything possible to increase our baby's chances.

Eight days had come and gone with no problems when my husband called to check on us and tell me he was coming for an unplanned visit.

Round two then began. Lauren's heart rate flattened out and the pain began. They wheeled me to surgery for an emergency C-section, and Lauren was born at twenty-seven weeks old, just as Keith arrived. She was so tiny—two pounds, twelve ounces and only sixteen inches long. Her frail body was strapped down, tubes dangling out of her everywhere. We only saw her seconds before she was whisked away. The doctors told us she was very big for her age, but a very sick little girl. She had hemorrhaging in her head and her lungs were not developed.

At about 4 A.M., I received a call from a doctor stating they had to insert two chest tubes into Lauren. It seems her lungs were leaking, endangering her heart. "She is a very sick little girl," the doctor stated once again. Still, somehow I knew she'd be all right.

I was dismissed from the hospital and told I had to go home and rest. It broke my heart to leave our daughter in the ICU. We visited twice a week and called at least two times a day. How I ached to hold and rock her. The doctors and nurses were wonderful, filling us in on every little detail. Lauren was a real fighter. She constantly pulled out her tubes and they had to put mittens on her hands. I remember thinking, *She's going to make it.* I just knew it.

After a few more setbacks, and a lot of prayers and love, we finally took Lauren home—one month earlier than the doctors had anticipated. As Keith held Lauren in his arms, I began packing. Among her many tiny Cabbage Patch preemie dresses was a small pink blanket.

"This pink blanket is not ours," I informed the nurse.

"Yes, I think it is," she answered.

"No, I would have remembered buying such a warm, fuzzy, tiny pink blanket," I insisted.

"No, you did not buy it," the nurse admitted, then slowly explained. "When a baby is not expected to make it, we wrap them in this blanket and let the parents hold them one last time."

Keith and I stared at each other and then Lauren. She was truly our miracle baby. We continued to pack her belongings and I cried most of the way home—it was all over now . . .

"Mommy, I said I saw Jesus in heaven when I was sick!" Lauren repeated.

"What did He say? What did He do?" I quizzed my four-year-old child.

"I went up to heaven when I was very sick in the hospital. Jesus walked towards me and held me," she answered as if it were yesterday. "He then told me I should go back. Jesus said 'You will be all right. Go back.' So I said bye and came back."

And so she did.

Sandy Deters

Hands

Hands speak themselves. By them we ask, promise, evoke, dismiss, threaten, treat, deprecate. By them we express fear, joy, grief, our doubt, assent, or penitence.

Quintilian

Twenty-four years ago, I attended my great-grandmother's funeral and was privileged to hear the eulogy of a pastor who knew her well. "Whenever I think of Lillian, I think of hands." I recalled her hands, twisted and swollen with arthritis for as long as I could remember. Yet she maneuvered her suffering hands to use knitting needles or a crochet hook. She kneaded dough for biscuits or pies. Never complaining, she made miracles with those hands. Rubbing my back, they would soothe wounds both physical and emotional. I witnessed her folding her hands both night and day in many prayers. I felt God's grace in the words this pastor spoke, and in time they brought me comfort. They helped to make me aware of the ways I could serve others with my own hands and use them as a reflection of my great-grandmother's love—an extension of the Lord's love.

Recently I faced a large pile of ironing with great trepidation. *Why had I let it sit for so long?* The Christmas season was upon us, and I had so many other things to do. The children needed outfits ironed for church, school concerts and holiday gatherings. Special holiday clothes had been unboxed and needed a year's worth of creases pressed out of them. Since music always soothes my soul, I put some on. As the joyful sounds of a choir singing "Joy to the World" rose above my own muttering, I felt the true meaning of Christmas open my heart and mind. I suddenly knew what I wanted to do. When I completed the tedious task at hand I would drive three and a half hours and visit my grandmother who lived in a nursing home. I always visited her prior to Christmas. We would spend part of the day together, and I'd bring her homemade goodies and Christmas presents.

My husband thought I was crazy to make this trip so impulsively, but my mind was made up. A close friend offered to make the journey with me. This appeased my husband's worries, and I knew it would make the long drive more pleasant.

We encountered a freak snowstorm halfway through our trip and nearly went off the highway. Slowing to a crawl, we arrived later than expected and checked into a small inn to spend the night.

The next morning I called my aunt to find out what time would be best to visit Gram.

"She's just been taken to the hospital," she told me. "It's her breathing again."

Gram had a long history of respiratory difficulties, so this was not out of the ordinary. Entering the tiny hospital room, I found my grandmother getting settled into bed. I helped my aunt move her into a comfortable position.

Her breathing was raspy and labored, but she was mentally alert. She winked at me, pointed to her cheek, and told me to "plant a kiss right here." I sat with her on the bed and held her hand.

Gram dozed off and on, never letting go of my hand. Her grip at times was stronger than I had recalled feeling it for many years. I stroked her face and head, smoothing her hair, and told her I would stay on the bed with her for awhile. She showed no signs of being anxious. She would awaken and smile, squeeze my hand and sleep for a few more minutes.

After this pattern had been repeated for an hour or so, I felt it best that we leave for home and let her get some good sleep. I kissed her forehead and told her I loved her.

In her wheezing breath she said, "I love you."

I met my aunt in the parking lot and transferred Christmas presents to her car. For my grandmother I had a beautiful snow globe depicting Jesus carrying someone. An excerpt from "Footprints in the Sand" was on the base. The snow globe played the "Lord's Prayer."

My aunt assured me my grandmother would love this gift. She would take them home and put them under her Christmas tree. I left feeling a little sad that Grandmother and I hadn't had the usual pre-Christmas fun, but pleased that our time spent together was quality time.

I arrived home at eight-thirty. My grandmother died about nine-thirty.

Suddenly the pieces fit together like that of a jigsaw puzzle, and I realized for the first time in my life that God's hands are upon all that we do. It was at His urging that I suddenly had the desire to make this trip. It was His will that I sat with her and noticed the strength in her frail little hands. She had said good-bye the only way she knew how.

At the funeral home I paid special attention to my

grandmother's hands. I remembered the years of hard work. I remembered her loving touch. As I touched them, I imagined the warm strong hands of the previous Sunday afternoon.

Before her casket was closed, my aunt wound the snow globe and placed it by my grandmother's side. The music to the "Lord's Prayer" seemed fitting, as we all recalled my grandmother kneeling beside her bed, her hands folded in prayer.

My grandmother's six children carried her casket. Her hands had carried them throughout their lives. And theirs provided her with the first leg of her journey home.

Kimberly Ripley

Coincidence on a Country Road

A coincidence is God's way of remaining anonymous.

Source Unknown

My mom was scheduled for serious brain surgery. I was so worried. She had already had one emergency surgery for a bleeding aneurysm. She almost died, and she was in the hospital for a long time with months of rehabilitation. Not only did she survive, but she was one of a small percentage of lucky patients who recovered completely.

This time, though, her aneurysm had doubled in size and so had the seriousness of her operation. The risks involved everything from needing mild rehabilitation, to brain damage, to death.

During this tense time, I took long daily hikes with my dog, my personal prescription for stress reduction. One day, on a deserted country road, an unmarked van pulled over and a man got out waving a sheet of paper. He seemed harmless, but my cautious heart was at its target rate.

"Do you know where Rock Hedge Road in Crystal Lake is?" he asked. We were nowhere near Crystal Lake, so I did not feel reassured. Then he gave me the name and address he was looking for. "It's an old delivery route that I used to drive. I'll know it if I get closer," he paused, "but I had brain surgery for an aneurysm in December," he explained. "I am doing great now, but sometimes, I have a little memory problem." He looked at me and smiled. "I'm really fine now, except for that. I'm just fine!"

Then I saw the pattern of a shaved head from a craniotomy and the gray stubble of new hair growth. I had seen that before on my mother. I recognized the familiar subtle swelling of scar tissue I would be seeing again.

"Here," I said. "Give me that paper and a pen." I eagerly drew him a map of where he wanted to go.

"What's your dog's name?" he asked.

"Bessie," I said.

"I walk two miles every day now, but I don't have a dog," he said, still smiling.

I really looked at him now, full in the face, and noticed his gentle brown eyes. They seemed to gleam with a secret message.

"You should get a dog," I smiled. "They're great walking companions."

"I might do that." He grinned and thanked me for my help. I wished him luck and he drove off.

I took several steps before realizing what had just happened on that empty country road. I burst into tears. That man must have been an angel. My mom? Her surgery was a textbook, "best-case" scenario, and they sent her home in only five days. This time, God did not remain anonymous!

Oh, and if that angel ever reads this, I have a message for him. Mom started walking every day, too, and her dog is named Casey.

Diana Mason Bruhn

A Daily Dose of Miracles

There are only two ways to live your life. One is as though nothing is a miracle. The other is as if everything is.

Albert Einstein

Having already experienced the death of my middle son to a rare congenital heart defect, I was devastated to learn that my beautiful, newborn baby boy not only had Down's syndrome but congenital heart disease as well.

"It's not the same thing that Travis had," my doctor assured me. "It's a hole between the chambers—probably a small one, which may even close on its own."

But at fifteen months old, the hole in Jay's heart had not closed and it was decided that open-heart surgery was the best course of action. A heart catheterization ("cath" for short)—a minor surgical procedure—would be done beforehand to note the extent of the problem and make sure the surgeon met no surprises.

On the morning of the cath, I held Jay's sleepy, sedated body in my arms as long as possible, then walked beside him as they wheeled him down the hall on a giant-size gurney into the cath room.

An hour or so later my husband and I were ushered in where Jay lay on the table, still sedated and nearly as white as the sheets that surrounded him. A nipple stuffed with cotton was taped to his mouth where a nurse had dripped sugar-water to pacify him. It was frightening to see him so still and pale. I wanted to pick him up and run home, but the doctor claimed my attention.

"I called you in here because I want you to see what we found. It's not good." The doctor explained that Jay had already developed pulmonary hypertension, a condition that made open-heart surgery so risky that the physician advised against it. "I don't believe he would ever come off the heart-lung machine," he said, apologizing for such devastating news. He had never known of a child so young to develop pulmonary hypertension. Without the surgery, Jay's life expectancy would probably be short. Barring any major respiratory infections, such as pneumonia, he might live into early adolescence.

I was in total shock. Was this a choice? Were they asking us if we wanted Jay to die now or die later? I was so tired, confused and frightened that I couldn't even cry.

We followed the gurney to Jay's room where we waited the next eight hours while he was monitored on a regular basis. I picked him up and rocked him, just wanting to hold him and protect him. I looked into his sweet, sleeping face, still pale and lifeless, and knew I could never send him into surgery where the odds were greater that he would die than survive. We would take what years we had with him, even if they were only a few, but my prayer was that God would perform a miracle in Jay's life and heal his heart disease. The Down's syndrome was no big deal to us. But I had learned from experience that heart disease is deadly.

In his first years of his life, Jay astounded all of us,

especially the medical profession, with his energy and vivacious personality—even though the heart disease progressed. Upper respiratory infections were rampant during the winter, and he had several bouts with pneumonia. Still, he survived. But he didn't just survive. Jay celebrated life! He would sing and dance to music, chase the waves at the beach, play T-ball with friends and aggravate his brother and sister.

By his teen years, Jay's skin began taking on a slightly dusky appearance, and he tired more easily. Doctors warned us of impending strokes or a fatal cardiac arrhythmia, but I continued to pray for a miracle. I wanted to walk into that cardiologist's office one day and hear him say, "Why, Mrs. Jones, we have no idea what has happened, but Jay's tests show that there is absolutely no heart disease present." That's what I prayed for—a real live miracle. But it didn't happen.

Soon Jay began to sleep with oxygen at night. But he still danced to his music during the daytime, dazzled friends at church every Sunday with his suit and tie, and often went bowling or rented favorite videos. He was a joy to be around, smiling and laughing, hugging and loving everyone he met.

We began schooling Jay at home to cut down on upper respiratory infections after an extremely serious episode with pneumonia and a week of recovery in the hospital. But we still gave him social interaction with other people, just making sure he wasn't around anyone who was sick. It became a way of life, but still I prayed for a miracle, and Jay continued to dance to his music and go out for his daily Coke at Sonic.

When Jay turned twenty we had a grand celebration, calling it his "Miracle Birthday." I visited his longtime cardiologist and said, "Tell me the truth. You never expected to ever see this day, did you?" He conceded that he did not. Perhaps none of us really thought we would. No one except Jay.

Jay never worries about tomorrow. He lives every day in the present, squeezing all of the life he can from it, then spreading it like sunshine to everyone around him. I feel blessed just being his mother. And somewhere along the way, in his now twenty-five years, I found that I had stopped praying for a miracle and began thanking God for the one I had. Though it wasn't the one big miracle that I had hoped for, I finally realized that we still got a miracle anyway. We just got it in daily doses.

Louise Tucker Jones

Santa Claus

My command is this: Love each other as I have loved you.

John 15:12

This was our first Colorado winter and we were excited about our first Christmas in our new home. We had just moved from the desert and my daughters, who were six and nine, had only seen a real winter once before in their lives. They were so little then, they didn't even remember it.

It was Christmas Eve. The girls and I were out and about, running holiday errands. We delivered treats to some of our friends and made a last minute trip to Kmart. My youngest daughter, Megan, was distracted by a simple jewelry box. You've probably seen them—the little square box with a dancer inside that twirls around when you open the box while sweet ballerina music plays. Megan and her big sister, Elizabeth, were enchanted. They each wanted to take one home. I just smiled and said, "Not tonight. Tomorrow is Christmas; let's see what Santa Claus will bring."

I, like thousands of other parents over the years, had

given my children the gift of believing in Santa Claus. I'd spent hours of their young lives telling them the stories, wrapping "Santa's gifts" in different colored paper and leaving milk and cookies. Among my favorite childhood memories that I share with them were those annual movies, *Rudolph the Red-Nosed Reindeer* and *Santa Claus Is Coming to Town.* I still love them!

I would really have liked to have sneaked those gifts into the shopping cart that Christmas Eve. The jewelry boxes weren't very expensive, but with our move to a new home that year, we were on a budget, and Christmas spending was done. Though I yearned for the day when we could afford such simple gifts, I was thankful to God for how far we had come. You see, there were Christmases past that the girls and I relied on the kindness of others. When Megan was born, we were living on public assistance, in an old trailer in a very small town on the prairies of the Midwest. We had struggled to make our lives better since then, and in answer to my prayers, my husband, Randy, came into our lives when the girls were four and seven years old. Yes, though times were frugal, life had become so much richer for us. There was a great deal to be thankful for.

We left the store that night without the jewelry boxes. Our errands were just about done. One last stop for gas on the way home, and then it would be time to tuck the girls in for the night, while Randy and I played Santa Claus. It was dark at the gas station at about eight-thirty. As I got out of the car to begin fueling, I was careful to be aware of my surroundings. You can imagine how nervous I was as a beat-up old truck pulled into the gas station right up next to my car and a gruff-looking man rolled down his window and beckoned me over. With a glance at the girls to make sure they were snug in the car with windows rolled up, I cautiously approached the truck.

The man looked like he had been working hard in filthy conditions all day and had not had a chance to bathe. I expected a question about where to find a hot meal or a warm bed and was prepared to direct him to our church or the police station. Imagine my surprise as the man held up two jewelry boxes almost exactly like the ones we had seen at the store!

"Ma'am, I won these two jewelry boxes at the movie theater," he said, "and I noticed you had two little girls. I don't have anyone to give them to and was wondering if your girls might like them."

I was speechless as I stood there, face-to-face with Santa Claus. Somehow I stuttered my way through thanks and gratitude, and assured him that the girls would be delighted to have the gifts he offered. I watched as he disappeared into the night—Santa Claus in an old, beat-up truck.

It has been four years since that night, and it still brings a tear to my eye as I tell the story. Who was that man? I don't know. I've never seen him again, but I do believe that God used him that night to answer my simple prayer. He opened my eyes to the true Santa Claus—the love of Christ shining through us to all the world.

Kimberly Henrie

9

INSIGHTS AND LESSONS

The end of learning is to know God, and out of that knowledge to love Him, and to imitate Him, as we may the nearest, by possessing our souls of true virtue.

John Milton

Caution: Follow Directions

I don't know about you, but I have a hard time reading directions. I'm embarrassed to talk about how many cars I have driven out of oil, or the sewing machine that locked up because I never oiled it, or the appliances I've burned up, or the clothing I've shrunk—simply because I failed to read the instructions. I seem to slip into a kind of mental sleepwalking when I try to read the directions for the VCR, CD player, cellular phone, pager or fax machine. God's good humor is solely responsible for me even turning on a computer.

One Christmas our son gave us a "New Age" clock radio. I describe "New Age" as anything that is new to me at my age! This radio has an extra feature. It's a menu from which you can select an assortment of relaxing sounds that are meant to serenade you into a deep, tranquil slumber. You can choose the sound of ocean waves, gently falling rain, a heartbeat, whales communicating, a gentle running stream, or a bird quietly singing. It was all I could do to keep from bursting into laughter as my son explained how to use the remote control to select these sounds and, better yet, combine them. I envisioned myself walking to the bathroom all night while listening to water running to the beat of a heart.

But the thing that made me giggle the most was that my son actually believed we could ever figure out how to actually use the remote control, or find it in the middle of a dark night!

Yes, following instructions is something I struggle with. I will do just about anything to get out of it. In fact, I'm reminded of the time my husband, Orvey (yes, that is his real name), and I decided to paint our house instead of hiring a painter. We couldn't wait to spend all the hundreds of dollars we were going to save by doing it ourselves. After all, we were young, industrious and energetic. Why hire a professional?

Orvey commuted every day into Los Angeles, which left him no time to pick out or pick up paint. That job was left to me. On the morning I was going to pick up the paint, Orvey had an idea. "Judy, why don't you rent a compressor? It will save us a lot of time and energy," he chirped.

Being the godly submissive woman I am (I just heard thunder), I dutifully trudged down to the paint store and picked out the paint. I also reserved a compressor to be picked up the following weekend. The owner of the store then introduced me to a man who would share his expertise on operating the paint compressor. But there was a slight problem. The man was drunk. I felt myself nodding off as he slurred his words and tried to flirt with me at the same time. I thought, *Get me out of here. We'll figure it out ourselves, for heaven's sake. If this guy can paint while he's drunk, surely my sober husband can manage this dumb thing.*

The next weekend, my husband completed his preparations for painting our house, while I picked up the compressor. He power-washed the siding, taped all the windows and covered the bushes with tarps.

I gave him a few directions on how to operate the compressor, and Orvey declared "Let the painting begin! I'll be done in no time." Little did he know!

Soon he was filling the large bucket with paint, ready to engage the compressor.

"Here she goes!" he bellowed.

He pulled the trigger on the nozzle, and the force from the compressor nearly knocked him off his precious little feet. Paint flew everywhere! It blew the plastic off the windows, the tarps off the shrubs and the newspapers off the cement. Within minutes, our home, yard and birds flying by were sprayed white!

Orvey hunkered down, tightened his grip on the nozzle and went forth like a soldier in battle. Paint blasted out a mile a minute. Everything in sight was turning white, and it looked like a blizzard had hit California. Our terrazzo front porch was covered in paint, as were the sidewalks, trees, shrubs and mailbox.

By now, both our moods had deteriorated to an ugly state. Our children quietly packed their belongings and moved in with the neighbors. I know I should have kept my mouth shut, but that's another lifetime.

"Honey, you are ruining our home!" I shrieked.

Orvey turned to me with a look that would have scared Hitler, pointed the nozzle at me (but didn't pull the trigger), and I ran into the house.

By evening the neighbors had bolted their doors, contacted Realtors and the street was silent. My husband was finished. He looked like someone out of a science fiction movie. Only the circles around his eyes, where his glasses had been, remained untouched by white paint.

When he returned the compressor, he told the store about his experience, and commented "I think this compressor must be broken. The paint shot out like a nuclear missile."

"Mister, why didn't you turn the pressure down with this knob here on the right?"

The blood drained from my husband's face. He didn't know about the knob. I never told him, because I hadn't listened to the man's directions.

We've had many laughs over that paint day through the years. It was harmless enough. All it cost us was a few gallons of paint and some marriage counseling.

I wish it were just as harmless and laughable to ignore the counsel of God's word and how important it is for my life. Oftentimes, when I read the Bible, I slip into my spiritual sleep mode and ignore God's directions. The consequences are not as harmless as a broken VCR.

Out of His marvelous grace and mercy, God forgives me when I stray. It has taken me years to understand how lifechanging His love and wisdom are.

And it sure beats listening to whales talk in the middle of the night.

Judy Hampton

Helen

Without kindness there can be no true joy.

Thomas Carlyle

What was that foul smell? We all turned toward the rank odor that wafted from the back of our small Bible study room. But we were not prepared for the sight of the woman looking back at us from the doorway. Filthy clumps of hair matted her head. Her badly wrinkled clothes were darkened with overlapping layers of crusted food stains. Each shuffling step she took toward us released the nauseating stench of someone who had not bathed in weeks.

We stared as she made her way to the last empty seat—right beside me. I edged away, overcome by her reeking odor. Finally, she settled herself and looked toward the front of the room where our teacher, Bea, patiently waited.

"Hello, Helen," Bea said, smiling gently. Helen returned a smile just wide enough to show residue-caked teeth. "It's good to have you here," Bea added softly.

It is? I protested silently. I wondered how Bea could know a woman who was so obviously disturbed, but worried more about how I would survive the lesson with her beside me.

For the next hour, my attention strayed from the lesson to fantasies of tackling Helen with a good scrub brush in a bathtub of hot bubbles. I closed my eyes and played her transformation through one complete soak and scrub cycle, then drained the tub and started again. I scrubbed her hair, brushed her teeth, doused her with scented powder and dressed her in clean clothes. It would be the ultimate makeover. Meanwhile, I tried not to breathe too deeply. As long as Helen sat perfectly still, her odor hung in her own space.

When the lesson ended, I rushed past Helen toward the church kitchen and the wonderful aroma of coffee. With a momentary twinge of guilt, I considered how we usually fussed over new visitors. Instead, Helen trailed slowly alone behind us, her head sagging on her chest. But, as she shuffled closer, I stifled my guilt and busied myself with the coffee.

I treasured these afterglow moments of personal attention with Bea as she talked us through our questions and problems. We all needed the love and mentoring she offered so generously. Today, however, I was annoyed. Helen was intruding, monopolizing Bea with her depressive monotone. The more patiently Bea listened to her endless story, the more Helen droned on with her negative complaints. There was nothing the rest of us could do but wait.

I turned back toward the coffee, only half-listening to Helen's monologue. But gradually, as her incredible account of heartache and pain unfolded, I forgot my resentment and began to feel a genuine stirring of compassion. Horrible circumstances had devastated her and left her severely depressed. As she struggled on with her story, I listened with new perspective and surprising tenderness to this lonely, hopeless woman.

Then, from nowhere, a quiet thought surfaced. *She needs a hug.* I froze. It was one thing to feel compassion—but hug her? Her filth and odor zoomed back into focus. I shifted uncomfortably, trying to imagine getting so close.

She needs a hug. There it was again. I considered a side hug—just a quick pressing squeeze across her shoulders. I could possibly manage that. Still, I hesitated.

Urgently, this time, the silent voice insisted, *She needs a hug.* But I didn't move.

Suddenly, while Helen was in midsentence, Bea crossed the space between them, stood squarely in front of her, and wrapped both arms tightly around her. For an instant, Helen seemed stunned, then collapsed onto Bea's shoulder with loud, racking sobs. Bea did not loosen her hug while Helen spewed tears and lonely pain from the deepest crevice of her soul.

After a long time, when her sobs had quieted, Helen stepped back, wiped her face with the napkin someone offered and blinked as though she just noticed we were there. I could think of nothing to say. Helen seemed strangely transformed. The heavy strain that had contorted her expression with misery had loosened its grip. Her deadened gaze had cleared just enough to reveal the dim silhouette of a different woman.

She panned our hushed little group, then looked gratefully to Bea. "Today, all I needed was a hug," she choked. "I knew if I came here, God would hug me."

Hot tears stung my eyes. God had whispered from beyond my comfort zone and invited me to join Him in one holy moment of transforming love. But I had passed up the opportunity. It was my loss, not Helen's.

While I hesitated, Bea stepped into the moment to lend God her arms.

Armené Humber

"I don't think people are all dressed up in heaven. 'Cause if they were, it wouldn't be heaven!"

Reprinted by permission of Goddard Sherman.

The Best Defense

. . . You are my fortress, my refuge in times of trouble.

Psalm 59:16

For the first time in eleven days, my husband searched the TV channels for a distraction from Ground Zero, the haunting graveyard of debris in New York. He settled on a football game featuring our hometown team, the Florida State Seminoles. I was glad to see the team back on the field, but I felt guilty for watching. Twenty-two boys chasing a pigskin seemed insignificant with our hearts buried in the ashes of the World Trade Center, our minds tangled in the wreckage at the Pentagon, and our souls poured out in a field in Pennsylvania.

Why watch at all? I wondered. The look of expectation on my husband's face gave the answer. We watched in hopes that the good guys, our guys, would win the game and things would get back to normal. At the kickoff, a flicker of hope in my own eyes—bloodshot from days of crying—reflected off the television screen.

Somehow, though, it wasn't the same. North Carolina's

cheers were deafening, but the Seminole fans seemed reluctant to commit to the game. I watched their uncharacteristic reserve and wondered if anything would ever be the same again. The thought of these same players battling to defend America's shores instead of Astroturf end zones, diminished the magnitude of the game, even for a devotee like me.

My husband was no exception. When Florida State's point deficit became insurmountable, he shrugged and headed to the kitchen for a snack. Our silent neighbors were further evidence that football had been dethroned. On our street, where the houses are inches apart, game day emotions are shared by everyone. Today, however, stillness replaced the cries of anguish that usually echoed through my walls by Tallahassee's fans. Their wells of pain had run dry days ago.

As another North Carolina offensive lineman crossed the goal line, I asked my husband, "What happened?"

"It was the defense," he said, between bites of his sandwich. "If your defense lets the other guys run up the score, you can't run your offense. By then you're desperate, and desperate people make mistakes."

The word "desperate" pulled me back to the hulking ruins lurking on the edge of my mind. The hijackers were desperate, and they had definitely made a mistake. They reminded us who and what we are—one nation, under God, indivisible. Their acts of cowardice transformed a land of self-seeking individuals into a melting pot of prayer.

While North Carolina celebrated their victory, I considered my own scorecard since the historic hijackings of September 11, 2001. Like Florida State's offense, I had dropped the ball. I had not returned to the daily grind like our determined opponents. Instead, I sat glued to the news, debilitated by grief, wading in a sea of unopened mail and unfinished manuscripts.

Now I felt inspired. North Carolina's victory was infectious. I decided I wanted to win again, too. It was time to get back to life and back to love.

Organizing bills and forcing thoughts onto my keyboard again would be the easy part of my resurrection. Jump-starting the stalled relationships with my family, however, proved more difficult. Unintentionally, I had turned inward in my sorrow instead of communing with my loved ones for strength.

I felt especially estranged from my children. On the day of the tragedy, I hugged each of them close. In the days that followed, however, I shooed away their crayons and unanswerable questions while my heart collapsed with the towers again and again. In my efforts to protect them, I denied them what they needed most—me. How long had it been since I brushed the hair back from their foreheads and planted an unexpected kiss? I couldn't remember.

I looked over at my husband, his brow creased from days of shock and concern. How long had it been since I whispered "I love you" to him in the middle of the night? Too long. It was time to get back into the game.

I'm back at work now as a wife, mother and writer. Most days, my mind still lingers on the victims and their families—and on those days I work the hardest. My children and I color flags and pray about our fears together. Only by living and loving can I truly be free again. Without realizing it, I'd given the terrorists what they sought more than anything—my freedom. By my inactivity, I relinquished my ability to honor my family, my country and my God.

I cannot be sure that such a vicious thing will never happen again, but I have decided to pass my life, once frozen with fear, back into the capable hands of my defender—Jesus Christ.

After all, He never fumbles.

Marilynn Griffith

It's Better to Give Than . . .

Give to them according to the work of their hands; render to them what they deserve.

Psalm 28:4

My parents were models of generosity. "It is more blessed to give than to receive," was the hallmark of their marriage. While growing up in their home, I watched them share their money, their time, their talent and their love with family, neighbors, friends. It seemed natural that I would do the same when I got married.

Years later, following a divorce, I met and married a man who had also been raised in a generous home. Everyone who came into his parents' house left with gifts of love, food and even spare cash when needed. We wanted that same spirit to permeate our marriage, so my husband suggested we establish a special checking/savings account and call it "God's Account." We deposited 10 percent of our income for church tithes, offerings and gifts to missionaries, family or friends in need. We donated from that account without fail—until my husband lost his job.

My freelancing opportunities also dwindled. We

prayed. We asked others to pray, feeling certain my husband would get back to work soon. Meanwhile, we drew on our savings account. We cashed in investments. We sold some property. Before long we were using the last bit of reserves we had—even money from "God's Account." I panicked. Then I became angry. Hadn't we followed the Lord's leading? Hadn't we obeyed and shared and given freely and joyfully? I felt cheated.

"Why this, Lord?" I asked. "What have we done wrong? We want to work and earn our way. And we want to give to others. Please provide jobs and income for us."

But the Lord didn't answer the way I had hoped.

One Sunday my husband, a deacon at church, found an envelope addressed to him in the deacons' mailbox there. It contained an encouraging passage from scripture, an anonymous note and enough cash to tide us over for a couple of weeks. About the time that cash ran out, people in our Bible study unexpectedly delivered gift checks.

The more people reached out to us, the more upset I became, and the more tension we felt in our marriage. I began to undermine my husband's confidence. I made it clear that I felt it was his job to get us out of this predicament—he was supposed to be the head of our family. He became depressed, and I became more demanding. We were at a breaking point. I thought about separating. Even thoughts of divorce crossed my mind. I blamed my husband for everything.

I began teaching part time, which helped keep us going a while longer, but I resented carrying the load. Soon our bills were greater than my income, so we began to slip again. Then one month, when our rent was due and our checking account empty, my husband appealed to the Deacons' Fund at our church.

The Deacons' Fund! That was the final blow. How humiliating. That was for people who couldn't make it.

People who didn't have skills. People who were poor. We had always given to the fund. I never expected to receive from it. People knew my needs. I didn't like it. Receiving didn't fit my self-image as a giver.

The following month we received a check from my parents who had not known the extent of our problems. On my husband's birthday, three gift checks appeared.

Then one afternoon just before Christmas, we received a money order for the exact amount we needed for our tree, holiday food and a few gifts. It was signed "Barnabas." In scripture, it was Barnabas who sold his property and gave the money to the apostles to do Christ's work.

That's when my hard shell crumbled. It was all coming clear at last. It was our season to receive, our time to be humbled before God, our turn to acknowledge our weakness and our neediness before our brothers and sisters and to one another. For an entire year God had kept us going, despite my clumsy attempts to interrupt the process. I apologized to my husband and to the Lord.

Shortly after Christmas, things began to turn around, almost as suddenly as they had fallen apart the year before. My freelance writing picked up, and my husband received several promising job leads. As I looked ahead with hope, I also looked back with thanksgiving for our season of receiving. I discovered that the lesson I had learned from my parents so long ago was just as true in the present as it had been in the past. It simply took hold in a new and deeper way.

It is more blessed to give than to receive. But giving has more than one dimension, as the Lord had shown us. The joy of giving also requires a humbled heart and a receptive spirit.

Karen O'Connor

Attitude Adjustment

My husband doesn't like that I travel. However, traveling has been a part of my life all my adult years. When I met him, I was teaching seminars all over the country. I think he should be used to it after seventeen years of marriage. Instead he likes it less and less.

On the plane on the way home, I often enjoy the relaxing escape of romance novels. As I read, I picture Chuck meeting me at the gate with roses in his hand. Or at least dropping what he is doing when I walk in the door to hug and kiss me and confirm how much he has missed me.

In reality, the plane lands, I deplane and walk alone through the terminal, get my baggage and go to my car. I wait in line to pay for parking and drive home. Because I like to get home from a trip as soon as possible, I frequently arrive late at night rather than the next day. Chuck is often asleep. I tiptoe in, drop my bags and undress in the dark. I crawl into bed beside him and he wiggles his foot against my leg to welcome me home. Hardly the romance novel scene I like to paint in my mind.

Recently, a scheduled trip had me flying home the day after the seminar, on our sixteenth anniversary. Now I really wanted that romance novel scene. The day before I was to arrive home, I arranged to have flowers sent to Chuck's office with a card that said "Happy Anniversary! Hurry home!" (I had the flowers delivered in the morning, in case he forgot what day it was.) I arrived home before he got off work, did the prep work for a lovely dinner and went into the bedroom. There I found something small and black hanging on our four-poster bed with an anniversary card. I relaxed in a bubble bath and put my present on. I lit candles in the bedroom and put two crystal flutes and something bubbly in a silver bucket next to the bed.

When it was time for Chuck to get home, I crawled up on the bed and read my romance novel. I waited. The dogs barked, and I heard his car door. I tucked the romance novel away and placed myself artfully across the bed. I could write a romance novel about the results of my efforts—the night left me breathless!

The next morning I thought it through. That was the reaction I'd like every time I came home. I knew it was my job to do the changing, not Chuck's. What could I change that would bring about the desired effect? First, I could change my schedule so I got home before he did, instead of after he was asleep. I could fix a special dinner and bring on the bubbly. I could put on one of the many "little somethings" he has given me over the years, and I could place myself across the bed as if in a lingerie catalog. Yes, I could do that.

My next trip I did. It worked again—even without the special day and the flowers. My next trip I tried it again. It worked again. I had created an attitude adjustment. While Chuck is still not crazy about my traveling, he loves my coming home.

Marita Littauer

My Menorah—The Little Tree of Life

I can remember, as a little girl, always searching for God. My childhood was lonely and filled with pain. I rarely had a place to find security and love. My mother was severely mentally ill and abusive, and my father barely hung on, trying to support our family and stay sane himself. I remember praying alone during my childhood, crying softly on my bed, hoping God, if He was real, would come to love and rescue me from my loneliness and fear.

At eighteen, I ran away from my unhappy family life, from my past and my Judaic heritage. When a friend invited me to a small church meeting, it was that night I first heard men and women worshipping God, and I felt a peace I had never known before. Soon after that experience I asked the Lord Jesus to come live in my heart. Though I was born and raised a Jew, I now had a new identity as a Christian. My conversion to Christianity greatly angered my father, who felt betrayed, and it deeply hurt my mother. In my parents' eyes I was disloyal to my heritage. I felt very confused about my roots as a Jew. Who and what was I? How could I reconcile my birth as a Jew and my new belief in Jesus? How could I explain my new spiritual beliefs and still cherish my rich ancient heritage?

At the age of twenty-one I married a quiet, loving, Episcopalian young man with a nondescript name to match. I hid behind that name and used it as a mask that would shield me for years.

One warm Sunday afternoon, my husband and I went for a drive looking for an interesting way to spend the day together without leaving Los Angeles. We decided to visit the Museum of Tolerance. I became so anxious and afraid that I almost asked my husband to turn the car around. He sensed my uneasiness and took my hand as we descended into a dark underground parking lot. I felt a sense of foreboding, of being captured in a dramatic life-changing experience.

In order to enter the museum, each of us in line had to step through an archway metal detector. As I passed through, the alarm system went off. My large silver earrings had triggered the detector. I felt shocked and humiliated as the crowd behind me stared. Then the security guard asked me to relinquish my purse for inspection. He emptied the contents onto a large table where everyone could see. He explained that spot inspections were done to prevent any violent acts or destruction of the Holocaust exhibition. In a strange way, I felt stripped and vulnerable.

To distract myself until the tour began, I went into the museum's gift shop. It was filled with many artistic and religious items from Israel. I spotted a table with an assortment of menorahs. Some were ceramic and painted with bright colors. Others were more traditional and made of metals. My eye was drawn to a little menorah that looked like a small silver tree. I picked it up and quietly held it, remembering a distant time in my childhood. Although raised in a nonreligious Jewish home, I was carried back to our celebration of Hanukkah and the small and simple menorah my mother filled with colorful candles.

My younger sister and I were allowed to light a new candle each night for eight nights. It was a rare and joyful time for our family.

Now I held the little silver menorah close to my chest and warm tears trickled down my cheeks. I decided to buy it—the first step in my repossession of my birth as a Jew. It was an amazing moment for me.

As we toured the museum, we came to a case filled with the personal belongings of an exterminated Jewish family from Poland: baby photos, an infant's shoes and a large china platter with the lovely little girl's photographed face in the center. I felt like an intruder sifting through the precious remains of an unknown family. Suddenly I realized that those Polish Jews were not strangers at all—we were connected by our mutual heritage. The little girl's face strongly resembled our own older daughter, Sasha. As I looked into the face of that innocent Jewish child, two opposing forces within me met for the first time in my life. It was as if the past and the present were face-to-face, and I felt complete. I no longer needed to struggle and hide, but I opened my heart to integration and to peace.

As we continued on the tour we saw walls covered with photos of many Gentile people who sacrificed their own lives to help hide Jews from the Nazis. I learned a powerful lesson about heroism that day. No longer will I dismiss the events of the Holocaust or the many souls who perished in vain. I will never again be ashamed to call myself a Jew, a member of a strong, surviving people.

Now, twenty-seven years later, I am able to see that I have not sold my heritage, but followed it to its prophetic conclusion. This Hanukkah my husband and I will once again light the candles of our menorah, blending my Jewish heritage and my Christian faith.

Judith Hayes

Refresher Lesson from Dad

The voice of parents, is the voice of God, for to their children they are heaven's lieutenants.

William Shakespeare

It was a typical school morning. Ashley, our ten-year-old, finished homework during breakfast. Tiffany, who is nine, was told three times to finish up in the shower. The school menu sounded terrible, so lunches were packed. Finally, with only minutes to spare, we jumped into the car and were on our way.

One mile from school, Tiffany informed me from the backseat, "Mom, I must have left my book bag at Grandma and Grandpa's. It's not back here."

During planting season, when my husband Alan and I were busy in the fields, the girls went to my parents' house after school. I knew Alan was waiting for me then to work the ground ahead of the planter. So I launched into a lecture on responsibility. Even though Mom and Dad's house was only three blocks from the girls' school, I didn't want to waste time on an extra stop.

As I turned into their driveway, my plans changed.

There was Dad, leaning all of his weight on the handle of a jack, trying to lift his boat of a car off a flat rear tire. Sweat beaded his forehead, muscles knotted in his neck.

Dad suffered from hardening of the arteries and high blood pressure. Medication kept it in check, but after a slight stroke, his activities were limited. Changing a tire was not on the "okay to do" list.

"Dad, why didn't you call us or a garage? You shouldn't be doing this." Boy, I was in the lecture mode that morning. He smiled like a little boy caught doing something he knew he shouldn't.

"I knew you were busy," he explained.

Hurrying, I grabbed the tire iron and began loosening the lug nuts. *Just like Dad taught me,* I thought. That had been the rule—if I was driving, I had to be able to do simple repairs and maintenance: check the oil and battery, and change a flat.

As I removed Dad's damaged tire, memories of my first lesson flooded my mind. The warm autumn sun glistened off Dad's farmer-tanned arms, and muscles rippled under his blue denim work shirt as he single-handedly jacked up the rear of my car. Then his heavy work boots stomped down on the tire iron. I, a skinny sixteen-year-old girl, struggled to lift the tire, until I felt Dad's sturdy grasp along with mine. He smiled as he wiped his callused hands on the ever-present red bandanna. He reminded me, "Take your time, Sis. Anything worth doing is worth doing right and more likely to turn out that way if you take your time."

But now, Dad stood back, a little hunched over, smiling apologetically. Where had the time gone? When did we change places?

Tire changed, I loaded the kids back into the car—with the book bag. Dad repeated, "Thank you, Sis."

"Thank you, Dad," I choked back tears. "I was just

remembering when you taught me how to take care of my car."

"Me, too," he said, his smile broadening.

We were late for school. Even a little later, because I took the time to apologize to Tiffany for being so impatient.

"You always say everything happens for a reason, Mom," Tiffany chided. "Maybe God knew that Grandpa needed you this morning."

Maybe so, Tiffany. And maybe He knew I needed a refresher lesson from my dad.

Pamela Bumpus

Getting Out of God's Way

I was leaving Christine's physical therapy office, my toddler in my arms, my oldest son by my side. Christine appeared again at the door to say my husband was on the phone.

"Honey, will you put Jonathan in his car seat?" I turned to eleven-year-old Joshua, everyone's right-hand man. "I'll be right back," I told him. Christine had asked Joshua to come to this weekly physical therapy session to distract Jonathan from the discomfort and tedium of his workout.

"Sure, Mom," Joshua said. I put his brother into his arms. At three, Jonathan was still too wobbly to negotiate the rocky parking lot. Down's syndrome meant that both his physical and mental development were delayed. For his family, however, his cute little face spelled courage and perseverance.

Christine's shriek sliced my phone call midsentence. "Barbara! Hurry! Your car's rolling down the hill!"

Throwing down the receiver, I spun and raced down the hall, hearing only the pulse surging in my ears. I begged, "Oh God, dear God, please let it be empty."

The car wasn't empty. Through the windshield, I could

see the top of Jonathan's blonde head, framed by his car seat. He was being carried backwards down the sloping driveway toward the two-lane road below. On the other side of the road was a thirty-foot drop to the San Francisco Bay.

"No! Oh, no! Oh, God, please, no!"

As though I were falling down it myself, I felt the agony of what would happen to my little boy in the minute ahead. If the car cleared the roadway without being struck, it would crash down the embankment and end in the Bay.

"Oh, Lord, not here, not now," I pleaded. Moments from Jonathan's brief but difficult life flashed through my brain. I could hear the beeps of the monitors in Intensive Care, see the tangle of cords and wires from the limp body, feel the tug on my heart when the doctors prepared us for the worst. So many times we had been through these things, with so many people praying for our special little boy. And, one by one, God had healed him of his frailties. For the past year Jonathan had been so healthy we had actually begun to relax.

Could God really choose to take him now, after all He'd seen us through?

Not if my son Joshua could help it. Horrified, I saw him behind the car, straining his ninety-five pounds against the ton of metal grinding him backwards. Running awkwardly in reverse as the car picked up speed, he was on the verge of being crushed any second.

I couldn't lose two sons! "Joshua, let go! Get away from the car!" I screamed. Christine was screaming, too. Even as we pleaded with him, I understood my son's heart. He always took responsibility. Everything within him would rage against giving up the battle to save his brother.

I screamed again, "Joshua! Obey me! Let go!"

At last, he jumped away from the car. As Joshua let go,

Christine and I stopped screaming. The quiet was eerie. The moment hung suspended. The car seemed to hesitate; the rear wheels shifted. It moved toward the edge of the driveway, lost momentum and ground to a halt. Almost gracefully, it came to rest against an old and faithful-looking tree.

I bolted for the car, flung open the door and found Jonathan unhurt, but bewildered. Catching sight of Joshua right behind me, he grinned and stretched his arms wide, his way of saying, "Life—what an adventure!"

"Mom, all I could think of was that I couldn't let him die," Joshua told me later.

Like Joshua, I've tried to pit my puny weight against circumstances that were way too big for me to handle. Perhaps that's why I understood Joshua's reaction all too well. I always overestimate my indispensability—even when I know I need God's help. In fact, I often act as though God can accomplish the supernatural only if I stay involved.

Maybe sometimes God is just waiting for me to get out of the way and let Him take care of things before I get myself hurt. Maybe God would like to do something truly miraculous: something I'd always remember, something I couldn't take credit for myself. Maybe God would like me to be more like Jonathan, just going along for the ride, a little worried perhaps, but remembering I'm in good hands and ready for the rescue.

Barbara Curtis

Sunset in the Rearview Mirror

Destiny is not a matter of chance, it is a matter of choice. It is not a thing to be waited for, it is a thing to be achieved.

William Jennings Bryan

It was almost dusk as I drove home from work one night, the setting sun on my left. With a slight headache, my thoughts drifted through my day at work at the domestic violence shelter, where we never know from one moment to the next what to expect.

As I drove I thought of my life and all the changes that had come about. I, too, had once been the victim of domestic violence. I was never beaten. I was threatened, yelled at, and had things thrown at me, but I never identified this as abuse. I'd always thought abuse was hitting and physical pain.

The sky was slowly darkening, and the feathery wisps of clouds turned to pretty pastels as I drove along. I continued to keep one eye on the clouds as I watched the road and let my mind wander. I had often tried to reason with my husband. I would say he didn't need to yell—I could hear what he was trying to say. I just didn't always agree with him. Did we have to think the same way about everything? Was that what it meant to be submissive? I usually acquiesced. My husband was the head of the household; I was the wife. That was my role. Often I felt put down and betrayed—the butt of my husband's jokes. But my own husband wouldn't want to do that, would he? He loved me! I must be the cause of our problems. Soon, it became easier to just agree with my husband, rather than fight. I wanted peace at any cost. I didn't know the cost was giving up myself. And no one else seemed to notice—no one but me.

My life had begun with so much promise. I'd been a good student. I hadn't made many of the mistakes my classmates did. I thought I was steady, reliable and a commonsense thinker. So why couldn't I do anything right in my marriage?

Thankfully, our three children were not the victims of my husband's violent temper—I was. And as long as that temper was directed at me, it didn't hurt my children, did it?

My car left the freeway, and I headed in the opposite direction of the beautiful sunset. I hated to leave the florescent sky behind, but my trip must continue. I was headed home.

Home, now, was not with that man. After sixteen years, I left him. Despite much counseling, I could find no way to reconcile our miserable marriage. When we sought the help of pastors and counselors, my husband always made it clear that I was the "bad guy." But by this time I was convinced that he didn't love me, and I realized how evil he had been.

My family was devastated by the divorce. No one in our family had ever divorced. It just wasn't done. My family's shame was almost worse than the bad marriage. There were secrets about my marriage that even they didn't know. I tried to explain, but I couldn't bring myself to relive the details. They didn't trust me, so I was on my own. I learned to live with that pain as well, but I had never felt so lonely.

Seven years after the divorce, home was now an eighty-year-old farmhouse on a beautiful country road. I was remarried to a peaceful soul like myself, whom I learned I could trust. We worked together on our home—remodeling, landscaping, building. We were constructing more than a house—we were building a new life. My family was more understanding now, and my kids had weathered the rough years after the divorce, much as our farmhouse had weathered the winds of time. They were doing very well. "Staying together for the sake of the children," simply doesn't work—it's a lie. My children now know that everyone deserves respect, even mom.

I'd learned what marriage was really all about. As head of the household, a man was meant to lead, but not bully, push, manipulate, threaten and criticize. My current husband was a gentle shepherd, not a drill sergeant. He was someone who could be respected and honored—a man of character and commitment. Power and control meant nothing to this man. He was committed to "love as Christ loved the Church."

Not far from home, I climbed a hill and suddenly was stirred out of my reverie. A brilliant sunset, more brilliant than any I'd ever seen, radiated in the rearview mirror. The vibrant oranges and vivid pinks held me spellbound. I rounded a turn at the top of the hill and pulled to the side of the road. With tears streaming down my face, I witnessed God's awesome creativity at work. I also knew exactly what he was trying to tell me at that very moment. While I was going through those hard times, God knew what I didn't. He knew that one day I would look back and see his brilliant master plan. God didn't put me through the abuse, but he used it to create a masterpiece—one I couldn't see at the time, but only when I looked back on it. I'd weathered the storm, and God was right there with me all the time. I was never alone.

I sat for several moments, drinking in the beauty of the incredible sunset. I eased back on the road and rounded another bend. That sunset was with me all the way home in the rearview mirror—just as God had been.

Sheryl Simons

Be Still with God

Rest and be still.

Jeremiah 47:6

All day long I had been very busy; picking up trash, cleaning bathrooms and scrubbing floors. My grown children were coming home for the weekend. I went grocery shopping and prepared for a barbecue supper, complete with ribs and chicken. I wanted everything to be perfect.

Suddenly, it dawned on me that I was dog-tired. I simply couldn't work as long as I could when I was younger. "I've got to rest for a minute," I told my husband, Roy, as I collapsed into my favorite rocking chair. Music was playing, my dog and cat were chasing each other and the telephone rang.

A verse from Psalm 46 popped into my mind: "Be still, and know that I am God." I realized that I hadn't spent much time in prayer that day. *Was I too busy to even utter a simple word of thanks to God?* Suddenly, the thought of my beautiful patio came to mind. *I can be quiet out there,* I thought. I longed for a few minutes alone with God.

Roy and I had invested a great deal of time and work in

the patio that spring. The flowers and hanging baskets were breathtaking. It was definitely a heavenly place of rest and tranquility. *If I can't be still with God in that environment, I can't be still with Him anywhere,* I thought. While Roy was talking on the telephone, I slipped out the back door and sat down on my favorite patio chair. I closed my eyes and began to pray, counting my many blessings.

A bird flew by me, chirping and singing. It interrupted my thoughts. It landed on the bird feeder and began eating dinner as I watched. After a few minutes it flew away, singing another song.

I closed my eyes again. A gust of wind blew, which caused my wind chimes to dance. They made a joyful sound, but again I lost my concentration on God. I squirmed and wiggled in my chair. I looked up toward the blue sky and saw the clouds moving slowly toward the horizon. The wind died down. My wind chimes finally became quiet.

Again, I bowed my head in prayer. "Honk, honk," I heard. I almost jumped out of my skin. A neighbor was driving down the street. He waved at me and smiled. I waved back, happy that he cared. I quickly tried once again to settle down, repeating the familiar verse in my mind: "Be still, and know that I am God."

"I'm trying, God, I really am," I whispered. "But You've got to help me here."

The back door opened. My husband walked outside. "I love you," he said. "I was wondering where you were." I chuckled, as he came over and kissed me, then turned around and went back inside.

"Where's the quiet time?" I asked God. My heart fluttered. There was no pain, only a beat that interrupted me yet again. *This is impossible,* I thought. *There's no time to be still and to know that God is with me. There's too much going on in the world and entirely too much activity all around me.*

Then it suddenly dawned on me. God was speaking to me the entire time I was attempting to be still. I remembered the music playing as I'd begun my quiet time. He sent a sparrow to lighten my life with song. He sent a gentle breeze. He sent a neighbor to let me know that I had a friend. He sent my sweetheart to offer sincere sentiments of love. He caused my heart to flutter to remind me of life. While I was trying to count my blessings, God was busy multiplying them.

I laughed to realize that the "interruptions" of my quiet time with God were special blessings He'd sent to show me He was with me the entire time.

Nancy B. Gibbs

Chapel of the Wash and Dry

There are moments when whatever the attitude of the body, the soul is on its knees.

Victor Hugo

Yes, I hear it, but I can't believe it's morning already. The alarm sounds thick and far away. My arms are at anchor and my eyelids are stubbornly half-mast. Six o'clock and already the day's not adding up: Although I went to bed at eleven, I feel like I've only gotten a few hours sleep.

With the shock of a shipwreck it hits me—I *have* only gotten a few hours' sleep!

Awareness comes in waves, with glimpses of scenes from the night before: Joshua coughing up a storm quelled only with cough syrup; Benjamin sobbing for a prayer to soothe away a bad dream; baby Jonathan calling for his lullaby tape; Zachary's wet bed. And how could I forget being startled at three a.m. to find Sophia at my bedside, waiting politely for her mommy to open her eyes? I guess she wanted quality time.

"Count it all joy," I mutter as I sit up and, not wanting to break my meager momentum, lunge for the laundry room.

The slick linoleum under my feet is a wake-up call. Once over the threshold, my body carries me through the familiar routine of stuffing sheets into the washer, measuring soap and setting dials. The whoosh of the water into the machine is refreshing, like a splash of cool water on my face.

Contemplating the mounds of clothes around me, I am reminded and reassured: *I lift up my eyes to the hills; where does my help come from? My help comes from the Lord, the Maker of heaven and earth.*

Here is where I get a second wind. Here is where, like a shipwrecked survivor, I grab the life preserver of the Lord. Because, Lord knows, He is the only one who can get me through this day.

It wasn't always this way. I used to think my laundry room was just a laundry room. Here is the story of how it became something more:

I was a new Christian nine years ago when I first heard the term "prayer closet" and began to feel inadequate. Someone said, "She fled to her prayer closet and poured her heart out to the Lord." I, too, wanted a prayer closet to flee to. So I hurried home to look for any previously uncharted territory to call my own. But with the hordes in my house, I could find nowhere with the sustained privacy necessary for even a prayer shoebox.

One day, as I was unrolling a multitude of balled-up socks for the washer, I prayed, "Lord, is there a prayer closet somewhere for me? And what about this thing they call quiet time?"

The answer, "Aren't you praying now?" was wordlessly impressed upon my heart.

"Yes, but Lord . . ." and things began to spill out of my heart that I hardly knew were there. I didn't have to tell Him how hard it was to feel like a lightweight when others had more spiritual muscle to flex. I didn't have to tell Him how much I wanted to be the best I could be, and how far from the best I often felt. I didn't have to tell Him because He already knew. But since God was listening, I told Him anyway. Somehow I was made to understand that a mother of toddlers just isn't like anyone else. I felt comforted and loved, and I felt like God cared for me just as I was. Maybe I cried a little. Probably I laughed as well. I did a lot of praying and a lot of laundry before we were through.

And so my laundry room became my prayer closet. This is where I meet the Lord each morning before my children wake, and at intervals throughout the day as I transfer clothes from baskets to washer, from washer to dryer and from dryer to baskets again. In these twelve- and twenty-minute snatches, I have found my quiet time.

I have never had any trouble finding God in my laundry room. He is always ready to receive my praise, my thanks, my prayers for family and friends, and my joys and heartaches, too.

My four-year-old son, Jonathan, spent his first two years in and out of the hospital. My laundry room, with its reassuring routine and memories of mornings with God, became the most comfortable place for me when I could not be at my son's side. People must have questioned my sanity when I staggered home from the hospital and made a beeline for the laundry room. How could I explain what it had become?

Many prayers and loads of laundry later, I now wonder if there are other mothers like me—mothers too busy wiping peanut butter and jelly off little faces and kissing "owies" to maintain the practice of what the less encumbered call "quiet time." I'm thinking of mommies who can't remember how it feels to sit when the sun is shining, who can't count on five minutes in the shower without the world falling apart.

Are there mommies whose prayer closets are buckets

and scrub brushes, sewing baskets, garden patches or car pools? Are there mommies whose prayer closets are assembly lines or switchboards or operating rooms? Are there mommies squeezing moments of quiet time between customer calls or the clamor of kids?

I wonder, because now I understand that God is bigger than any place I set aside to meet Him, and is as near as I invite Him to be.

Before too long, the hum of my steadfast machines is joined by the predictably unpredictable noises of my many children. I'm ready for those precious sleep-snatchers now; ready for whatever the day will bring.

Barbara Curtis

More Chicken Soup?

Many of the stories and poems you have read in this book were submitted by readers like you who had read earlier *Chicken Soup for the Soul* books. We publish at least five or six *Chicken Soup for the Soul* books every year. We invite you to contribute a story to one of these future volumes.

Stories may be up to 1,200 words and must uplift or inspire. You may submit an original piece or something you clip out of the local newspaper, a magazine, a church bulletin or a company newsletter. It could also be your favorite quotation you've put on your refrigerator door or a personal experience that has touched you deeply.

To obtain a copy of our submission guidelines and a listing of upcoming *Chicken Soup* books, please write, fax or check one of our Web sites.

Chicken Soup for the Soul
P.O. Box 30880 • Santa Barbara, CA 93130
Fax: 805-563-2945
To e-mail or visit our Web sites:
www.chickensoup.com
www.clubchickensoup.com

Just send a copy of your stories and other pieces, indicating which edition they are for, to any of the above addresses.

We will be sure that both you and the author are credited for your submission.

Passing It On

Out of our commitment to tithing, both personally and organizationally, it has become our tradition to donate a portion of the net profits of every *Chicken Soup for the Soul* book to charities related to the theme of the book. Past recipients have included The American Red Cross, The Wellness Community, The Special Olympics, Juvenile Diabetes, The Breast Cancer Research Foundation, Feed the Children, and Habitat for Humanity, to name a few. We also support a project called Soup Kitchens for the Soul, which donates *Chicken Soup for the Soul* books to individuals and organizations that cannot afford to purchase them. Tens of thousands of copies of *Chicken Soup for the Soul* books have been given to men and women in prisons, halfway houses, hospitals, churches and other organizations that serve adults and teenagers in need.

Due to the miraculous personal and spiritual transformations that have occurred for many inmates as a result of reading *Chicken Soup* books while in prison, Jack and Mark—along with prison volunteer Tom Lagana—undertook the compilation of *Chicken Soup for the Prisoner's Soul.*

Chicken Soup for the Christian Family Soul, published in March 2000, funded the first printing of 50,000 *Chicken Soup for the Prisoner's Soul* books in August 2000, which we distributed free to people incarcerated in America's prisons, jails and youth detention centers. Since then, more than 200,000 additional books have been requested by chaplains for the inmates they serve across the U.S.

A portion of the proceeds from *Chicken Soup for the Christian Woman's Soul* will fund distribution of additional *Chicken Soup for the Prisoner's Soul,* as well as *Chicken Soup for the Christian Woman's Soul* books free to incarcerated women.

It is our hope and dream that we can use this tool that God has given us to change the lives, one story at a time, of those who desperately need to change.

> *For I was hungry and you gave me something to eat, I was thirsty and you gave me something to drink, I was a stranger and you invited me in, I needed clothes and you clothed me, I was sick and you looked after me, I was in prison and you came to visit me.*
>
> *Matthew 25:35–36*

Who Is Jack Canfield?

Jack Canfield is one of America's leading experts in the development of human potential and personal effectiveness. He is both a dynamic, entertaining speaker and a highly sought-after trainer. Jack has a wonderful ability to inform and inspire audiences toward increased levels of self-esteem and peak performance.

He is the author and narrator of several bestselling audio- and videocassette programs, including *Self-Esteem and Peak Performance, How to Build High Self-Esteem, Self-Esteem in the Classroom* and *Chicken Soup for the Soul—Live.* He is regularly seen on television shows such as *Good Morning America, 20/20* and *NBC Nightly News.* Jack has coauthored numerous books, including the *Chicken Soup for the Soul* series, *Dare to Win* and *The Aladdin Factor* (all with Mark Victor Hansen), *100 Ways to Build Self-Concept in the Classroom* (with Harold C. Wells) and *Heart at Work* (with Jacqueline Miller).

Jack is a regularly featured speaker for professional associations, school districts, government agencies, churches, hospitals, sales organizations and corporations. His clients have included the American Dental Association, the American Management Association, AT&T, Campbell Soup, Clairol, Domino's Pizza, GE, ITT, Hartford Insurance, Johnson & Johnson, the Million Dollar Roundtable, NCR, New England Telephone, Re/Max, Scott Paper, TRW and Virgin Records. Jack is also on the faculty of Income Builders International, a school for entrepreneurs.

Jack conducts an annual eight-day Training of Trainers program in the areas of self-esteem and peak performance. It attracts educators, counselors, parenting trainers, corporate trainers, professional speakers, ministers and others interested in developing their speaking and seminar-leading skills.

For further information about Jack's books, tapes and training programs, or to schedule him for a presentation, please contact:

The Canfield Training Group
P.O. Box 30880 • Santa Barbara, CA 93130
Phone: 805-563-2935 • Fax: 805-563-2945
To e-mail or visit our Web site: *www.chickensoup.com*

Who Is Mark Victor Hansen?

Mark Victor Hansen is a professional speaker who, in the last 20 years, has made over 4,000 presentations to more than 2 million people in 32 countries. His presentations cover sales excellence and strategies; personal empowerment and development; and how to triple your income and double your time off.

Mark has spent a lifetime dedicated to his mission to make a profound and positive difference in people's lives. Throughout his career, he has inspired hundreds of thousands of people to create a more powerful and purposeful future for themselves while stimulating the sale of billions of dollars worth of goods and services.

Mark is a prolific writer and has authored *Future Diary, How to Achieve Total Prosperity* and *The Miracle of Tithing.* He is coauthor of the *Chicken Soup for the Soul* series, *Dare to Win* and *The Aladdin Factor* (all with Jack Canfield), and *The Master Motivator* (with Joe Batten).

Mark has also produced a complete library of personal empowerment audio- and videocassette programs that have enabled his listeners to recognize and use their innate abilities in their business and personal lives. His message has made him a popular television and radio personality, with appearances on ABC, NBC, CBS, HBO, PBS and CNN. He has also appeared on the cover of numerous magazines, including *Success, Entrepreneur* and *Changes.*

Mark is a big man with a heart and spirit to match—an inspiration to all who seek to better themselves.

For further information about Mark write:

P.O. Box 7665
Newport Beach, CA 92658
Phone: 949-759-9304 or 800-433-2314
Fax: 949-722-6912
Web site: *www.chickensoup.com*

Who Is Patty Aubery?

Patty Aubery is the vice president of The Canfield Training Group and Self-Esteem Seminars, Inc. and president of Chicken Soup for the Soul Enterprises, Inc. Patty has been working with Jack and Mark since the birth of *Chicken Soup for the Soul.*

Patty is the coauthor of *Chicken Soup for the Surviving Soul: 101 Stories of Courage and Inspiration from Those Who Have Survived Cancer, Chicken Soup for the Christian Soul, Chicken Soup for the Expectant Mother's Soul* and *Chicken Soup for the Christian Family Soul.* She has been a guest on over 150 local and nationally syndicated radio shows.

Patty is married to Jeff Aubery, and together they have two wonderful children, J. T. and Chandler. Patty and her family reside in Santa Barbara, California, and can be reached at:

The Canfield Training Group
P.O. Box 30880
Santa Barbara, CA 93130
Phone: 805-563-2935
Fax: 805-563-2945

Who Is Nancy Mitchell Autio?

Nancy Mitchell Autio is the Director of Story Acquisitions for the *Chicken Soup for the Soul* series. She graduated from Arizona State University in May 1994 with a B.S. in Nursing. After graduation, Nancy worked at Good Samaritan Regional Medical Center in Phoenix, Arizona, in the Cardiovascular Intensive Care Unit. In September 1994, Nancy moved back to her native Los Angeles and became involved with the *Chicken Soup* series. Nancy's intentions were to help finish *A 2nd Helping of Chicken Soup for the Soul* and then return to nursing. However, in December of that year, she was asked to continue on full time as part of the *Chicken Soup* team. Nancy put nursing on hold and became Director of Story Acquisitions, working closely with Jack and Mark on all *Chicken Soup for the Soul* projects.

Nancy says that what she is most thankful for is her move back to L.A., where she could be there for her mother, Linda Mitchell, during her bout with breast cancer. Out of that struggle, Nancy coauthored, along with her sister, Patty Aubery, *Chicken Soup for the Surviving Soul: 101 Stories of Courage and Inspiration from Those Who Have Survived Cancer.* Little did she know that the book would become her own inspiration when her dad was diagnosed with prostate cancer in 1999.

Nancy also coauthored *Chicken Soup for the Christian Soul, Chicken Soup for the Christian Family Soul, Chicken Soup for the Expectant Mother's Soul, Chicken Soup for the Nurse's Soul* and *Chicken Soup for the Sister's Soul.* Nancy resides in Santa Barbara with her husband, Kirk Autio, daughter, Molly Anne, dogs Kona and Cora, and three cats.

You may contact Nancy Mitchell Autio at:

P.O. Box 30880
Santa Barbara, CA 93130
Phone: 805-682-6311
Fax: 805-682-0872
E-mail: *nautio@chickensoupforthesoul.com.*

Who Is LeAnn Thieman?

LeAnn Thieman is a nationally acclaimed professional speaker, author, and nurse who was "accidentally" caught up in the Vietnam Orphan Airlift in 1975. Her book, *This Must Be My Brother,* details her daring adventure of helping to rescue 300 babies as Saigon was falling to the Communists. An ordinary person, she struggled through extraordinary circumstances and found the courage to succeed. *Newsweek* featured LeAnn and her incredible story in its *Voices of the Century* issue.

Today, she shares life-changing lessons learned from her airlift experience. Believing we all have individual "war zones," LeAnn inspires audiences to balance their lives physically, mentally and spiritually; truly live their priorities; and make a difference in the world.

After her story was featured in *Chicken Soup for the Mother's Soul,* LeAnn became one of *Chicken Soup's* most prolific writers, with stories in eight more *Chicken Soup* books. That, and her devotion to thirty years of nursing, made her an ideal coauthor of *Chicken Soup for the Nurse's Soul.* Given her devotion to God and her lifelong practice of her Christian faith, she is overjoyed at the opportunity to be a coauthor of *Chicken Soup for the Christian Woman's Soul.*

LeAnn and Mark, her husband of thirty-two years, reside in Colorado where they enjoy their "empty nest." Their two daughters, Angela and Christie, and son Mitch have "flown the coop" but are still drawn under their mother's wing when she needs them!

For more information about LeAnn's books and tapes or to schedule her for a presentation, please contact her at:

LeAnn Thieman
6600 Thompson Drive
Fort Collins, CO 80526
Phone: 970-223-1574
www.LeAnnThieman.com
E-mail: *LeAnn@LeAnnThieman.com*

Contributors

Many of the stories in this book were taken from books we have read. These sources are acknowledged in the Permissions section. Some of the stories and poems were contributed by friends of ours, who, like us, are professional speakers. If you would like to contact them for information on their books, tapes and seminars, you can reach them at the addresses and phone numbers provided below.

Many of the stories were also contributed by readers like yourself, who, after reading other volumes of *Chicken Soup for the Soul,* were inspired to submit a story out of their life's experience. We have included information about them as well.

Candy Abbott is a speaker, bible study leader, founder of Delmarva Christian Writers' Fellowship and author of Fruit-Bearer. She and her husband Drew are partners in Fruit-Bearer Publishing, a desktop publishing service for beginning writers. Candy can be reached at P.O. Box 777, Georgetown, DE 19947 or *dabbott@dmv.com.*

Sandra P. Aldrich, president and CEO of Bold Words, Inc., in Colorado Springs is a popular speaker who talks from experience—with humor and encouragement—about the serious issues of life. She also is the author or coauthor of fifteen books. Please reach her at *BoldWords@aol.com.*

Sandy Austin is a counselor at Green Mountain High School in Lakewood, Colorado. She has a master's degree in counseling, and has worked in education for eighteen years. Sandy has written two books, *Angry Teens and Parents Who Love Them* and *Focus on Your Future.* Sandy's Web site is at *www.home.att.net/~sandy-austin.*

Barbara Baumgardner and her golden retriever Molly live in Bend, Oregon, when not motor-homing across America gathering stories. Barbara, a widowed hospice volunteer, has written three books and is a columnist for *RVCompanion* magazine. She can be reached at *barbarab@bendcable.com.*

Michelle Beaupre Matt is a freelance writer and speaker. She has been published in a variety of local and national magazines and has won numerous awards for her writing. She resides in southern Maine with her husband, their five children and many litters of cocker spaniels. E-mails are welcome at *micmatt@cybertours.com.*

Glynis Belec is a freelance writer and author, nurse, homeschool mom, private tutor for special needs children and youth drama ministry leader. Her days are filled with children, challenges and sunshine and she looks forward to the door God will open for her tomorrow! You can reach Glynis at *gbelec@sgci.com.*

Martha Bolton is the author of forty-six books. She was a staff writer for Bob Hope for over fifteen years, and has been nominated for both an Emmy and a Dove award. She is The Cafeteria Lady for *Brio* magazine, and is a popular speaker and teacher of comedy.

Henry Boye is a professional writer/cartoonist whose works have appeared in many leading newspapers and magazines. He is the author of several books and though retired, still continues to work at his craft. He can be reached at 112-D Amberly Drive, Manalapan, NJ 07726.

Marty Bucella is a freelance cartoonist/humorous illustrator whose work has been published over 60,000 times through magazines, newspapers, books, greeting cards, etc. To see more of Marty's work, check out his site at: *www.members.aol.com/mjbtoons/index.html.* Marty can be e-mailed at: *mjbtoons@aol.com.*

Pamela Bumpus and her husband Alan farm in east central Illinois. Tiffany and Ashley are their beautiful daughters and Morgan their wonderful granddaughter. Pam's story, *Something Special,* appeared in *Chicken Soup for the Soul of America.* Look for her book Backside of the Storm or contact her at *pamela@mcleodusa.net* or (217) 348-7734.

Karyn Buxman, R.N., MSN, CSP, CPAE, is an internationally recognized expert in therapeutic humor. She works full time as a professional speaker, writer and consultant. Her primary topic is humor as it relates to health and business professionals. For more information about Karyn or for articles relating to humor and health, visit: *www.HUMORx.com,* email: *Info@HUMORx.com* or call: 800-8HUMORx or (800) 848-6679.

Dave Carpenter has been a full-time cartoonist since 1981. His cartoons have appeared in a number of publications including *Reader's Digest, Harvard Business Review, Barrons, Wall Street Journal, Better Homes & Gardens, Good Housekeeping, Saturday Evening Post* as well as numerous other publications and *Chicken Soup for the Soul* books. Dave can be reached at *davecarp@ncn.net.*

Candace Carteen received two B.A.s from UNLV in 1980 and 1981. She worked as a technical writer for eleven years before pursuing her career in creative writing. Candace enjoys rafting, singing, fishing with her husband and playing with her young son. Contact her at *scribecandace@netzero.net* or visit her Web site at *www.geocities.com/keefersmom/.*

Arlene Centerwall is a retired R.N. with years of nursing experience in all fields of nursing, including teaching and supervision. She currently lives in Surrey B.C. Canada and spends her time writing true inspirational stories and pet sitting. She has traveled extensively in many places of the world.

Joan Clayton has recently been included in *Who's Who Among America's Teachers* for the second time. (1994 and 2002) She has over 450 published articles and six books to her credit. Her Web site is *www.joanclayton.com.* Joan says Emmitt is God's gift to her.

Bonnie Compton Hanson, editor, artist and author of several books, is also included in two other *Chicken Soup for the Soul* books. Her lively family includes husband Don, children, grandchildren, birds, cats and possums. You may reach Bonnie at 3330 S. Lowell St., Santa Ana, CA 92707; phone (714) 751-7824; e-mail: *bonnieh1@worldnet.att.net.*

Jeanne Converse lives in upstate New York with her husband John. They have seven children, twenty-one grandchildren and two great-grandchildren. Her articles have been published in newspapers, magazines and *Chicken Soup for the Christian Family Soul.* She's published a book about organizing on *Booklocker.com.* She can be reached at *jconver1@tweny.rr.com.*

Barbara Curtis is an award-winning freelancer with two published books as well as 500+ published articles. Mother to twelve—including three adopted sons with Down's syndrome—Barbara holds a B.A. in philosophy as well as an AMI Montessori teaching credential. Visit her at *www.barbaracurtis.com.*

Lynn Dean is a Colorado writer and the mother of three children ages eleven, fourteen and sixteen. Lynn has written over 500 parenting articles which have appeared in more than 100 national and regional publications in thirty states. You can contact Lynn by writing to her at P.O. Box 146, Timnath, CO 80547.

Sandy Deters resides with her husband, Keith, and their five children: Megan, Lauren, Ashley, Justin and Brittany (twins) in Sigel, Illinois. Sandy became a home-based computer consultant in 1989 after the early arrival of Lauren. Keith farms and the family helps out with chores. The family enjoys playing and watching basketball and baseball.

Peter Dow currently lives in Pottstown, Pennsylvania. He's a sergeant in the U.S. Army reserves. At his local church, he preaches in children's church and works in the bus ministry. He wants to go into evangelism.

Rosey Dow is a popular speaker, author and writing instructor. She won the coveted Christy Award for her historical novel about the Scopes evolution trial, *Reaping the Whirlwind,* a factual account of the trial with a compelling fiction mystery. She is a pastor's wife and homeschooling mother of seven children. Visit her Web site to learn more about Rosey's many books and current projects. *www.roseydow.com.*

T. Suzanne Eller is the author of Real Teens, *Real Stories, Real Life* published by RiverOaks Publishers. She is a freelance writer, author and inspirational speaker, ministering to teens, churches and women on how to impact a real world with their faith. She can be reached at *tseller@daretobelieve.org* or *www.daretobelieve.org.*

Linda Evans Shepherd, (*www.sheppro.com*) is a radio talk show host who speaks nationally for women's groups. She authored *Heart-Stirring Stories of Love* and *Teatime Stories for Women.* Linda founded the Advanced Writers and Speakers Association (*awsawomen.com*) as well as Right to the Heart Ministries and Winning Women for church ministry leaders (*www.righttotheheart.com*).

Susan Fahncke is a freelance writer living in Utah. Author of Angel's Legacy, she also writes for inspirational books and magazines and runs a Web site and daily list of inspirational stories. You can find her stories in other *Chicken Soup for the Soul* books. E-mail: *Editor@2theheart.com.* Web site: *www.2THEHEART.com.*

Barbara Fisher was published in sixteen magazines, published five books and has been published in several *Chicken Soup for the Soul* books. Her first novel, *Stolen Moments,* portrays many of her personal emotions stemming from illness in her own life. She uses the feelings of her heart to touch and inspire other's hearts. *mentorsfriend@cros.net.*

Elaine F Galaktionova, M.A., is a Russian freelance writer, journalist and translator. Her family was among the survivors of the Siege of Leningrad. Based in France, Elaine writes on the subjects of travel, history, culture and self-improvement. Her current projects include *900 Days: When Death Surrendered,* a book based on the Siege survivors' accounts. You can contact Elaine at *baltimpex@wanadoo.fr.*

Shirley Garrett, Ed.D., a professional speaker, writer, and facilitator, works with organizations that want to create a new sense of spirit in the workplace and community and with people who want to work and live together better. Shirley makes learning fun through her use of southern humor, wit and wisdom. *drshirl@mindspring.com.*

LaDonna Gatlin is a keynote speaker whose personal story of faith to "sing her own song" apart from her brothers (country music's Gatlin Brothers) is the cornerstone of her presentations. Her unique blend of music, humor and content not only entertains but also delivers a powerful message on leadership, change and personal development. Contact: *www.ladonnagatlin.com.*

Carol Genegels and her husband have three grown children and five grandsons. They live on scenic Hood Canal near Seattle. Carol's adventures in faith give her much to write and speak about. She's the cofounder/director of A Woman's Touch Ministry. She enjoys traveling, writing, teaching and prayer. Please contact her at: *awtcarolg@juno.com.*

Nancy B. Gibbs is an author, writer and religion columnist. Her stories have appeared in over thirty books and dozens of magazines including *Chicken Soup for the Nurse's Soul, Stories for the Heart, Guideposts* books, *Woman's World* and *Family Circle.* She may be contacted at *Daiseydood@aol.com.*

Sharon Gibson and her husband adopted four abandoned teenagers. She stays at home to care for them and write her stories. She was raised in Africa by missionary parents, servered in the Kansas legislature as a state representative, owned two Christian stories and worked for DaySpring Cards. E-mail her at: *sharongibson@cox-internet.com.*

Marilynn Griffith lives in Florida with her husband and six children. Her recent credits include *Honey for a Homeschooler's Heart, Crumbs in the Keyboard, Comfort for a Grieving Heart* and *Proverbs for the People.* Marilynn can be contacted at *mgriffith32@aol.com* or through *www.marilynngriffith.com.*

Carol Hamblet Adams, a heartwarming, fun-loving motivational speaker, inspires audiences to believe in themselves and in their dreams. Her book, *My Beautiful Broken Shell,* shares God's message that there is profound beauty in our brokenness. Carol can be reached at P.O. Box 1234, Attleboro, MA 02760 or at *chadams@naisp.net.*

Judy Hampton is a wife, mom, grandmother, businesswoman, keynote speaker across the U. S., frequently published freelance writer and author of the book *Under the Circumstances,* published by NavPress. Her testimony has aired on several radio programs, including *Focus on the Family,* and *Decision Today,* as well as television. E-mail: *judyjudyjudy9@juno.com.*

Jonny Hawkins has been cartooning professionally for sixteen years. His work has appeared in *Barron's, Saturday Evening Post, Guideposts, Harvard Business Review* and over 250 other publications. His comic "Hi and Jinx" has run for nine years in newspapers around the country. He lives in Michigan with his wife, Carissa, and two boys, and can be reached at (616) 432-8071 or *jonnyhawkins2nz@yahoo.com.*

Judith Hayes has been a published freelance writer since 1995, which has been the fulfillment of a life-long dream. She is the mother of two adult daughters, Sasha Beebe and Annabelle Shoemaker. Judith is the proud new grandmother of baby grandsons Devin and Shane. She is a certified childbirth educator, with sixteen years of teaching experience, and hopes to become a birthing doula (helper of women) in the near future. You can contact her at: *gdsangl@msn.com.*

Sara Henderson received her bachelor of arts from Illinois Wesleyan University and her master of education from Bethel College in St. Paul, Minnesota. Sara has taught kindergarten and second grade and is currently serving as the elementary principal in a private Christian school in Minnesota.

Kimberly Henrie is a radio personality, voice talent and freelance writer. She lives with her family in Colorado and is active in her church and community. Through her work, Kimberly hopes to inspire young women to live happier, fuller lives. You can reach Kimberly via her Web site at: *www.kimberlyhenrie.net.*

Dorothy Hill has worked with children both as an educator and a foster parent. As a single parent, she raised three adopted daughters. Dorothy has written articles about her home state of Mississippi for the Internet and is currently working on a children's book. She can be reached at *missisip@dixie-net.com.*

Nancy Hird continues to practice her leadership abilities: producing church dramas, organizing pastors' breakfasts and teaching Sunday school. She also writes. Her articles have appeared in *Discipleship Journal, The Lookout,* and *Moody Magazine.* Her books for children are *Marty's Monster* and *Jessica Jacobs Did What?* She can be reached at *hirdne@christcom.net.*

Armené Humber teaches career transition classes at University of California Extension in Irvine, California. In addition to working toward a master's degree at Fuller Theological Seminary, she freelances as a writer and editor. Her work has appeared in numerous publications. Please contact her at: WORDable SOLUTIONS, (714) 775-6705 or *armhumber@aol.com.*

Ellen Javernick is a first-grade teacher in Loveland, Colorado. She is the author of fifteen books for children, and her inspirationals have appeared in numerous magazines and anthologies. Ellen enjoys playing tennis and spending time with her five grown children and their families. She can be reached at *javernicke@aol.com.*

Jewell Johnson is a wife, mother of six children, grandmother of six and a registered nurse. She writes personal experience articles, curriculum and nonfiction for children. Jewell enjoys reading, walking and quilting in Arizona. You may reach her at: *tykeJ@juno.com.*

Bil Keane created "The Family Circus," based on his own family, in 1960. It now appears in well over fifteen hundred newspapers and is read daily by 188 million people. The award-winning feature is the most widely syndicated panel cartoon in America. Check out The Family Circus Web site: *www.familycircus.com.*

Vicki Kitchner has been teaching in the Sarasota County School system for eighteen years. She has a master's degree in motor disabilities and holds a national board certification in exceptional student education. She wrote the lyrics for an educational children's CD entitled: *It's Circle Time!* that will be published in 2001. Kitchner has also been a fitness instructor for seventeen years. She lives with her husband of thirteen years. Please reach her at: *vkandjb@aol.com.*

Lee Kochenderfer and her husband, retired Lieutenant Colonel Harold Kochenderfer, live in California. "ReConsider the Lilies" is a memory from their Kindley Air Force Base, Bermuda days. Lee, professor emerita, Riverside Community College, and author of a children's novel, *The Victory Garden,* holds a Ph.D. from the University of California, Riverside.

Darlene Lawson and her husband live on a farm in Atlantic Canada. She credits her writing ability to being in touch with the beauty of God's handiwork that surrounds their farm. Darlene enjoys gardening, walking, singing in the church choir and the farmhouse filled with family and friends. E-mail: *antenna@nb.sympatico.ca.*

Marita Littauer is a professional speaker with over twenty-five years of experience. She is the author of ten books including *Personality Puzzle, Talking So People Will Listen* and her newest, *Love Extravagantly.* Marita is the president of CLASServices Inc., an organization that provides resources, training and promotion for speakers and authors. Marita and her husband Chuck Noon have been married since 1983. For more information on Marita and/or CLASS, please visit *www.classervices.com* or call (800) 433-6633.

Patricia Lorenz is an art-of-living writer and speaker, the author of three books; over 400 articles; a contributor to ten *Chicken Soup for the Soul* books; thirteen *Daily Guideposts* books; numerous anthologies; and an award-winning columnist for two newspapers. For speaking engagements phone (800) 437-7577 or e-mail *patricialorenz@juno.com.*

Caron Loveless is a wife and mother who knows to expect surprising encounters with God. Bestselling author and coauthor of nine inspirational books, she writes for magazines including *Today's Christian Woman* and speaks on radio and television, and at seminars and retreats. Caron serves as creative director at Discovery Church in Orlando, Florida. Her next book, *Honey They Shrunk My Hormones* arrives March 2003. Contact Caron at *www.caronloveless.com.*

Susan Lugli is a Christian speaker and author. In 1998 she wrote "Out of the Fire" and it was published in the *Today's Christian Woman's* Magazine. That same year she was profiled in the *Woman of Faith New Testament Bible.* Susan is now living on a ranch in Lompoc, CA. Please reach her at *suenrusty@aol.com.*

Diana Mason-Bruhn lives in Woodstock, Illinois, with her husband, three beautiful teenaged daughters, horses, dogs, cats, birds and bunnies. An addicted reader of fiction for all ages, she has recently completed a novel in which the heroine's adventures are loosely based on her own youthful escapades. Reach her at *horsingarounddmb@aol.com.*

Nancy Massand received her B.A. in English at Gordon College and M.S. in secondary education/English at Queens College. A teacher in New York City, she and her husband Mike have three daughters and two sons-in-law. Nancy is working on a collection of short fiction. You may contact her at *Malemud@aol.com.*

Carol McAdoo Rehme finds her inspiration in stories, and she chooses to share it as an author, speaker and professional storyteller. With a lasting passion for the elderly, she creates and presents her model, grant-driven program, "Silver Linings for Golden Agers," in long-term healthcare facilities. Carol can be reached at: *www.rehme.com or carol@rehme.com.*

Walker Meade started writing at the age of fourteen. His first story was published in *Colliers* magazine when he was twenty-two. He wrote short fiction for the *Saturday Evening Post, Gentlemen's Quarterly, Good Housekeeping, The Ladies' Home Journal* and nonfiction for *Cosmopolitan, Redbook* and *The Reader's Digest.* Later he took a position in publishing and became managing editor of *Cosmopolitan* and then managing editor of *The Reader's Digest Condensed Book*

Club. His last position in publishing was as president and editor in chief of *Avon Books,* which he continued to do for ten years. His first novel titled *Unspeakable Acts* it is available from *Amazon.com.*

DiAnn Mills is the author of eight novels, six novellas, short stories, articles, devotions, and contributor of ten nonfiction anthologies. She is on the board of the newly formed American Christian Romance Writers and does speaking and writing workshops. DiAnn can be contacted at *diann@rehobothministries* or *www.rehobothministries.com.*

Janet Lynn Mitchell is an inspirational speaker and author of numerous articles and stories in compilations. Her being a victim of medical fraud resulted in the signing into law California Assembly Bill AB2571. Her story, "Taking a Stand," has inspired thousands. Janet can be reached at *Janetlm@prodigy.net* or faxed at (714) 633-6309.

Denise Mizell is mother of three successful children and grandmother of three. Office manager for a neurosurgeon, she lives along the Florida Space Coast. Since her husband's death, she has been chairperson of a singles support group and a grief counselor. This is her first attempt at writing. E-mail her at *nisimizell@aol.com.*

Howie Mullis, originally from Monroe, Michigan, lived in Winder, Georgia for ten years before moving in 1996 to Greeneville, Tennessee. Howie makes all-natural herbal soaps as a hobby under the name, Lye'n Around Soap'n, and is now pursuing her dream of becoming an inspirational writer. Contact Howie at: *heyhowiejo@yahoo.com.*

Adele Noetzelman, a freelance writer, is the assistant director of Write the Vision (*www.visionretreats.com*), which offers retreats and resources for Christian women writers. In both active and support roles, Adele and her husband, Jim, have been involved in international missions for twenty years. They now live in Snohomish, Washington.

Dawn Nowakoski, along with her best friend and husband, John, make their home in Indiana. They have been abundantly blessed with eight little people between the ages of four and fourteen, all of who teach them lessons daily and remind them of God's plan. You can reach Dawn at: *eightsenuf@hotmail.com.*

Karen O'Connor is an award-winning author of thirty-seven books for children and adults, a popular speaker at women's events and a writing instructor with the Long Ridge Writers Group. She enjoys hiking, walking on the beach, singing in the church choir and being with her family. Contact her at: *karen@karenoconnor.com.*

Susan Titus Osborn is director of the Christian Communicator Manuscript Critique Service. She is a contributing editor of *The Christian Communicator* magazine and an adjunct professor. She has authored twenty-four books and is a publisher's representative for Broadman & Holman Publishers and Concordia Publishing House. Contact Susan at *Susanosb@aol.com.*

Donna Partow is a Christian communicator with a compelling testimony of God's transforming power. A popular conference speaker, she's been featured on 200+ radio shows, including *Focus on the Family.* Her bestselling books include *Becoming a Vessel God Can Use* and *Walking in Total God-Confidence.* E-mail *donnapartow@cybertrails.com* or call 928-472-7368.

Chris Patterson's whimsical style of cartoons have been commissioned to illustrate books, and have been published in many trade journals around the world, thanks to the WWWeb. Familiar names would include *Family Digest, Lutheran, Mature Living, Reader's Digest* and *Woman's World,* to name a few. As a freelance cartoonist/illustrator, he enjoys creating other's ideas to paper and can be reached for your next project at: *CartoonsByChris@aol.com.*

Rebecca Price Janney is the author of fifteen books, including *Harriet Tubman and Great Women, Great Stories* and *Great Letters in American History.* She lives near Philadelphia and enjoys speaking about history to all kinds of groups. Please reach her at: *ppbkrtr@hotmail.com.*

Harry Randles lives in Hot Springs Village, Arizona. Born in upstate New York in 1919, he "flew the Hump" in World War II. Later, the GI Bill provided his education. Since earning a Ph.D., his career has been in education: public schools, Syracuse University and Vanderbilt. Now retired, he spends his time reading and writing.

Rhonda Rhea is a pastor's wife, mother of five, conference speaker and an inspirational humor columnist for *HomeLife Magazine* and other Christian newspapers in the U.S. and Canada. She has also written scads of feature articles and her first book, *Amusing Grace,* is due out in early 2003. *Rhonda@RhondaRhea.net.*

Carla Riehl is a speaker/author touring nationally speaking on *Calm, Confident, and Assertive for Christian Women* and *The Blueprint Factor: Living the Power of Your Uniqueness.* She has been awarded three Clio awards (advertising's Oscar) and an Emmy for singing TV and radio commercials. Her pop/rock Christian albums have been heard nationwide. She can be reached at *carlareal@msn.com.*

Kimberly Ripley is a freelance writer and published author from Portsmouth, New Hampshire. Her writing workshop, Freelancing Later in Life, will visit cities across the United Sates in 2002. A wife and mother of five, Kim is an avid school volunteer and an active member of her church.

Julie Saffrin lives in Excelsior, Minnesota. A freelance writer of numerous articles, Julie has just finished *That Summer Place,* a contemporary inspirational novel, and is at work on her second novel, *One Blood.* Stop by and say hi at *www.home.talkcity.com/BookmarkBlvd/juliesaffrin* or e-mail her at *ssja@qwest.net.*

Lisa Scheepsma-Beuter lives in Millerton, Pennyslvania, with her husband Steve and two sons, Justin, sixteen, and Casey, thirteen. She is disabled with a severe neck injury caused by domestic violence in a previous relationship.

She loves to write poetry and would like to write a book someday. Her e-mail address is *beuterski@hotmail.com.*

Debra J. Schmidt, a.k.a. "The Loyalty Builder," works with businesses and people who want to sell more products and services by helping them build customer and employee loyalty. Emmy nominee, author and entrepreneur Debra is in demand as a speaker and well known for her humorous programs. Please visit her Website: *www.theloyaltybuilder.com.*

Barbara Seaman is a graduate of the Conservatory of Music, Wheaton College, Wheaton, Illinois. Her stories, articles and poems have appeared in mainstream and literary magazines such as *Modern Maturity, Marriage Partnership, Troika* and *Image.* She lives in Lawrence, Kansas.

Duane Shaw has been previously published in *Chicken Soup for the Nurse's Soul.* He is currently writing an autobiography of short stories about his combat experiences in Vietnam. God blessed Duane with his supportive wife, Jennell, and their loving family, Tony, Rob, Chelsea, Loretta and Salome'. *Dbshaw1947@aol.com.*

Goddard Sherman, Th.D., is a retired United Methodist minister with a longtime hobby of cartooning. His work has appeared in many major magazines. He was a pastor in Florida for over thirty years and taught history of world religions for seventeen years in community colleges and the University of South Florida, Tampa.

Robin Lee Jansen Shope received her bachelor of science, with honors, from the University of Wisconsin in Whitewater in 1975. She teaches middle school in Lewisville, Texas. Robin enjoys reading, writing and working with children and young adults. Saturday mornings you will find her perusing flea markets or rummaging through local garage sales. Her dream is to have a novel published. She would enjoy hearing from you at: *hi2Robin@attbi.com.*

Gloria Cassity Stargel, contributing writer to *Guideposts, Decision,* and other Christian publications, had urgent need to know: "Does God still heal today?" The answer? Read her award-winning book *The Healing, One Family's Victorious Struggle with Cancer*—an unforgettable true story of faith, hope and love. Call (800) 888-9529; or visit *www.brightmorning.com.*

Kimn Swenson Gollnick is a wife, home-schooling mother and award-winning writer specializing in essays, children's topics, nonfiction and op-ed pieces. She's a popular speaker at retreats and writers' conferences. Contact: 550 Edinburgh Ave., Marion, IA 52302-5614, (319) 373-9760. Visit *www.KIMN.net* or send e-mail to *gollnick@gte.net.*

Nanette Thorsen-Snipes has published more than four hundred articles, columns, devotions and reprints in publications such as *Woman's World, Power for Living, Breakaway, Home Life, Chicken Soup for the Christian Family Soul,* Honor Books, Multnomah Publishers and others. Contact: P. O. Box 1596, Buford, GA 30515 or e-mail: *nsnipes@mindspring.com.*

Louise Tucker Jones is a Gold Medallion award-winning author and inspirational speaker, sharing God's love and grace through difficult times. Married to Carl, and mother of four, Louise lives in Edmond, Oklahoma. She is the author of *Dance From the Heart* and coauthor of *Extraordinary Kids.* Contact her at: *LouiseTJ@aol.com.*

John P. Walker began his professional life as a radio announcer. He left broadcasting to pursue a call to pastoral ministry in 1982. His passions include writing, photography and skydiving. John's writing has appeared in magazines, periodicals and inspirational books. You may contact him at *john1walkr@aol.com.*

Rachel Wallace-Oberle has an education in radio and television broadcasting as well as journalism/print. She is a freelance writer/editor and has written for numerous publications. She cohosts a weekly Christian radio program and loves walking, classical music and canaries. Rachel can be reached at: *rachel w-o@rogers.com.*

Maggie Wallem Rowe is a graduate of Wheaton College and a former college communications instructor. After twenty-five years of ministry in New England, she now lives in Wheaton, Illinois, where her husband is senior pastor at First Baptist Church. A writer, dramatist and conference speaker, Maggie may be reached at *maggie.rowe@verizon.net.*

Sharon Wilkins is an educator, author and speaker. Her book *Ready for Kindergarten,* has 157 fun activities to give preschoolers a giant head start (*Zondervan,* 4th printing, Spanish edition 2002.) Sharon's experiences include: teacher, nominee for Walt Disney's Teacher of the Year, writer of numerous articles and national speaker for parents/teachers on *Raising Kinder, More Capable Kids.* Contact her at (480) 892-6684 or by e-mail: *swilk44@aol.com.*

Permissions *(continued from page iv)*

The Song in You. Reprinted by permission of LaDonna Gatlin. ©2001 LaDonna Gatlin.

God Listens. Reprinted by permission of DiAnn Mills. ©2000 DiAnn Mills.

A Thousand Ways. Reprinted by permission of Susan Titus Osborn. ©1995 Susan Titus Osborn.

A Special Lady. Reprinted by permission of Joan Clayton. ©1982 Joan Clayton.

Living on the Ledge. Reprinted by permission of Denise C. Mizell. ©2001 Denise C. Mizell.

Startled by a Dream. Reprinted by permission of Sharon Gibson. ©1999 Sharon Gibson.

Hanging on to Hope. Reprinted by permission of Martha Bolton. ©2001 Martha Bolton. Excerpted from *Still the One.* ©2001 Revell.

The Egg. Reprinted by permission of Dorothy M. Hill. ©2001 Dorothy M. Hill.

It Can Happen. Reprinted by permission of T. Suzanne Eller. ©1999 T. Suzanne Eller.

The Wedding. From *God Allows U-Turns,* published by Promise Press, an imprint of Barbour Publishing, Inc., Uhrichsville, Ohio. Used by permission.

Bringing It to Pass, Football and All. Reprinted by permission of Patricia Lorenz. ©1995 Patricia Lorenz.

You Did Good. Reprinted by permission of Carla S. Riehl. ©2002 Carla S. Riehl.

The Plan. Reprinted by permission of LeAnn Thieman. ©2002 LeAnn Thieman.

Come to Our House. Reprinted by permission of Maggie Wallem Rowe. ©2001 Maggie Wallem Rowe.

Love Lives Forever. Reprinted by permission of Peter Dow and Rosalie M. Dow. ©2001 Peter Dow and Rosalie M. Dow.

Love That Lasts. Reprinted by permission of Barbara Seaman. ©1995 Barbara Seaman.

Crisis on the Court. Reprinted by permission of Gloria Cassity Stargel. ©2001 Gloria Cassity Stargel.

A Mother's Intuition. Reprinted by permission of Glynis M. Belec. ©2001 Glynis M. Belec.

Daddy's Gift. Reprinted by permission of Shirley D. Garrett. ©1996 Shirley D. Garrett.

Make a Wish, Mommy. From *God Allows U-Turns,* published by Promise Press, an imprint of Barbour Publishing, Inc., Uhrichsville, Ohio. Used by permission.

Unconditional Love. Reprinted by permission of Carol Hamblet Adams. ©2002 Carol Hamblet Adams.

My Turn. Reprinted by permission of Barbara Jeanne Fisher. ©1996 Barbara Jeanne Fisher.

A Treasured Gift. Reprinted by permission of Kimn Swenson Gollnick. ©1998 Kimn Swenson Gollnick.

The Breathin' Part. Reprinted by permission of Sandra P. Aldrich. ©1999 Sandra P. Aldrich. Adapted from *Will I Ever Be Whole Again?* (Howard Publishing)

Love Bugs. Reprinted by permission of Darlene Lawson. ©2001 Darlene Lawson.

By Their Roots Ye Shall Know Them. Reprinted by permission of Carol McAdoo Rehme. ©1998 Carol McAdoo Rehme. Originally printed under the title: *"How Does Your Garden Grow?"* Excerpted from *Whispers from Heaven,* April 2000, pg. 50.

Blossoms for Belle. Reprinted by permission of Carol McAdoo Rehme. ©2001 Carol McAdoo Rehme. Excerpted from *An Angel by Your Side,* PIL (Publications International, Ltd.), 2001, pg. 263.

A Small Unsteady Light. Reprinted by permission of Walker Meade. ©2001 Walker Meade.

Meeting God at 30,000 Feet. Reprinted by permission of Caron Loveless. ©1998 Caron Loveless.

The Healing Power of Forgiveness. Reprinted by permission of Karen O'Connor. ©1982 Karen O'Connor.

Healing at Columbine. Reprinted by permission of Sandy J. Austin. ©1999 Sandy J. Austin.

Mercy's Time. Reprinted by permission of Julie A. Saffrin. ©2001 Julie A. Saffrin.

Forgiveness Tastes Sweet. Reprinted by permission of Elaine Freeland. ©2001 Elaine Freeland.

The Ride. From *God Allows U-Turns,* published by Promise Press, an imprint of Barbour Publishing, Inc., Uhrichsville, Ohio. Used by permission.

The Purpose of My Soul. Reprinted by permission of Duane Shaw. ©2001 Duane Shaw.

That's What Friends Do. Reprinted by permission of T. Suzanne Eller. ©2001 T. Suzanne Eller.

Prayer Pals. Reprinted by permission of Ellen Javernick. ©2002 Ellen Javernick.

Tammy and the Diamond Dress. Reprinted by permission of Robin Lee Shope. ©1998 Robin Lee Shope.

Strengthened By Angels. Reprinted by permission of Sharon A. Wilkins. ©1996 Sharon A. Wilkins.

Wigged Out! Reprinted by permission of Bonnie Compton Hanson. ©2001 Bonnie Compton Hanson.

Rhythms of Grace. Reprinted by permission of Marilynn Griffith. ©2001 Marilynn Griffith.

God's Timing. Reprinted by permission of Rebecca Price Janney. ©2001 Rebecca Price Janney.

Ivy's Cookies. Reprinted by permission of Candace F. Abbott. ©1998 Candace F. Abbott.

An Unexpected Moment. Reprinted by permission of Sara L. Henderson. ©2001 Sara L. Henderson.

Miracle on Mercer Street. Reprinted by permission of Carol L. Genengels. ©2001 Carol L. Genengels.

Eulogy to a Stranger. Reprinted by permission of Carol Hamblet Adams. ©2002 Carol Hamblet Adams.

Never Too Late. Reprinted by permission of Debra J. Schmidt. ©2001 Debra J. Schmidt.

The Woman Who Wouldn't Pray. Reprinted with the permission of Scribner, a Division of Simon & Schuster, Inc., from *THE CATHOLIC DIGEST BOOK OF COURAGE* edited by Rawley Myers. Copyright © 1988 by Rawley Myers.

Take My Hand. Reprinted by permission of Barbara J. Baumgardner. ©2001 Barbara J. Baumgardner.

The Ministry of Life. Reprinted by permission of Karyn Buxman. ©2002 Karyn Buxman.

Flying a Kite. Reprinted by permission of Vicki L. Kitchner. ©2001Vicki L. Kitchner.

All God's Children. Reprinted by permission of Carol McAdoo Rehme. ©2001 Carol McAdoo Rehme. Excerpted from *Whispers fom Heaven,* August 2001, pg. 116.

Leadership Material. Reprinted by permission of Nancy E. Hird. ©2001 Nancy E. Hird.

Miracle of the Stray E-Mail. Reprinted by permission of Barbara J. Baumgardner. ©2001 Barbara J. Baumgardner.

Love's Power. From *God Allows U-Turns,* published by Promise Press, an imprint of Barbour Publishing, Inc., Uhrichsville, Ohio. Used by permission.

Happy Heart Day. Reprinted by permission of Jewell F. Johnson. ©1996 Jewell F. Johnson.

Apron Time. Reprinted by permission of Donna Power Partow. ©1999 Donna Power Partow.

Tough Love. Reprinted by permission of Nanette Thorsen-Snipes. ©1996 Nanette Thorsen-Snipes

Mother's Day Angel. Reprinted by permission of Jeanne Converse. ©2001 Jeanne Converse.

Disaster on the Mountain. Reprinted by permission of Patricia Lorenz. ©1996 Patricia Lorenz.

Angel in Black. Reprinted by permission of Nancy E. Massand. ©2001 Nancy E. Massand.

Where There's a Wheel There's a Way. Reprinted by permission of Barbara Jeanne Fisher. ©1999 Barbara Jeanne Fisher.

But You Are Beautiful. Reprinted by permission of Sandra P. Aldrich. ©2002 Sandra P. Aldrich.

Desires of Your Heart. Reprinted by permission of Susan Kay Lugli. ©2001 Susan Kay Lugli.

The Gift. Reprinted by permission of Linda Evans Shepherd. ©1996 Linda Evans Shepherd.

In God's Eyes. From *God Allows U-Turns,* published by Promise Press, an imprint of Barbour Publishing, Inc., Uhrichsville, Ohio. Used by permission.

The Blessing Jar. Reprinted by permission of Janet Mitchell. ©2001 Janet Mitchell.

The Flood. Reprinted by permission of Howie Mullis. ©2001 Howie Mullis.

Judging a Book by Its Cover. Reprinted by permission of Adele M. Noetzelman. ©2001 Adele M. Noetzelman.

And the Little Child Shall Lead Them. Reprinted by permission of Dawn F. Nowakoski. ©2000 Dawn F. Nowakoski.

Journey to the Depths of My Purse. Reprinted by permission of Rhonda S. Rhea. ©2001 Rhonda S. Rhea.

The Miracle of Medjugorje. Reprinted by permission of LeAnn Thieman. ©2002 LeAnn Thieman.

Casey. Reprinted by permission of Lisa K. Scheepsma-Beuter. ©1999 Lisa K. Scheepsma-Beuter.

Reconsider the Lilies. Reprinted by permission of Lee Kochenderfer. ©2001 Lee Kochenderfer.

The Birthday Gift. Reprinted by permission of Arlene Centerwall. ©1995 Arlene Centerwall.

Do You Believe in God? Reprinted by permission of Lynn M. Dean. ©1999 Lynn M. Dean.

Our Little Pink Blanket. Reprinted by permission of Sandra J. Deters. ©1998 Sandra J. Deters.

Hands. Reprinted by permission of Kimberly Ripley. ©2000 Kimberly Ripley.

Coincidence on a Country Road. Reprinted by permission of Diana Mason Bruhn. ©2001 Diana Mason Bruhn.

A Daily Dose of Miracles. Reprinted by permission of Louise Tucker Jones. ©2001 Louise Tucker Jones.

Santa Claus. Reprinted by permission of Kimberly K. Henrie. ©2001 Kimberly K. Henrie.

Caution: Follow Directions. Reprinted by permission of Judy Hampton. ©2001 Judy Hampton.

Helen. Reprinted by permission of Armené Humber. ©1998 Armené Humber.

The Best Defense. Reprinted by permission of Marilynn Griffith. ©2001 Marilyn Griffith.

It's Better to Give Than . . . Reprinted by permission of Karen O'Connor. ©1987 Karen O'Connor.

Attitude Adjustment. Reprinted by permission of Marita Littauer. ©2001 Marita Littauer.

My Menorah—The Little Tree of Life. Reprinted by permission of Judith Hayes. ©2001 Judith Hayes.

Refresher Lesson from Dad. Reprinted by permission of Pamela Bumpus. ©2002 Pamela Bumpus.

Getting Out of God's Way. Reprinted by permission of Barbara Curtis. ©1995 Barbara Curtis.

Sunset in the Rearview Mirror. Reprinted by permission of Sheryl A. Simons. ©2001 Sheryl A. Simons.

Be Still with God. Reprinted by permission of Nancy B. Gibbs. ©2000 Nancy B. Gibbs.

Chapel of the Wash and Dry. Reprinted by permission of Barbara Curtis. ©1996 Barbara Curtis.